A POW DIARY

My Father's Struggle

To: C.J. Bamford,
My father often spoke
fondly of the "Brits" he
served with. He always admired
their sense of honor. As we celebrate
the 4th of July I am reminded of all
the things that our two peoples
have in common. A sense of freedom
and the determination to fight for that
priviledge. Please accept my deep
appreciation for all your sacrafices
that have meant so much to
the U.S. and the U.K.
Thanking you
George J Matta Jr
4 July 2000

CMSgt (Ret.) George J. Matta Jr.

DarRyan Press
Hoover, Alabama

Other copy George sent me has been placed in Feltham Library for all to read + find out about the forgotton war

First printing 1997

Library of Congress Cataloging in Publication Data

Matta, George J. Jr.
A POW Diary - My Father's Struggle

1. History
I. Matta, George J. Jr. II. Title.
Library of Congress Catalog Card Number: 97-66742
ISBN 0-9658080-0-9

Printed in the United States of America

DEDICATION

This book contains a first hand account of the experiences of my father and the other brave Americans held in captivity with during the Korean War.

I grew up never realizing the true character of the man who raised me. I had known that he was a prisoner during the war but like most repatriated POWs, the years spent in captivity were not a subject for discussion. As children we never asked for any details, not out of disinterest, rather out of respect for his feelings.

It wasn't until much later in my life that I realized that publishing the accounts of his experiences in the Prisoner of War (POW) camps had been a life long dream for my father. Not for the money, it will never be a best seller. Not for the glory, thoughts of glory faded upon his return from Vietnam. No, he has held this dream for so long to ensure the sacrifices of so many Americans would not be lost as the years past. The men and women who served in the Korean War have often been referred to as "The Forgotten People of the Forgotten War". As a country we can not afford to forget, it is our legacy. Most importantly, we can not forget the thousands still listed as Missing in Action (MIA) from both Korea and Vietnam.

I wrote this book to honor my father and his dream. But more importantly, it was written as his lasting tribute to all of those who gave their freedom and their lives so my family and many families like mine can live free. It is intended to honor the over 1250 men listed in the back of this book and all of their comrades in arms. Their sacrifices have not been in vain and will not be forgotten.

George J. Matta Jr.

Table of Contents

CHAPTER 1

The Capture

If I had known what was in store for me on the day I was captured, and the 802 days that followed, I would have continued to fight, even though there was no chance of survival.

The damaged weapons carrier slid to a halt, and we piled up against the cab. The noise was deafening and we could have been yelling at each other but I don't remember hearing anything but the noise of the mortar rounds. The next round came in close and we dove over the tail gate and headed for the ditch. Wherever we looked there were Chinese. They swarmed at us like ants coming out of the side of the hill.

I was scared, damned scared, but I knew we had to fight. I remember men running and then spilling into the snow as they were hit, some quietly, others screaming. I looked over my shoulder and watched one of the men on the other side of the truck disappear in the middle of an explosion. When I turned back the man next to me had been hit shattering what had once been his face.

Oh God, why couldn't we have made the other 100 yards to the bridge and the safety that lay on the other side? I wiped the sweat from my eyes and fired three rounds at the enemy on the hill just across from us. I can remember saying to myself hell, I missed him. This time I took careful aim and he went skidding sideways as the bullet plowed into his side. While he lay there on the ground two of his comrades stopped to help him. Seconds later they also fell.

Please God, don't let me get hit. I rested my head on the stock of my rifle and took a deep breath. *I can't stay here. But I can't run. They'll get me for sure if I run.* I took another look at the bridge.

Over to the left some guys got one of our heavy guns into action. I don't think they got off more than four bursts before they were all dead. It was just as though every damn Chink in North Korea was shooting at them. I tried to get closer to the ground and I remembered, for no apparent reason, the story we use to tell on Okinawa during the last war. When you're in the infantry, don't carry your cigarette papers in your breast pocket – it keeps you from getting close enough to the ground. I have never felt so alone in my life. But even in the panicky feeling that goes with a battlefield, I was conscious of other M-1s firing on both sides of me. *God, I wonder if they're as scared as I am.* My heart was pounding so hard I thought I would choke. I tugged at my collar trying to get a deep breath. Smoke and dirt from the exploding rounds made it tough to see, but there wasn't much to see anyway. They were still swarming over the hills straight at us. I fired my last round and then rolled to get the next clip out. As I did I hit the motionless body laying next to me. I felt like I was going to get sick. Please God, don't let me get hit. I took another look at the bridge. My mind calculated the chances of making a dash for safety. *If I get up and run to the back of the truck, and then if I haven't been hit, run to the rock. And then if I haven't been hit, run down the road to that spot in the ditch. Then, if I haven't been hit, take off for the bridge for all I'm worth.*

Don't be a damn fool, you'll never make it. Their rifles can't hit me if I stay in this ditch. But they had a lot more than rifles out there and they were using them all. I can't stay here forever; I decided to try it. It felt like I had been thinking about it for hours, but in reality it had only been minutes since the first round hit. I struggled to get to my feet to make the dash for the rear of the truck. As I looked towards the vehicle, a machine gun stitched a pattern through the side of the truck. Another crew was methodically working the area between me and the rock. *You'll be killed, don't try it. Hell, you're going to be killed right here if you don't do something quick. This can't last forever.*

Why didn't I go out with the first truck? I would have been across that stupid bridge and still had a chance to see my wife and kid again.

The sight of one of our gunners standing up walking for the truck woke me up. *Get down you crazy fool! Get down!* He kept walking, just like he was taking a walk in the park. His carbine was gripped in his fist, hanging by his side. Little puffs kicked up beside him. He hunched his shoulder and winced in pain. He just stood there then finally crumbled to the ground. His eyes were looking straight at me. *You dirty, rotten...* I fired wildly into the hill ahead of me. I got off about eight shots before I realized my gun was empty. I reached for my cartridge belt to get another clip. I couldn't find one, so I rolled over to get one out of the right side of the belt. Suddenly another loud burst and I felt blood splash on my arm. At first I starred at it in fascination thinking it was my blood. The whine of a ricochet brought me back again. Then I realized the blood was from one of my buddies about 25 yards from me. I pushed the clip into my rifle and moved my gloved thumb out of the way of the bolt, then kicked the operating rod forward with the heel of my hand and looked up again. It was the same sight I had seen earlier. The only difference was they were closer to us now. I thought again about running to the bridge. The final answer was given to me when three mortar rounds hit in succession between me and the bridge. I ducked down again, wanting to cry. For some reason the tears wouldn't come out.

Oh, please God, don't let me die here. Where the hell are we anyhow? I remember someone telling us last night that we were in Hangseong. That's just north of Wonju. What a hell of a place to die. Another Chink stuck his head out from behind a rock on the hill. He carefully looked around and then signaled for those behind him to move forward. I fired and he rolled down the steep slope. Then there was silence. It was shocking, no rifles, no mortars, nothing. I looked over my shoulder and froze.

Okay you dirty bastards, shoot me. Go ahead get it over and shoot me. Twenty gun barrels were pointed at us. *How did they get there? Where did they come from?* I had looked over there just a few minutes ago, and our guys were there. Now just 15 feet away from us were 20 Chinese soldiers. They didn't say anything, but we knew what they wanted. I lifted my rifle. They tensed. I could almost feel their trigger fingers taking up the slack. I nervously looked around me. *God, there are only four of us left.*

"Drop guns."

I could feel the eyes of the other three looking to me. I could commit suicide by making the wrong move. All of them will shoot at once and maybe I won't feel it. There was a pleading in the eyes of the man closest to me. I looked the Chinese soldier nearest to me right in the eye and squared my shoulders. The muzzle of his gun came up and he pointed it right at my gut. I was sure that he was going to shoot me. I could almost read his mind.

He wanted me to make a break, any move, so he could shoot me. His leering made it plain that he was playing for keeps. Every muscle in my body tightened. I remember how tired he looked. We were all tired and almost relieved that it was coming to and end. I dropped my rifle into the muddy ditch, and the other three followed suit. The tangled nerves started to unravel, and the screams that eluded me earlier were now released in an unintelligible growl. That was all that came from my throat. It was over. I was still alive and it was all over.

As of that day, 12 February 1951, my freedom came to an end. If I had known what the next 26 months would bring, I would have invited the quick, certain death further resistance would have brought.

At a signal, we fell into line and were marched across the street and up a hill. The same hill the Chinese had swarmed down to capture us. There was still a lot of fighting taking place on the other side of the hill, so they sat us down to wait it out.

There were two guards assigned to us and they would not let us talk to one another. All we did for the next two hours was wait, each of us sure that we were waiting to die.

I thought about my daughter, my wife, my mother, and the guys in my outfit I had seen massacred this day, and worried. I said a few prayers and tried to keep warm.

The scream of jet engines overhead brought us abruptly back to reality again. We dove into the hill side from habit – our guards did the same. For the next few minutes all hell broke loose just over the crest of the hill as jets cascaded streams of rockets onto the Chinese below.

"Thank God those guys are on our side," I mumbled, mostly to myself. Then I thought that it might be much better if they were somewhere else right now. *Wouldn't it be awful to get killed by our own forces after living through the nightmare of the past few hours?*

Now with their ammunition expended the jets went topside and headed south. Except for scattered rifle fire off in the distance, all was quiet. As the smoke and dust settled on the mountain from the initial shock of an aerial attack, the awesome sight of rockets fired upon exposed troops could be seen. Now screams of the survivors echoed between the hills. Our two guards motioned for us to get to our feet and we started back towards the top of the hill and the nearest Chinese stronghold.

The Chinese must have been very busy the next two days, because not one of them came near us, except the two guards. We had assumed that we would be interrogated immediately, but I guess they weren't too interested in us at the moment. They were preoccupied with pouring more and more of their troops at the American lines.

It was cold that night, awfully cold. About 50 of us were lying on the dirt floor, huddled together for warmth. One of the guards motioned to a pile of hay outside the door. We grabbed handfuls and tried to keep some of the penetrating cold out. We were hungry, but there would be no food this day.

The next day came, and we still were waiting for something to happen. A flight of our jets hurdled the hills and headed for the valley beyond. They caught about fifteen of the Chinese out in the open and the lead jet dropped a tank of napalm. All fifteen disappeared as the jelled gasoline mushroomed into a wall of flames.

With no food or water we were pretty weak when they decided to move us, but even if we had been in good shape the ordeal we were about to face would have worn us down. We didn't know it at the time, but we were the victims of a deliberate attempt to weaken us to the point where we could not go on. Then we would be left to die or be shot. This valley would later become known as Massacre Valley, not without good reason.

On the third day it started. We were lined up, all the prisoners taken the past week, and we started walking. Helping each other as best we could, constantly prodded by the evil-looking guards, we traveled about 20 miles that day. That night we had our first meal since our capture, plain cracked corn. We were so hungry that even it tasted good.

From that point on, we didn't measure time in days, but distance. We marched over many hills and on many roads. We crossed scores of streams, some choked by ice, some shallow enough that we could walk across on the stones. It comes back to me as a nightmare of cruelty and torture, during which the strong turned weak, and the weak were no longer with us.

It must have been about the tenth day when we saw our first chance to escape. Five of us passed the word quietly and decided to take a chance. Anything was better than this constant process to wear us down. One of the five was South Korean. If we got caught it was sure death for him, and possibly for us as well. The North Koreans weren't doing too much for their southern countrymen those days, and the Chinese were doing less. We nicknamed the South Korean "Stewart". The only thing that had kept him alive thus far was the fact he spoke excellent Japanese. Posing as a Japanese-American he was able to stay alive, at least for a while. For the purposes of our escape plan he was to play the part of a North Korean guard.

I passed the word. "When we get out of this village, wait until the guards are far enough up the line and drop out. Pretend you're taking a crap." The four nodded, Stewart even smiled.

The long line of prisoners, with a machine gun armed guard every 50 yards, wound its way through the small village. The few civilian inhabitants that remained came out into the darkness to insult and taunt us. As we left the other end of the village, I looked both ways and stepped into the bushes to the right of the road. The others followed.

The five of us pulled down our pants and squatted. Either the guards didn't see us, or they didn't care, at least they didn't bother us. The column went on past us, hundreds of men, and gradually we relaxed. Guards further to the rear looked at us and probably figured we had the permission of the guards in front. The prisoners in line were too tired to even look our way.

We stayed in that position for about 40 minutes and were only disturbed once. Stewart saw the guard coming, and stood up with a stick in his hand. The guard assumed he was assigned to watch us and turned back to the column. Once the column had passed we stood up.

We carefully checked the trail over which the column had passed and then headed for the main road. We had gone only about half a mile when we ran into a Chinese guard and North Korean civilian. Before I could say a word, Stewart touched me on my sleeve as a warning and spoke to them in Japanese. The Chinese guard looked at the North Korean who acted as interpreter. He then painstakingly advised Stewart, through the North Korean, how Stewart could return his "four prisoners" to the column of captives. Stewart thanked him profusely and we passed on.

"What did he say" I asked.

"Him say Merican prisoners go on right road up ahead. We go left instead, huh?" Stewart whispered back.

I asked, "Why weren't they suspicious when you spoke to them in Japanese?"

Stewart explained that the North Korean thought he was speaking Japanese because he was Chinese and couldn't speak Korean. The Chinese, on the other hand, assumed he was North Korean speaking Korean.

"Never mind, you have me all mixed up now," I said with a grin. "Just keep talking buddy, and see if we can talk our way out of this mess."

We deliberately made the turn in the opposite direction from the one the Chinese soldier had pointed out and found ourselves in a solid stream of Chinese soldiers, heading south. We just fell in along with them and nobody asked any questions, figuring Stewart was our guard.

A varied assortment of men and material flowed over the road that night. The heavy movement of troops, trucks, mule carts, and motorized guns kept the Chinese so busy thinking of the battle that was to come, that we went virtually unnoticed.

A few times when a particularly large unit of Chinese soldiers passed, Stewart would talk to us in Japanese and we would move off to the side of the road and wait until they passed. We were still pretty scared, but very happy to have made it this far. We kept heading south.

We entered a pass about five miles long with steep cliffs on one side and even steeper mountains on the other. This left us no options, we had to stay close to the road until we got out of the pass. Once through, we could head into the hills and away from the enemy column.

We did fine until we neared the end of the pass. I figure we were within a few miles of our lines at that point. But as we turned into the valley, two Chinese guards were waiting for us. The sight of them coming out of the bushes, guns aimed straight at us, brought us to an immediate stop. They were in front of us before we ever saw them. They challenged Stewart for his authority to transfer prisoners.

Stewart did his best to talk us out of this one too, but since he was taking prisoners south rather than north they insisted on seeing his pass. He went through the motions of searching his pockets, but they were suspicious enough to realize he was bluffing. If he had even had a scrap of paper on him we could have been on our way, we knew they couldn't read Korean, but without it we were recaptured.

They tied our hands behind our backs and headed us north once again. While it was obvious these guards meant business, they were not as abrupt as our previous captors. They seemed unconcerned with our conversations. Stewart began to tell us what had taken place in his discussion with them. It seems that these two Chinese soldiers belonged to an outfit that had captured two American soldiers earlier that day. The two had escaped by overpowering their guards, tied them up and taken their weapons. The two guards who had caught us were waiting for them to try to make their way out of the pass. If this earlier chain of events hadn't taken place we would have never been caught.

At first, our two captors seemed confused. They had been ordered to look for two American soldiers armed with a machine gun and a pistol. Instead they had captured five unarmed escapees. They finally decided to abandon their post and return us to the holding area. This probably meant that the other two American prisoners would make it to safety. The thought of this, and the fact they didn't decide to shoot us and wait for the other escapees, lifted our spirits a bit.

It was a feeling that would only last a short time as we realized the position that Stewart was in. As long as they were convinced that he was an American soldier he was not in any more danger than the rest of us. But if they found out that he was South Korean, coupled with the fact he was helping us escape, it would be curtains for him. I could see he was worried about it as well.

As we trudged northward, our hands lashed behind our backs, I began to tell Stewart about California to take his mind off his predicament, but more importantly to give him information to keep up the charade.

"Tell them you are a Jap." I explained. "Tell them you were born in Reedley, California. Your mother and father are American citizens. Tell them you worked in a grape packing house in Reedley. You understand?" He nodded.

I gave him the address of my aunt in Reedley and described the entire countryside in that part of the country, including all the surrounding towns. I had visited that area for a year just after my return from World War II, and I used my experiences there to give him some facts to back up his story. We knew it was a long shot, but we were desperate, it had to work.

We walked for about ten miles that night. Then they locked four of us in a big concrete vault-like structure. It was about ten feet square, no windows, and a big steel door. The door was solid except for a four inch hole at about eye level. Stewart was taken away to be questioned.

After about two hours the door clanged open and Stewart was thrown in. He was badly beaten. One eye was closed and there were long strips of skin missing from his cheek and chin. But through it all he was still smiling.

"I am an American soldier," he said, and then simply passed out. He had passed another test. At least for now Stewart would be treated as an American, a member of the U.S. Army. I felt sure that given enough time to brief him, he could pass any interrogation they threw at him - or answer any questions they tried to beat out of him. Since I was from Massachusetts they would never connect the incidents of Stewart's new life with my own.

Over the next three days, they really put the pressure on us. I guess they were hoping one of us would crack. But none of us did. At all hours of the day and night, at an irregular schedule, they would bang on the steel door with clubs until the noise was unbearable. We couldn't hear ourselves think. We tried to figure out how they were timing their noise barrages, but I guess that was part of the "treatment", wondering how long it would be until the next assault. We might get one hour, or three. We had two hours without noise once and then the pounding every eight to ten minutes for the next hour.

During those three days we were fed only once. The meal consisted of sorghum and soybeans rolled into a ball about the size of a baseball. The door remained locked and by the end of the second day the stench was unbelievable. We were forced to relieve ourselves inside the room, and the four inch opening in the door provided very little ventilation. We felt like animals. By then we were probably acting like animals as well. It was all a part of their softening up process to make sure we understood who was in charge. This was all intended to get us to the point where we would answer any question just to be relieved from the noise and horrible living conditions. It was as though they expected us to develop the attitude that hitting ourselves over the head with a hammer was good because it felt so good when we stopped.

At the end of the third day they took us to something they called a hospital. It more closely resembled a morgue. It was where the seriously wounded were left to die. God only knows how many of our men did just that in this place. Since none of us were badly injured we weren't there very long. Just long enough to rip up our undershirts and shorts to make bandages for those in the worst condition. We knew full well that most of them would eventually die. The real tragedy is that it would have taken so little to save most of them, just simple medical attention. But the communists were not about to go out of their way to save these poor souls.

Out of this mass, about fifty of us were capable of walking and were started on a march where most were to suffer the same fate as those left behind - death.

After marching for hours without a break we were all pretty weary. They said that we were going to the rear, but in reality we were going up, moving uphill ever since we started. Breathing was difficult and the muscles in my legs were tied up in knots. I was on the tail end of the line. The guard behind us was getting on my nerves.

I stumbled. "Move, keep moving. No lagging!" he shouted.

"Get off my back you son of a bitch or I'll kill you," I said, mostly to myself. *Where the hell are they taking us now?* A couple of the guys up ahead were really having a rough time. We were all deliberately walking as slowly as the guards would allow. We tried to give them a break. We knew if they fell out of line it would be over for them.

Tired as we were, four of the men ahead of me helped the two exhausted men, supporting them on each side despite the narrow trail. They continued to stumble every few yards. The guards never let up.

"Move, keep moving. No lagging!"

I was beginning to think that was the only English they knew. The prod of a bayonet convinced me I couldn't stall much more. I moved up with the rest of the pack.

We were a few hundred yards passed a small village when the guard grabbed me and the four men just ahead of me.

"You, all of you, go back down the road. Bring up the food." Food, did he say food? We hadn't had a meal in so long I'd forgotten what food tasted like. One of the men said "Ya jerk, why didn't you let us stop while we were in the village?" I knew how he felt. A few hundred yards felt like miles at this point. But I told him to stow it. I knew this guy was crazy enough to shoot.

We started back down the trail towards the village. We didn't talk too much, we were too tired. We got to the village and a guard came running up with his gun at the ready.

"You halt!" he commanded. "Where you go?"

"We were sent down to get food," I explained.

"You lie, there is no food. Go back."

Hell, here we go again. We started back up the trail.

Then a shot rang out, then another. "Hit it!" I yelled and we dove for the bushes. I figured they were shooting at us. We lay panting on the ground for a few minutes, but nothing happened. We couldn't hear anything. So we started up the hill again. If we delayed much longer it would have meant trouble.

As we approached the column I spotted the guards moving something into the bushes. I paused. *Oh no, Mother of God, no.* I whispered to the other four, "Quick follow me, don't look around. Keep coming. Keep coming."

I took a closer look and saw that what the guards were putting in the bushes were two bodies. There was blood on their heads. Now I knew what caused the shots we heard earlier.

We caught up to the rear of the column and the interpreter hurried back to meet us.

"What did you see? Tell me what you saw." His tone was very insistent.

"What do you mean?"

"Did you see soldiers back there?"

"You mean the soldiers back there where there wasn't any food," I said.

"No," he answered, "The other ones."

"I didn't see any other ones. Why, did some get lost?" I hoped the desperation I felt wasn't reflected on my face.

"Never mind, That's okay." He headed forward again.

"What happened?" I whispered to the man ahead of me. He didn't even look around at me, just remained silent.

A few seconds later he replied, "They couldn't keep up with us. They had to fall out. That dirty bastard said they were going to put them in a house until they got better. Then we heard the shots. Are they...?"

"Yeah. Both shot."

"The dirty, rotten, sonofabitches..."

"Stow it, they'll hear you," I whispered fiercely.

"You're lucky. If they found out you saw it they would have shot you too."

"Yeah, I suppose." I still hadn't come to the point where I understood that the Chinks were capable of such things without giving it a second thought. Thank God, I'm still alive.

One thing I did realize now was that we had to learn real soon when to fight back and when not to. I don't think we ever really stopped fighting back - when we had a chance to gain something. We had to be smart enough not to fight back against hopeless odds to stay alive. The feeling of complete despair, along with the horror and torture we had seen to this point had proven to us that we had to take the path of least resistance, at least for now. Giving in on some minor point today meant that we would live to see tomorrow, and tomorrow might give us the chance we need.

The main problem with the situation we now found ourselves in was that the life and death decisions had to be made quickly, leaving little time to distinguish the minor points from the major ones.

The distinction was also blurred by the fact that we were so sick, tired, and hurt that even the most outrageous indignities, that would have appalled us earlier, now didn't even penetrate our feelings.

It was at our next stop that I found that we still were fighting the wrong battles.

Four Chinese guards came into the building they had thrown us in to search us. Some of us got real smart, yeah, real smart. We took off our rings and watches placing them on the dark floor and sat on them. Our judgment was so clouded we didn't realize that even if they weren't found during this inspection, they would be on the next. The searches came all to frequently. For less than fifty bucks in jewelry each of us were risking the beatings that were sure to come.

When the beatings did come they taught us a lesson in relative values - the only thing really important was our lives and the lives of our buddies. Nothing else mattered, nothing else was worth the risk.

During the next few days we came to find out how animals in the zoo feel. After assuring themselves that we were beaten, mentally and physically, they made a point to parade us through the town and call out all the townspeople to see us. It wasn't a pretty sight. It surely wasn't the parade we thought would be awaiting us when we entered this "police action". It was the parade of some pathetic human beings who were fighting for survival, not of a heroic army fighting for freedom. It was however a good show for the citizens.

The show finally ended when some of the Korean people didn't react the way the communists had expected, throwing us tobacco and cigarettes. We were to spend the night in the home of some of the Koreans. It was apparent that they were forced to open their homes as much as we were forced to stay there. It was in some of these homes that we experienced the first acts of kindness we had seen since our capture. We were given some food out of sight of our Chinese captors. Some of the North Koreans had found that their Chinese allies were treating them as badly as they were treating the Americans. They seemed to know that the members of the Chinese army were invaders, not the friends from the north they pretended to be. They had seen too many of their countrymen pushed aside by the Chinese in their ruthless attempts at conquest.

Eventually our pitiful group reached the "Bean Camp," so called because all we ever got to eat there were bean balls made from sorghum and half cooked soy beans. It was April 17, 1951 and only 35 of the fifty that began this journey were still alive.

CHAPTER 2

Bean Camp

They joined us in with some other unfortunates and then separated us into groups of ten. We dragged ourselves into our assigned huts. I don't know what we expected, and God knows we had seen enough Korean huts, but this one was particularly lousy.

I can remember all the times we complained about how bad the Army supplied us. Looking back on it from this vantage point, I realized how wonderful the Army's logistics system was. Even when things were really tough in combat we got food, when it was cold we got blankets, when sick we got medicine. Even if things just cooled off a bit we got shelter. It may be a hole in the ground, an elaborate sand bag bunker or a pup tent. Now all we got were Korean huts. No matter where we went, it was a dirty, filthy Korean hut.

This one amounted to two rooms constructed out of packed mud. One room served as a combination living room, dining room and bedroom. The other was a tiny kitchen. The ten of us would live in this eight foot square patch of earth. The only equipment provided to us was an improvised table and crummy blankets, absolutely nothing else. We slept on the dirt floor and would make shelves by digging out an area in the mud walls. We were surprised to find an electric light supported by a mostly bare wire. We also found that the Koreans had long ago learned an ingenious way to heat their huts by building a series of tunnels under the floor.

The fire in the kitchen was made in a fireplace fashioned from mud and rocks. The tunnels under the floor were connected to this fire source and drew heat from it forming an elaborate, if not primitive, heating system. A cast-iron pot hung over the fireplace and we used it for everything.

"Well, well, well, home at last – at least until they decide to move us again."

"Call this dump home, hell, I've seen more comfortable foxholes."

"I'll bet these knockers won't even let us try to clean it up."

The rest of us were much too tired to even comment about the accommodations. It was a place to rest, and God knows it was time to rest.

I took off my uniform for the first time in weeks. I couldn't remember the last time I had clean clothes. As I took my pants off I stopped and just starred at myself. Being of Lebanese decent I naturally had a lot of hair on my body, chest, back, shoulders and legs. I stood in shock as I found that all the hair on my body was gone. Instead of hair I found my body was now covered with blood sucking lice. Once I was finally able to look around the room I found that the other men were making the same discovery.

As part of my training I remembered reading that epidemics can be carried through lice and I began to worry. "Here's the first thing we've got to do," I commented to the room in general. "These damned things will kill us if we don't get rid of them fast."

"Let's get to it then, I want to see if I have any skin left," one of the boys said. There were a lot of wise cracks while we killed the lice, but we all knew how deadly serious it was. We agreed on the spot – "anybody that doesn't clean the lice off of them can get the hell out of this hut." We meant it and everyone got the message without further elaboration.

It took hours working with fingernails, picking one off, capturing it between our fingernails and squashing it. My hands looked like I had dipped them in my wife's red nail polish before I was half finished. My wife, I wonder what she is doing now. I wonder if she knows I'm alive. I wonder if the Army's telegram told her that I was killed, missing in action, or POW. Oh, dear God, take care of her and my little girl. Please let me get back to them safely. Please let me live through this hell. I can't let go, they need me so much. I was sure the family would look after them till I got home. But my daughter won't even know me when I get home, if I get home.

It took days to completely rid ourselves of all the lice and at that it took every minute of our time. By then one pest was replaced by another. Flies so thick we had to keep our hands moving back and forth over our food to get it into our mouths. They would swarm onto any open cut or bruise. They covered our dead buddies. The smell of death hung in the air. Death is the only smell you can taste. Anyone who has lived near a dead body knows what I mean.

I began to wonder when you become immune to human feelings. When do you look at a bloated body, the skin so tight it is ready to burst, without getting sick? When do you pass a skeleton without wondering who he was, what did he look like? I didn't know the answer to these things yet and hoped I never would. But if I ever did find these answers I was sure they would be found in a place such as this.

The latrine at Bean Camp was a hundred yards from our hut. It didn't take us long to learn that unless you had dysentery you would be better off to make as few trips out there as possible.

One of the guys from the 187th Airborne learned this lesson the hard way. He started out one night and as he approached the latrine, he heard; "Halt, where you go?" It was the guard.

"Right out there to the latrine, " he replied.

"Take off your boots," the guard demanded.

"You go to hell buddy, I ain't taking these things off in this weather for nobody."

"Take off your boots, now!" the guard got rough.

"Now look, what's the idea, I need these boots." He said pointing to the jump boots on his feet. "What will I use for shoes?"

"I give you my sneakers," the guard replied. He held up a beat-up pair of tennis shoes, the foot gear of oriental soldiers.

"Oh, no you don't, I'll be damned if I freeze my feet just because you want a pair of jump boots...Ohhh" The guard had swung the butt of his rifle against the soldier's head. He fell to the ground fighting to stay conscious.

We heard the commotion and looked out the door. The guard was getting furious because each time he reached for the boots he was kicked by the still resistant soldier. "Beat me, you sonofabitch, but you'll have to fight me for these boots, I ain't gonna freeze my feet."

One of the guys in the hut took off to get the interpreter. He yelled at the interpreter, "You told us we were going to be treated as prisoners of war, not slaves. What the hells the idea of that guard stealing those boots?"

The interpreter ran to the seen of the incident as the guard climbed off the top of the soldier. I don't know what the interpreter said to the guard but from the looks he was giving us it must of been hell.

The interpreter then helped the soldier off the ground and said, "So sorry, it was a misunderstanding. The guard did not want your boots. It will not happen again."

Yeah, it won't happen again – not until the next time. The guards continued to try to force us to give up what little clothing we had every chance they got. Sometimes they would strip us down to our underwear, but they were mainly after good boots, watches, wallets, and rings.

Everyone was a target of opportunity for the guards, dead or alive. In combat you never get use to watching someone die and be carried off the battlefield, but at least you know he will get a descent burial. Even when you are not in combat, because of the way we live, you expect some kind of funeral – or at least some respect. You never get use to seeing a man laying stiff on the ground. You know that no matter what your circumstances are something must be done – he has to be buried.

Our problem in the camp was finding out when we had one to bury.

One night I started for the latrine and had walked about fifty feet when I saw him. He was not only dead, but naked.

I can't tell you how I felt. It was a mix of embarrassment and shame. Nakedness on a living being is one thing, but on a dead man, laying on the snow covered ground, frozen solid, is something that defies description. I looked around for something, anything, to put over him. I finally took my jacket off and laid it over his head. What entered my thoughts next made me realize the effect this place was having on me. I remember saying to myself, "Take back your jacket, the Chinks will just steal it if you leave it here." I stifled a sob, grabbed the jacket, and stumbled back to the hut.

That night we made a decision. Whenever one of our buddies died, we would appoint an honor guard to stand watch over him until we were given a chance to bury him.

The first few nights we had to fight with our bare fists to keep the Commies from undressing the dead. But those soldiers were buried with their clothes on – but then we found another striking character flaw in these Chinese.

Less than a week later. We were carrying a dead sergeant up the hill to lay him to rest. Four of us carried the body and two others followed with a shovel – we had insisted that the company commander furnish us with one.

None of us were prepared for the sight that met us at the top of the hill. All the bodies we had buried the past three days were dug up. They were all naked.

Callous as it may sound, we wouldn't have minded too much if they had only buried them again, but as we now knew, they had absolutely no respect for our dead.

If this is communism, and I think it is, they can have it. When we protested to the Chinese commanders they had the gall to tell us the dogs had dug them up. Some smart dogs that can dig up a body and undress it.

It was also here that we had our first experience with brainwashing.

In those days we weren't familiar with the term. What we did know was that they did their best to get us as physically and mentally exhausted as possible and then would drum in the same bits of propaganda over and over. Eventually it was hard to tell the fact from the fiction. In the beginning their efforts were careless and laughable. It was easy to fight back.

Our first lecture was on combat situations. They drilled it into us that the Chinese People's Volunteers and the North Korean People's Army had pushed the United Nations troops all the way back to Pusan. One of the "Facts" they gave us was that the U.S. troops would be pushed all the way back into the sea. One of the men decided to dispute this fact. He jumped to his feet and yelled, "The only way you bastards will ever get to Pusan is the way I got to this Goddamned hole – as a prisoner."

They were very patient. He didn't get any food that night. The following day they spent hours "convincing" him that they were right.

We soon found that we could use this process to our advantage. If we pretend to accept one of their "Facts" we could get a meal, some sleep, and they would leave us alone for a while. Our education on which battles were worth fighting was beginning to pay off.

Each of us knew where we stood. Life here is unbearable. Tell them yes to anything to make it a little easier. Tell them anything, we know you don't mean it.

The knowledge that we stuck solidly together in this little scheme made it easier to fight back when we felt we could no longer sell our dignity. Every now and then we each had to take a stand. If for no other reason than to reassure ourselves that we were worthy of survival. When one prisoner was told he would not get any supper because of his arguments against the "party line." The defiant one knew that meant he would get more to eat than the rest of us in the hut. Each man in our hut would sneak a mouthful of their meager rations to the disobedient soldier. It was our way of paying tribute to him.

Infections, beatings, starvation, and exposure, all served to thin out our ranks over the next few weeks. It was more than just one or two now and then. It was ten or twelve men each day. More than anything else it was the lack of proper food and medicine that took it's toll. We begged for more food for the starving and more medicine for the sick, promising to work even harder to make it up. Our efforts resulted in even less food and even less attention being paid to our sick and wounded. We hated ourselves for even thinking that our begging would accomplish anything.

Their excuse was always the same. "Sorry, we would like to feed you and give you medicine, but your planes bombed train with your supplies."

After hearing that excuse over and over in answer to our pleas, I decided it was my time to assert my dignity. I challenged, "It's damned funny that our planes bomb our supply train and let yours come through. How stupid do you think we are?" That cost us some more food and some more sleep.

The march to our next location was the longest and by far the toughest. This one lasted twenty-three days and it seemed to have only one objective – to get rid of as many of us as possible.

It began on the 24th of April, 1951, when 760 of us were formed up and told to walk. That first day we walked about 30 miles and most of the weaker ones died that day, being shot as they fell out of line. It wasn't anything we hadn't seen on our way to the Bean Camp, only the numbers were larger.

At the end of the first day we stopped in a small village. To hide us from air attacks they jammed us into small huts. There were about fifty of us to each structure. Those of us that were able stood in order to allow the sick and wounded enough room to lay on the ground. Some of the men would collapse from sheer exhaustion and fall on the wounded men at their feet. The interpreter laughed as he called, "Get all the rest you can, we move out early."

The day that followed was even worse. We needed water desperately. We protested to the guards who finally stopped us a short distance from a well. We became delirious at the thought of getting a cool drink. Each of us that were in fairly good shape took the canteen of a wounded man and headed for the well.

As we approached the well the guards pushed us back using their bayonets for emphasis. We got the message, we were to go no further.

"We want a drink!" we yelled.

"You wait!" the guards said, pushing us back with sadistic grins.

Actually we didn't mind too much at first. After all we were the captors and they had a right to drink first. We stood silently watching as they each took their turn at the well, the first clean water we had seen in days.

As they finished, however, we were stunned when they ordered, "Get back in line, we march."

"Hey, we need some water. Those men are dying. We can't go any further without water." They laughed at us as if it was some big joke. One of the men screamed, "You dirty bastard, I want a drink", and headed for the well. He was struck by a blow from one of the guards and now lay helpless on the ground just a few feet from his goal. The rest of us turned toward the column of thirsty men and we went on without the water.

We had barely started moving forward again when another man began cursing the guards for not giving us water. He received the same reward - a rifle butt to the head. It was no use, these beasts lacked human emotion. To them this was simply another step in their methodical process to break us down.

I think we marched all over Korea, at least we felt that way. I honestly don't know what kept us going. Maybe it was seeing that many of us who couldn't go on were left to die or be killed.

The next day we stopped marching and rode - if you can call it that. We were packed, standing up, in a railroad coal car and traveled in that position for the next three days. There was no room to lie down or even sit. We were packed so tightly into that car that as men fell asleep or worse yet died, they would do so remaining upright.

During the second day on the rails, just before daylight, the train stopped. They were afraid of air raids so they pulled the train into a railroad tunnel. This proved to be worse than the ride because they deliberately left the smoke from the stack of this old locomotive pouring out smoke. The black smoke was scolding hot and suffocating. We remained in the tunnel for hours. We waited in terror for something to happen, knowing that whatever was to happen would mean death to more of us who had already seen our share of ordeals. By noon we were all more dead than alive as the bitter fumes choked off the breath of already sick men. By early afternoon three men had died in my car alone. We could stand it no longer, climbing through the thick smoke, over the walls of the train car, we dropped to the tracks below. From there most of us were barely able to crawl the few feet to fresh air.

We carried the three dead men, along with many more from other cars, to a bomb crater about seventy-five yards from the track. We intended to bury these poor souls but the guards wouldn't allow that. We were made to leave them lying there as we were forced back to the edge of the tunnel.

Later they brought us some sorghum which we attacked like the starving animals we had become. Then we were placed back onto the train to continue our miserable journey. On the fourth day we started on foot once again.

They kept telling us we were being taken to the rear where we would be safe from our planes. At times I was sure that we had walked far enough to be half way into China by now. I'm sure we were taken around in circles most of the time. It was a process that was reaching it's intended outcome - turning us into zombies.

On May 17th, my birthday, I found out how it feels to be dead. I thought I was and by all rights should have been.

It started as we climbed a long mountain trail. It must have been a mile straight up. Even though I was sure I couldn't make it another hundred yards, I kept myself going by telling myself over and over, *Gee, this will be easy going down the other side.*

But as I soon found this was another of Korea's one-sided mountains. When we reached to summit there in front of us was another hill just a little higher than the one we just struggled up.

Oh, God, I'll never make this one. It became an endless routine, dragging one foot in front of the other, stumbling, half falling, slipping backwards on the muddy trail.

Half way up this second hill I had given all I had to give. I couldn't force myself to take even one more step. I was too tired to think of the consequences. I had to stop, to rest just for a minute. I eased my exhausted body to the ground. *All I need is a minute or two then I can make it.*

But one of the guards spotted me before I saw him. Even though I knew he was coming for me I couldn't move. He took his rifle by the barrel and with a full swing hit me across the head with the butt of the gun. I rolled face down to the ground. I was still conscious, but all I could see were lights, and my head felt as though it had been ripped right off my shoulders.

Oh, my God, I'm heartily sorry for having offended thee. I confess all my sins... Jesus Christ, just get it over with - shoot me and get it over with... what are you waiting for? Even though I couldn't see him I knew he was still standing over me with his rifle. I had seen this act played out too many times before, I knew what to expect. I tensed up waiting for the bullet to hit and extinguish what little life was left in me.

I was surprised to feel a pair of hands lifting me to my feet. *Why didn't they kill me like they had killed so many others?* It was Pete Murphy, he was carrying me the rest of the way up the hill.

But I had already given up, I thought it was over, I wanted a quick escape from this torture. "Let me go, don't try to carry me," I mumbled. I could feel the blood running into my eyes and my stomach turning inside out.

"Hold on sarge, I'll help you," a voice whispered in my ear, "Keep moving, sarge, I'll take care of you."

"No, I can't. I can't walk any more, they'll kill you too," I moaned. But he dragged me over the top of the hill and my head began to clear.

God was with me that day. Half way down that hill, the hill I thought was my final resting place, our "Death March" came to an end. God must have heard my prayers when he arranged to have Camp No. 1 located just a mile from where I had my head knocked in. Having to endure even one more hill would have meant the end for me.

CHAPTER 3

Camp No. One

There it stood at the bottom of the mountain looking just like all the other Korean villages we had seen. Camp No. 1 was a mass of mud huts with straw roofs. The huts were positioned so they formed a large semi-circle.

We were led over a bridge and passed some of the huts occupied by Korean civilians inside the compound. I kept hoping they would let us stop for a rest. As soon as we spotted American prisoners on the other side of the road we knew we would get a rest. Our next hope was that this would be our last stop and there would be no more marches from this place.

As the column began to slow it's pace I picked up a tin can that was lying on the side of the road. Then we moved slowly toward a group of empty huts and I began picking dandelions that were growing in little patches. I had filled the can with these buds before we reached the huts. Other than my rosary beads these were my only possessions.

The huts were pretty well beat, no windows, no doors, sagging roofs. Finally we stopped and the guards started separating us into groups of twelve. Each group was assigned to a hut.

The prisoners that were here before we arrived were only fifty yards away and were pressed against the barbed wire staring at the new tenants. Some tried to sneak under the wire and come over to us but the guards moved them back.

Someone on the other side yelled, "Anybody from Connecticut?"

"No I don't think so," was the reply from one in our group.

"Where are you coming from?" came a query from the other side.

"Damned if I know," someone said. "Where are we now?"

"Camp No. 1" he answered.

"Where's that?"

"Damned if I know," he called back.

At that point I was shocked to see one of the prisoners on the other side of the road try to get to the latrine. He was pulling himself along the ground with his hands, two stumps dragging out behind him.

"What happened to him?" we yelled.

"Him, that's Tulley from Alabama. His legs froze off."

We stared in silence. This was an indication of the treatment we could expect in Camp No. 1.

We didn't have much else to say, we were too tired.

At that point a Chinese guard ordered us inside. The twelve of us entered the ten by ten foot hut and dropped to the ground. The guard came in, counted us, then left. It was mid afternoon, not a typical time to stop during our march. We began to wonder if this would be just another rest stop or if we really were going to stay here.

We sure weren't much to look at. We hadn't shaved or changed clothes in more than three months. But we didn't try to clean up, we just sat and waited for something to happen. We gradually fell asleep.

Of more than seven hundred that started this terrible march only around one hundred were still alive.

As one day stretched into two, then days into weeks, we realized that at least for a while we were going to remain here.

It didn't take long before the brainwashing, something they called indoctrination, began. We treated it in this camp just as we had in the Bean Camp. At the start it was so clumsy we treated it as a joke, then we got indignant-trying to tell them off. That got us into trouble. Finally we tried to make it into a game, and our game was discovered quite by accident.

We had just gotten settled into Camp No. 1, settling into our day-to-day routine. The twelve of us were sitting in the hut when the commissar came in. The first time I met him I didn't think it would be possible for a guy like him to get on my nerves, but after lectures two or three hours a day, every day, telling the same lies, he really got to be a pain.

In perfect English he started. "Good morning, sergeants." He bowed low.

"Good morning, teacher," I muttered and the gang caught on. We all bowed low and parroted like schools kids, "Good morning, teacher."

"Ah, so," he smiled, obviously pleased with the progress he was making this day.

"Ass hole, yourself," I mumbled, mockingly.

"Our relationship will not be the usual one between prisoner and captor. You are to consider me your friend. I am your instructor, you are my students. If you cooperate, attend to your studies, you will find certain advantages that will make your life here in camp a lot more agreeable. If you don't...if you persist in reactionary attitude, you must be prepared to suffer the consequences. I hope my meaning is clear."

We didn't take his opening remarks to kindly. Here we are half starved, more dead than alive, and this clown is calling us students.

He pulled out a typewritten sheet of paper and started his lecture. This one was a hodgepodge of lies, as they all were. So began the hours of misery during which we dared not fall asleep. To sleep meant the guards standing behind us would start clubbing the insolent student.

"You..." He pointed at Carlie Duggan.

"Me?"

"Get up!"

"Why did you come five thousand miles to fight the peace loving people of North Korea?"

"Come again," said Carlie.

"You heard the question. Answer it!"

"Hell, I came because I was ordered to. I'm a soldier. I go where they tell me."

"You were duped by the capitalists who are false to the masses. You were sent here to fight so they can make more money. That is why the warmongers in America invaded the land of the peace loving North Koreans. They told you lies."

"That's a crock..." I said.

"What's that?" he screamed at me. "What does that mean?" I noticed that two of the guards had their rifles raised and were closing in on me. I put an innocent expression on my face and replied, "It just means, if you say so, I didn't mean any harm."

One of the men started to giggle, but stopped when I gave him a worried look. The whole hut was in silence. The instructor tried to make sense of the two phrases. He decided he had not been insulted and waved the guards off. I let out a sigh of relief. So this was how it was going to be.

The remainder of the lecture that day covered many subjects but mainly focused on a few areas. Russia was wonderful. It is China's friend. It's everybody's friend. The collective farmers are much better off than the U.S. farmers. New farms are going up all the time. A Russian worker can easily afford a fur coat or diamond ring for his wife. He makes over $400 a month. America grinds all the Negroes into the dirt. America discriminates against all minorities – the Catholics, the Protestants, the Jews, the Italians, the Irish, the Poles, the veterans, the workers, the...well you get the idea. He also insisted that the U.S. is attempting world domination, is imperialistic, and is trying to add Korea and Japan to it's conquests. Morgan and Dupont control the country, Russia and China won the last war, and on, and on, and on.

I must admit the commissar did a marvelous job of controlling his temper most of the time. He was doing his best to make friends of us. He was intelligent enough to expect arguments. He remained very calm as long as the arguments consisted of words he understood. It was only when we talked in slang that he started to worry and would become angry. He wanted to make damned sure he knew what we were talking about. It was obvious that he was firmly convinced he was right.

He knew a lot about America, but from a distorted point of view. He was so sure what we told him were lies.

It was when we wouldn't allow him to distort our truths that the threats of punishments would come. That happened at the end of this lecture.

The instructor had been going on and on about the capitalists "exploiting the workers."

"Things were so bad in the United States in 1949 that the capitalists had to make more money. So they flooded the market with automobiles, just to make the workers spend their money. And of course, the workers couldn't afford these new automobiles," he smiled and looked around the room.

"Isn't that true?" he asked Carlie.

"That ain't the way I heard it." he replied.

"What do you mean?" the instructor asked.

"Well, back in 1949, I wanted to buy a car and I had to put my name on a waiting list."

"You lie, you lie" the instructor said.

"Ok, I lie, if you say so, but it seems to me that I can remember putting my name on a list and waiting a long time before I got the car I wanted."

"You don't understand," the instructor went on. "You were just waiting for an old car. The market was flooded with new cars. The capitalists wanted you to spend your money for a new car which you couldn't afford. That was to keep you poor. The waiting lists were just for old cars."

Then he decided to strike back at Carlie.

"What is your name?" he asked.

"Sgt. Duggan."

"You've been in trouble before, haven't you?"

"No, Sir."

"Weren't you in jail once for destroying property?"

"Oh, that. Yes, sir."

"I see. You are just trying to be funny. How much education have you had?"

"I finished high school – twelve years," Carlie replied.

"You see, you are just plain stupid."

"I may be stupid buster, but I did put my name on a list. I waited six months for my NEW car, brand-spanking NEW, Buick convertible. And it didn't break me. I could have paid cash, but I financed it just to keep some money in the bank while I paid for it." He sat down.

"Guards, guards, take that prisoner away and teach him a lesson." The instructor was mad now. He had lost his point.

"Wait a minute," I yelled. The instructor looked me dead in the eye and kept on talking.

"Look, first you say we're students, then you say we're prisoners. Make up your mind. If you want us to discuss these things, say so. Otherwise, we'll just shut up and let you spout. You asked Sgt. Duggan a question and he answered it. Why don't you let him alone. So he bought a Buick, so what. Is that any reason to lock him up?"

"Ah, so," the instructor queried, "and what is your name?"

"I'm Sgt. Matta," I replied, angrily, "and what's so surprising about buying a car in 1949? That's a lot of hogwash about flooding the market. Sgt. Duggan is right. We had to wait in line to get a car that year. And we didn't have to be capitalists to get one. Hell, my family owns five cars and a truck and we're just plain, ordinary Americans."

"Aha, I see." the instructor said. He seemed to be amused. "You are all going to keep lying just to protect one another. I see I will have to do a lot of work with this class. You just don't understand. Class dismissed." He strode from the room.

We sat there and looked at each other. What gives with this guy? We tell him the truth and he thinks we're stupid. We tell him more truth and he thinks we're lying. How are you going make any sense out of a guy like that?

It got worse, and worse, each day. These Communists believe lies about America so fervently that they could not handle the little bits of truth we dared tell them. They were so completely snowed under with all the garbage they were spewing that even if we gave them detail, point by point, they thought we were lying. It just didn't make sense to us. It didn't make it any easier to live there either.

During the remainder of that summer we did our best to stay alive. We knew many of us would not make it. It seemed that every day we lost a few more, some to neglect, some to beatings, and some were killed outright.

Something else that was hard to live with was the lack of medical attention. We thought the maggots we found at the Bean Camp were bad but even they couldn't prepare us this.

The activities that were common place before our capture, keeping clean and simply taking care of oneself, were now a life and death struggle. These things that now meant so much were not easy to accomplish in this environment.

One of the hazards we now had to battle was the dysentery that the blow flies spread, and that the Chinese did little or nothing about. If someone were too weak or neglected to take care of himself, the flies would lay eggs in any opening in his body they could find - nose, ears, eyes - and then their maggots would go to work on him. Sick call was held about once every two weeks. If someone were really bad off we would keep him away from the hospital on purpose. Whenever someone was placed in the hospital they inevitably died shortly thereafter. Some six hundred men had gone into the dungeon, as we called it, and I can remember only one of the seriously injured who ever come out alive. There really wasn't much sense in going to sick call anyway. You would be lucky to get any medicine at all and even if you did the dose was too small to do any good. Most of the medicine consisted of hot water and powdered charcoal administered by Dr. Haung (the water doctor) who was anything but a good representative of the medical profession.

During one period of dysentery I got so bad that I was passing blood. I guessed my insides were all messed up. I knew from the first aid training the army gave us that salt water will heal a surface wound. I figured that maybe eating salt would help heal my stomach. Since self aid was only aid we received I would have to find a way to get some salt on my own. But where could I get some salt?

The so-called hospital was about a mile up the road. Other than Dr. Haung the staff consisted of his assistant, and eight Chinese girls who tried to act like nurses. I forced myself to hobble to sick call hoping I would get an opportunity to do some exploring. My chance came as they were examining a group of other prisoners that just entered. There were plenty of them so I knew I would have enough time.

I snuck out the room and down to the kitchen and without any trouble located and stole some salt. I rolled it into some balls and took one about four times a day. Along with the salt I burned some maize down into a black charcoal-like mixture and ate it. This unorthodox prescription cured my dysentery within two weeks.

These home made remedies were great when they worked and when they did we passed them along. Unfortunately some of the medical problems that developed in the camp we could not cure.

One of the guys named George Sparks fell into this category and is a vivid reminder of their brand of medical care.

We all had something that served as our personal connection back to the world we had left. For George it was a replica of the U.S. flag he had fashioned on a small piece of cardboard. He always had it with him.

George had severe boils on his feet from the long march to the camp. These boils would normally be harmless, but here they became infected.

"We've got to do something with George's foot," I whispered one day as we left the hut. "It's swollen so badly that he'll lose his foot if it isn't stopped soon."

"He'll lose his life you mean, did you see those maggots? What can we do?" a friend of mine from New York whispered back.

"We'd better go see the water doctor, maybe he'll give us some medicine. Hell, one shot of penicillin would probably clear it up," I said.

"I just can't see that sonofabitch giving us anything," he said resignedly, "but come on, let's give it a try."

We headed for the hospital and asked to see Dr. Haung. After a long wait we were allowed into his office. I said, "Doctor, one of our men is dying from a foot infection and we can't get any medicine for him. He needs it badly. Can we have some?"

We could see the negative answer forming in his face before he even said a word. It was all we could do to contain our temper.

"He should have taken better care of his feet," he said. "We have no medicine except for those in the hospital."

"But he needs it," I pleaded.

"So sorry, but our records do not show anybody in the camp in need of medicine except those in the hospital," he dismissed us. I choked back the urge to tell him what I was thinking. He doesn't dare go into the hospital, at least he's got a fighting chance with us to take care of him." We left, furious at ourselves for even having lowered ourselves to the point of pleading for a favor. We should have known better.

Our only recourse was to try any remedy we could think of, most of which would never have been recommended by a member of the medical profession.

First we tried some tobacco leaves soaked in warm water. We applied them to the wound as a poultice. It apparently did some good because it drew out some of the puss and maggots and allowed him to sleep a little better that night. After two days we ran out of tobacco leaves and had to come up with something else.

We decided on onions. That night as the guard slept outside our hut, we snuck into the nearest Korean family's garden and stole some onions. We boiled them and put them on the badly swollen leg. The onions also seemed to help, but he was losing his strength and we could tell that blood poisoning was just about to infect his entire blood stream.

"Look, we've got to at least get some alcohol to wash out this mess," I said the next day, "he hasn't got a chance unless we can clean it up."

"What the hell can we do, we can't go to the hospital..." he paused and snapped his fingers, saying, "Wait! I've got an idea."

"Let's have it," I urged and he began to describe his daring scheme. He would pretend like he was sick and go to sick call. Once in the hospital he would steal a bottle of alcohol.

"Look, they guard that stuff with their lives," I said, "You'll never get away with it. Besides, all they will give you is charcoal or hot water if you complain of diarrhea, you won't even see any alcohol. It's not like the salt, this stuff they really control." We finally gave in - it would be a gamble, but it had to work. He tried it the next morning.

Later we learned just how close he came to pulling it off. He had found the alcohol and had a small bottle under his shirt when he left the hospital. Coming out the door the Chinese guard caught him and he was taken to jail.

The rest of us protested to the Chinese company commander. "Look, he was only trying to get some medicine for one of our men. He's dying with a foot infection, he's got to have some medicine. There's no reason for you to lock one of us up just for doing something your own doctors should be doing."

"Your sergeant is guilty of stealing from the Chinese People's Volunteer medical service. Only the Chinese soldiers may have that medicine, you have your own medicine, get out!" he coldly stated.

Despite our best efforts, the soldier we called George died four days later of what would have been corrected with little effort in the states. It upset the entire hut a great deal and we let the good Dr. Haung know it.

The next time we had a chance to see the "water doctor" we reminded him of our requests for medicine that fell on deaf ears. "You could have saved that man's life," we told him, "but you refused our pleas. I hope you are satisfied."

He simply flashed a thin smile which hardly hid the fact that he was very satisfied with the outcome and attempted to walk past us.

"God will take care of you," we shouted after him. That turned his satisfaction into rage and he turned to us and shouted, "There is no God. Stop talking about God. I do not worry about any God. Go back to your huts, now!"

I'd guess that there were now about 1800 of us at any one time in Camp No. 1. Probably six hundred or more died during the first few months of captivity. They were buried in shallow three foot graves without any indication of who they were. The stronger of us would occasionally sneak up the hill some nights and erect crude crosses over their graves.

CHAPTER 4

Segregation - Communist Style

It didn't take long before we were on the move again. This time there wasn't any long march to some unknown camp. We simply moved to different quarters within Camp No. 1.

"Holy Moses, home was never like this," I remarked as I entered the dust filled building.

"You said it," Carlie replied, "This place looks like the wreckers left it here by mistake. Why the hell didn't they leave us where we were?"

"Haven't you got that figured out yet?" I asked.

"What do you mean?" he replied.

"Well take a look around...take a look at the stripes in here and then figure out who was left on the other side of the street."

"You mean all sergeants? Yeah, that's all we got here, huh, just sergeants."

"That's it, Carlie my boy, nothing but high ranking sergeants...we ain't allowed to associate with the lower class of people you know."

"Yeah, but what the hell difference is forty yards going to make, we can still associate with the corporals and privates from here," he said.

"Not when they put guards into those two huts there," I said, pointing to two empty buildings between us and the rest of the POWs. "But I guess we can manage to find some way of keeping in touch if we try hard enough."

The men assigned to our new quarters were a diverse group. The main characters were a couple of Brits, Spud Murphy (a notorious wise cracker) and Bill who was to become the unofficial squad leader. There were also a few guys from New York, John Sobierk from Long Island, and Ray from the Bronx.

We took another look around the building. It had been a Korean home, but the Chinese had moved most of the families out of the area to make room for prisoners. This was a larger hut divided into two sections, a squad of twenty men in each section. It was about twenty by ten feet in size. The only furniture was a small table and the straw mats on the floor.

It was as dark as hell. There were no windows or other openings, other than the doorway, to allow any light to enter.

"Try opening the door," Carlie said, "That should help a little."

"Yeah, that'll be fine until it rains or gets cold," I smirked.

"Hey in there," came a call from outside. "Give me a hand with these litters, will ya?" We went to the door.

"Come on, help us carry these guys into that house over there," one of the sergeants requested. There were eight litters. Each litter carried a poor guy who had been stricken with one of the many contagious diseases making their rounds about the camp.

"Don't tell me they're moving these guys too," I asked. "Hell they were all right where they were."

He answered, "Yeah, but they figure they may contaminate some of the boys they're trying to work on over the other side of the street. It doesn't look so good to have sick men on your hands when you're trying to sell their fouled up brand of communism, you know."

"Yeah, I suppose not," I replied. "Come on, let's move them inside."

We got through the narrow doorway as best we could. The men were placed on the floor as gently as we could. They too, had to sleep on the straw mats. Some of them look pretty sick. We were trying to get out of there as fast as possible to reduce our chances of becoming one of their bunk mates.

"Hey, look," Carlie exclaimed before we made it outside, "There's somebody living on the other side."

We peeked through a small hole in the wall. Sure enough, a Korean woman about forty years old, and her four children were living in the room on the other side.

"I thought they moved all the Koreans out of this area," I said.

"I guess they forgot this one."

Behind us one of the British chaps started to sing as he arranged the blanket for one of the sick men. The Korean woman came over to the hole in the wall and forced a book through to our side. Carlie grabbed it from our end and pulled it through.

"Well, I'll be damned. Well, will you look at this," he said.

"What is it?" I asked. "Well, will you look at that. I wonder where she got it?" In his hands Carlie held an old English hymn book.

"Hey, mamasan, where you get?" Carlie called through the small opening. She didn't seem to understand his question. "Somebody go get someone that can speak Japanese or something," Carlie suggested. This part of Asia had been under Japanese control for so long some of the older Koreans understood a little of the language. One of the other soldiers came up and said, "let me give it a try." He jabbered at her for a minute or two and then turned to us.

"She says the book belonged to her husband. The Chinks killed him for being pro-American."

"God damn!" Carlie muttered.

"She says they are going to move her out of here this afternoon. She would like to help us, but she is afraid. She says she has to think of her children. The baby is just two and the little boy is six. The two girls are ages four and ten. She doesn't like the idea of moving. That book is all that she has to remember her husband by."

That afternoon we were cleaning up our hut when one of the guys noticed the poor Korean woman moving to her new home. It was only about 200 yards down the road.

Her new home was nothing more than a tumbled down shack about three feet back from the dusty road. It was considerably smaller than the one she left, only about five feet square. She was carrying the sum total of their possessions on her back. The kids followed carrying what little was left of their meager belongings.

"Come on, gang, let's give her a hand," someone called out. Everyone in the hut fell out to lend her a hand. Singing, "I Got Two Pence" at the top of our lungs, we carried her goods to the new location. The guards came running as soon as they noticed us. By the times the guards reached us a large number of native civilians had also gathered around us. They more than liked the idea of us helping the poor woman. The Chinese guards now realized that it would not create a favorable impression if they stopped us now so they left us alone. We also carried with us a load of firewood from our hut. The tears of happiness in her eyes were our thanks.

I guess most of the 500 families that lived in Changsong saw us help that woman. It didn't hurt our cause at all. We really felt good on the walk back to our hut. Of course that was mixed with a feeling of sadness at the tough time her family would have in the cramped confines of their new dwelling.

Once we returned to our area we resumed our clean up duties. We got some water from the brook which was about fifteen feet behind our hut. The water was all right for cleaning, but none of us would dare drink it. We washed off the dust from inside our hut. The stream would come in handy to wash our clothes.

We spent a lot of time on our clothing, besides washing there was also mending or making our clothing from scraps of material we could find. Since needles were a prohibited item they were in great demand. I hid mine in the binding of my bible. The Chinese didn't issue much clothing to us. We got a pair of sneakers in the spring and fall, one set of underwear a year, a thin blue uniform for the warm weather and the padded uniform for winter. We each had one thin blanket and one pair of socks issued to us. The socks, which were the only thing they gave us from the Red Cross packages, would usually only last a month, after that we had to improvise. Stockings were made from everything imaginable.

Just as we were finishing arranging the hut so it would be somewhat bearable two jets flew overhead. We hardly had time to run out and find them in the sky before they were gone. They were our jets, and as they passed they tipped their wings back and forth. They must have known that they were over a POW camp.

"Boy," I said, "Look at those lucky bastards. They'll be back in Pusan or some place in just a few minutes heading to the club for a steak."

"Or a drink," someone piped up.

"And tonight they'll be headed for the high spots. Gee, think of it, for a short moment they were only a few thousand feet away...so near and yet so far. I guess we can expect the same old bowl of slop tonight."

The Chinese guard came running over demanding, "What did he say? What did he say?"

"What did who say?" Carlie asked.

"What did plane signal, I saw! The plane signaled by waving wings. What did he say?"

"Well, I'll tell you," Carlie said as we laughed. "He just told us that MacArthur is coming up this way to get us very soon, see?"

The guard became so mad he couldn't respond. We laughed all the way back into the hut. The next thing to catch our attention was a truck that came roaring up the road. We noticed that as it passed the new home of our Korean friend the house disappeared in a cloud of smoke.

"Boy, is she going to have trouble keeping that place clean," Carlie said.

"Hell, she's so close to the road she's going to have a rough time keeping that place, period," I replied.

"That is a hell of a thing to do to that poor woman," he added.

"Why couldn't they have just left her alone, we could have doubled up some of the guys to make room for her to stay."

"You know the communists don't forgive or forget. Her treatment has a lot to do with what her husband had done, and nothing else," Carlie said.

"For that matter, what the hell did they have to move us over here for anyhow, we were all right back on the other side of the street," I said.

"Ah, but we must not bust up their plans for indoctrinating the youngsters, you know," he answered.

"Bust up their plans my foot. You know something? We gotta find a way of keeping in touch with those guys. We have to keep track of what's going on."

"That ain't going to be easy, though, not with two Chink shacks between us and them," he pointed out.

"Awe, hell, don't worry about it, we'll figure out a way...we always have before. Hey, look, there is Joe down there in Seven Company now. I wonder how they're making out. Hey, Joe! Joe! Up here!" I called.

"How are you guys doing for space down there?"

"Hey, We're doing fine now that you guys have moved. How's everything up that way?" he yelled back.

"Not bad. What did you get for dinner today?"

"Pork. How about you?" he asked.

"Pork! Well, I'll be damned. All we got was rice again. You guys must rate..." Two of the guards rapidly exited one of the huts between us to see what the yelling was about. They both headed in our direction and we waited to see what they wanted.

"What you call about?" one of them asked.

"Nothing, we were just asking that man how things were over there. Nothing wrong in that, is there?"

"You no call no more. You stay up here and don't call down to Seven Company. You understand?"

"Sure, sure, I understand. Don't get excited," I said.

Carlie and I walked back inside and when the guards had departed I said, "You're right, this is going to be harder than I thought. They can hear everything we try to call over to them."

That evening we got rice again for our supper. We raised hell.

We caught Black Shoes and one of the guards outside and asked, "Hey, how come Seven Company had pork today and we got nothing but rice?" Black Shoes got his name because he covered his Chinese army issue sneakers with tar in an attempt to keep the moisture off his feet.

His face reflected a mixture of surprise and interest as he asked, "Ah, so, did Seven Company get pork today?"

"You know damned well they got pork today. How come?"

"Ah, yes, I remember, they did have pork today. Do not worry, you will get pork tomorrow, we didn't have enough to give it to everybody today." His expression turned thoughtful and he inquired, "How did you know Seven Company had pork?"

"A little birdie told us," I taunted.

He gave a puzzled look to the guard and said something in Chinese, then, turned back to us and said, "Well, we will see if we can keep that little birdie from telling you anything else."

Once they walked away I said, "I wonder what he meant by that crack."

"Nothing good, I'll bet," my buddy replied.

The next morning we were up as usual, at 05:30, and were out in the company area for roll call. It was a cold damp morning and we shivered as they went through the list of names, one by one. Once the list was exhausted they began to identify the work details. I generally didn't get very many details because of my head wound. I usually helped with the cleaning around our hut and was given the lighter details that didn't require much walking.

I did participate in the morning exercise walks whenever I thought I could make it. Going on these walks was better than sitting around with nothing to do. This morning I felt pretty good and decided to go. We walked down the street and passed the miserable hut we moved the Korean woman into.

As we passed her three oldest children were out on the damp ground. They were lying there because she had been unable to find room for them in the small hut.

"Ain't that a crying shame," someone remarked.

"Yeah, I can see that the Chinese are going to have a difficult time selling communism to folks in this neighborhood. Not when they have to put up with crap like that."

"They don't sell communism buddy, they cram it down your throat with a bayonet."

"I'll bet that poor woman doesn't even have a few crumbs to give those children for breakfast," I said.

"Probably not," another soldier answered.

"Can you imagine our families living in a dump like that," asked one of the younger boys.

"Our family wouldn't let our chickens sleep in a place like that," came the reply. We continued to walk past and then turned around and went back to our huts. The kids were awake on our way back and they shyly waved to us as we walked past. They were kids, just like kids anywhere else in the world. They didn't look as if they enjoyed communism any more than we did, if they even knew what communism was. For the most part they had always lived under this communist regime and knew no other way.

We spent most of the remainder of the day making our hut a little more livable. We created some shelves, piled up the firewood, mopped up the dust, and picked up the debris in the yard.

It was later that afternoon that we learnt the meaning of Black Shoes comment yesterday. The guards were out in force. They were using branches, twigs, and leaves to obscure our view through the barbed wire fence that separated us from Seven Company. They obviously felt if they could cut off our line of sight they would also cut off our communications.

We began experimenting with a number of grapevine methods that had worked in the past. Outright yelling was no longer possible. They now posted a guard every thirty feet along the fence line and more of them understood English. When they heard us they were now putting an immediate end to our clandestine conversations. For a short time we tried leaving notes hidden in the branches and leaves in the fence. But to reach them Seven Company had to pass the two huts that housed the guards. This soon became more of a risk than it was worth. They weren't kidding around this time, they really didn't want us to have any contact whatsoever with Seven Company. We were now totally segregated.

After many attempts, and many failures, we came upon a method that seemed to work, at least for now. We didn't have carrier pigeons, but we did have plenty of rocks. Hiding behind one of our huts, we would tie a note to the rock and then throw them over the two Chinese huts to a point in the field near the Seven Company huts.

"Hell, this is like throwing one in from right field," a tall lanky Texan declared. He was always able to come closest to the desired landing spot than the rest of us. He was now our unofficial communications technician.

Once Seven Company caught on they would send us information using the same procedure. Our mail service was now back in business.

The following morning we started our exercise walk just like every other morning The only exception was our determination to take another poke at the communists.

As we passed the dust covered hut that housed the Korean woman and her kids, we threw small bundles of food into the yard. We had to be careful, insuring that the guards didn't see our CARE packages. Each contained either bits of bread, sugar, or candy.

By the time we made our return trip through the village the word of our assistance had spread through the civilian population. The Koreans greeted us with cheers along the entire route. As we passed the little woman and her family they were beaming with happiness. As far as these Korean civilian families were concerned communism and the Chinese were their enemies, not the U.S. Army.

We got even bolder as the day went on. We asked Black Shoes about moving her back into her own house.

"...we could split up the sick men living there now and move them into our huts. How about it?"

"Oh, no," he replied, "We could not do that. We do not have anything to do with the civilians."

"What do you mean," I challenged, "It was you how moved her out, wasn't it?"

"That was different," he continued, "We had to do that."

"This is bull, you can move her back if you want to and you know it," I said.

"Buddy, your just plain chicken. For my money you don't have the guts to move her back into her own house." I thought if I could challenge his manhood and authority he would do it just to prove me wrong.

"What are you saying? Do not forget, sergeant, that you are a prisoner. You can't do things your way around here. Do not forget this!"

At that remark we gave our usual response, yelling, "Make up your mind, are we prisoners or students?" "Okay, that's good, we are prisoners, so stop teaching us your foolish lessons, only students have to learn, not prisoners."

"Wait, wait," he interrupted. "Let us not talk about it any further for now. We will take it up with the regiment commander later. Now go to your hut."

As we dispersed, accomplishing nothing, I remarked, "I can just imagine what will happen to her if she has to spend the next winter in that shack."

That would not be our last encounter with Black Shoes that day. Just after supper we heard through the grapevine that Seven Company had received apples and peanuts. As usual we got nothing of the kind.

Black Shoes just about blew his stack when we asked him about it.

"How did you know that," he demanded.

"The same way," I replied.

"What do you mean, the same way?" he asked.

"Why a little birdie told us," I laughed. "Now tell us. Why didn't we get any apples and peanuts?"

He gulped and replied, "Your company has not earned luxuries yet. You are not behaving as you should."

"I don't know what that means," I replied, "But how about what you teach us about communism. I thought we were all suppose to be treated the same."

"Well you are," he answered.

"Yeah, as long as we go along with your screwball ideas, is that it?" I queried. "Fellows, I think we had better see the camp commander about this. What do you say?"

Everyone was in agreement.

Black Shoes said, "No, you can not see the camp commander about so trivial a matter. He is a busy man."

"Brother, he is going to be even busier. If you don't let us talk to him, we'll get him the next time he shows up at one of our lectures. You can't stop us then."

Black Shoes left it at that. The next morning we were spared the trouble of broaching the subject when the camp commander ordered us to the field for a lecture. We listened to his long drawn out spiel that told us in essence, from now on things would be different, we would all get the same food.

"Not only will you get the same food," he said, "but you will all have the same privileges. We will start today. Today you will have milk, and when the baking powder comes in from China, you will have doughnuts."

We cheered the prospect of getting decent treatment.

Well, they kept their word. That night we got milk. Not many of us could drink it though, it was made from soy beans. It took a whole sugar ration to get it sweet enough to even try to swallow it. Since we couldn't afford to be so extravagant with our sugar most of their milk was dumped on the ground. As for the doughnuts, the baking powder must have been well inside China because we never did see any of it.

This segregation was one of many paradoxes we found with the communist system. How could a society that was suppose to be all struggling for the same goal, all sharing the labors and benefits equally, be so divided. How could this classless society be separated into so many diverse groups. There were more similarities than differences to this system and the democracy we enjoyed in the states. Both systems and societies contained people who had everything and those that had next to nothing. The main difference being that in the communist system a persons position was determined by an elite group of military and party officials, while in our democracy an individual had more control over their destiny and surroundings. While many in our system do suffer from poverty and racial discrimination, it is not a perfect society. However, it is a society in which the people have hope and a chance to make things better. In the communist society many things are lacking but possibly the worst of these things is the total lack of hope for the future.

CHAPTER 5

Korean Cuisine

Asking the Chinese for food was about as useless and undertaking as asking for medicine or common decency. The response was always the same, "Ma Mon Dee". We would wait for five minutes, an hour, a day and then realize that we weren't going to get what we asked for. We figured that Ma Mon Dee meant anywhere from five minutes to never.

Once while at the hospital for another of my bouts with severe headaches I was able to turn the tables on them. It was common practice for them to try to solicit a written statement from us while at the hospital. An instructor asked me to write a letter telling how well we were treated by our instructors, not wanting me to use the term captors. I was also told to mention the excellent food we were provided.

"Ma Mon Dee," I replied.

He smiled. "I leave paper and pen for letter," he said as he departed. I knew to resist would mean punishment of one type or another. I also knew to comply meant giving up my dignity.

The instructor returned the following day. "What's the matter?" he asked.

"Oh, nothing, Ma Mon Dee," I said. He left obviously disappointed that I had not completed my work of fiction. The next day he approached me once again. Now he was visibly angry that I had not written anything yet.

"I told you Ma Mon Dee," I said.

"Okay. Now you write article. I wait for you to finish."

"What do you mean, wait for me? I told you Ma Mon Dee. Doesn't Ma Mon Dee mean no?"

"No, it means pretty soon," he replied with a tone of frustration.

"You must be mistaken," I stated. "Whenever I ask for decent food or some medicine, I am told 'Ma Mon Dee', and I never get anything. So see, what I am telling you is that I am not going to write any such letter for you."

Now the instructor was outright furious. He bolted out the door, but soon returning with the doctor. The doctor shouted "Write statement or you will leave the hospital now." Before he could change his mind I threw my meager belongings into a blanket and returned to my hut.

Soon we found the source of some of the food we were receiving. This realization was to quell any of my demands for food for quite a while.

I couldn't understand it the first time I saw a North Korean chasing a dog. I noticed that every time a North Korean or Chinese soldier saw a dog they would chase the poor critter. If they caught it the would kick it half to death.

I thought that all Koreans and Chinese simply hated dogs, maybe because they scrounged for what little food there was. Well that was part of it, they did have a burning hatred of dogs, but they also had another reason.

The entire time we were on the marches we ate plain sorghum, but after our arrival at Camp No. 1 the sorghum was frequently served with a sauce. We were also given cracked corn on occasion. The sauce was thick, pasty, and hotter than hell to taste. One day we asked the Chinese waiter-master what it was. When he explained that it consisted of dog meat ground up with red hot peppers our stomachs did flip-flops. That ended the "dog sauce" for us, though I must admit there were previously times in our awful hunger, that it did add taste to the sorghum and corn.

Dogs were not the worst bit of meat offered us by our captors. We often caught them peddling skinned rats to us insisting that they were squirrels. For that matter, one of our fellow prisoners tried that little trick on us once. We spread the word about him quickly. Tiny, as we called him, did his best to trade his "squirrel" for some tobacco or sugar. Failing this he and some of the guys in his hut finally cooked the rat and ate it with a bunch of dandelion greens. That was the extent of our hunger. That civilized men were brought do the depths of willingly eating dogs and rats to satisfy the emptiness in their stomachs, told the whole story.

Now we actively began to barter and do a little trading for the few possessions we had. Cans of beef were very rare items and could command a price of $120 or $60 for each half of the can. For these prized items the men from various huts would pool their resources to get a chance at even the smallest of portions of these great treasures.

Most of the time our meals were at the mercy of the Chinese cooks. In our world we didn't worry about nutrition, calories, or appeal. Substance was the thing that mattered. The only goal was to get enough into your body to make it to the next meal. Needless to say there was very little we would turn down.

"Awe now, we can't eat this stuff, it's rotten," I said to Carlie as he ladled out the small ration of rice that was our supper this day. It was rotten, so rotten that it turned our stomachs just to look at it. We were in some kind of a fix all right.

We had learned long ago that if we turned back any food, or left any on our plates, we were sure to get the exact same thing for our next meal. Usually without it being reheated.

"I'll take care of this," Carlie said, headed for the door with his bowl of rice. He marched right up to the Chinese platoon leader and shoved the bowl right under his nose. "Here, let me see you eat this crap. It stinks."

"Go back, you go back and eat it. That is all there is. Go back." This was the guards only reply.

"Brother, we ain't going to eat this stuff even if we all starve to death. Besides, I'd rather starve than be poisoned."

"Go back, go back," the head guard now screamed.

Carlie came back to the hut. There was no need to tell us what happened we had heard.

"Well, what the hell are we going to do with it?" he asked.

"Let's bury the stuff."

"Good idea, it will be dark soon and we can bury it right outside. I'll be damned if I'm going to eat any of it."

At nightfall two of the British, Spud and Bill volunteered to do the burying. We dumped all the rice back into the big pan they snuck out the door. The moon was pretty bright so they hid in the shadows of the hut to do their digging.

Just as they got the hole dug and were dumping in the rice one of the guards, Detective Louie as we called him, came around the corner of the building.

"Dammit, we're caught," Bill whispered, "Don't move."

"Ah so, what are you doing?" challenged Louie.

Spud and Bill stood up and Spud started dreaming up a story.

"Well Louie, it's like this. When we were kids we always believed that if we dug far enough we would come out in China. We're just trying to see if that works in reverse."

"What," Louie asked puzzled. Then he realized he was being made a fool of and shouted, "Here, let me look." He reached down into the hole and stuck his hand in rice, up to his wrist. That did it. Our two mates were marched up to the regiment office. We thought for sure that they were in for it. But they had just instituted a "Lenient Treatment Policy" and after a long lecture, they were sentenced. Their punishment was to criticize themselves in front of the whole company.

But we knew from past experience that the Chinese had no sense of humor when it came to food problems. We were all tense that next morning. One false move and Spud and Bill would be in big trouble, lenient policy or not. The only one who still appeared defiant was Spud.

He was a man of high principles and staunch loyalties, as were most of the British. He was not about to do any more than was necessary to appease our captors. He was betting that if he spoke fast enough even the few Chinese that understood English would have difficulty reading between the lines.

Spud was doing the talking. He announced in a loud, rapid tone.

"We are confessing to the terrible crime of destroying some of the rotten rice provided us by the freedom loving people of North Korea. After special consideration, we decided to dig two small holes in which to dispose of the much soured rice which was not fit for the pigs to eat inasmuch as we didn't desire to become as sick as the porkers undoubtedly would have become had they tried to eat it..." A chorus of snickers arose from the prisoners. We cut it off as soon as it started with a few warning looks. Whether most of the prisoners, or even Spud realized, he was playing a deadly game. One which could easily have killed the two lads.

"Spud continued, "...Of course we did not calculate the risks of apprehension, but we did not expect to be caught in the dastardly act of burying the rotten rice by the number one Detective Louie, the clever sleuth. And of course after he had caught us red handed, there was little we could do but promise that we would do our very best not to get caught the next time we find it necessary to bury the rotten rice given to us by the freedom loving people of the People's Republic."

We all held our breath. The Chinese were all wearing smiles. He had gotten away with it. They had swallowed the whole pitch without a glimmer of suspicion.

The regiment commander spoke. "I am glad that you have realized your mistake. Because you have criticized yourselves so well, we will not punish you. This will be all."

Those of us that had been here long enough to know how dangerous his speech had been were visibly relieved.

A few days later I had another bout of dysentery. My head was splitting. I attempted to pull my blanket over my head as a shield against the pain but it didn't work. Nothing seemed to work. Even the home remedy I created to cure my last spell of dysentery was not working now. All I could do was lay still and try to make my mind a blank. If I couldn't stop feeling the pain maybe I could at least stop thinking about it. After sleeping on the ground for so long the floor of the hut was much more comfortable but I still could not dose off. Oh, if I could only sleep. Each time I came close to sleep the searing pain in my head would jolt me back to consciousness.

I wasn't the only one in bad shape though. I could hear Al moaning softly at my side. God, his hand must hurt something awful. His hand was so swollen that it looked just like a big Kosher sausage. The swelling came from the infection that was spreading to his arms. They had done nothing to help him. Nothing! Just thinking about Al's hand, with the visible blue line now running clear up to his armpit, made me think a little less about my own pain. Oh, if I could only sleep.

Gosh, I'm hungry. Our meals were now brought to us by a Korean named Suzy. Well, by God, she's not going to pull what she did last night. Yesterday they passed out small bowls and then brought the rice in. It was watery, soupy, and hot as hell. Suzy had promised us seconds after she had passed out the first helping. But there was a catch. We could only get the second helping if our bowls were finished by the time she came around again. Well it didn't take long to get the first helping served around the hut and she immediately began checking our bowls. This stuff was just too hot to get down quickly no matter how hungry you were. Suzy laughed loudly as she walked out with the big serving bowl almost as full as when she came in.

"No sir, she won't get away with it again tonight. I'll get seconds tonight if it kills me." Then I realized that I must have been thinking out loud because Al said, "Jesus, I hope so, I'm starving."

"Take it easy Al, relax and take it easy," I said trying to soothe him. Al was awfully sick.

"I can't take it easy, George," he replied. "I just can't. I feel terrible. Oh God, I feel terrible."

At that moment Suzy pushed through the door with her bowl of rice. "Here she comes guys, grab your bowls."

There were now sixteen of us in our hut and at meal time we would line up eight on each side of the floor. Today Suzy brought a helper, we called her Shakie Lil. Suzy took one side and Lil took the other. Suzy started on our side and ladled out the meal that was again more water than rice. She moved as fast as possible. We got the idea. She was going to gyp us out of seconds again. I shoved the bowl to my face and forced the liquid through my burning lips as quickly as possible. I felt it searing down through my body. I was hungry. Out of the corner of my eye I could see Al desperately holding out his bowl. Suzy ladled in the rice and Al tried to support the bowl with his infected hand while he ate with the other. The hot bowl was more than he could stand. He dropped it.

Al stared dumbly at the spilled rice while Suzy screamed curses at him in Korean. Without a word Al reached out and grabbed the empty bowl and held it up to Suzy.

"You get no more, eat that," she said pointing to the puddle the spilt rice made on the floor. She then moved on next man. Al was hungry but not about to plead with her for more food. We knew pleading with these animals was useless. But his lips moved silently with the pain.

A wave of rage came over me and I stumbled to my feet. I never in my life had wanted to hit a woman, but at that moment I wanted to hit her so bad I could taste it. Al could see my face as I moved toward Suzy.

"Don't," he whispered. "Then she won't feed the others." I stopped just short of her. Suzy had heard and looked at me defiantly then continued to ladle out the rice.

I handed Al what was left in my bowl and headed for the door. God, if I stay here much longer I'll beat the hell out of that woman. I stumbled out into the night air and sat on the bottom step of the temple, our new name for the hut. My head felt as though it would push right through the top of my skull. I hurt so bad my eyes were watering, or maybe it was my rage that brought on the tears.

Shakie Lil came softly down the stairs and touched me on the shoulder. I could tell she felt badly.

"Whatsa matter, you sick?" she asked.

"Sick, hell, did you see what Suzy did to Al. She didn't have to do that, did she? She could have given him some more rice. Hell, Al's starving to death, and he's sick. She could have given the poor guy some more rice."

"Where's your rice?" she asked.

"I gave it to Al, of course, what do you think, hell, the poor guys hungry."

"You come back inside and eat, huh. You hungry too," she gently insisted.

"No the hell with it, I don't want to go back inside," I muttered.

"Come now, you come back in and eat, you need to eat." she lifted at my arm.

"Let me alone, will ya, I don't want to go back in. So help me, if I go in I'll punch that Suzy right in the face."

"You wait, I come back," she said and was gone.

A minute later she came out again with a bowl of rice. She handed it to me, saying simply, "Eat it."

"Thanks Lil, but honest, I couldn't eat it now," I said, cooling off a little bit. Lil stood there holding the out the bowl. I reached out and took it, and she walked away. I guess she could tell I wanted to be alone right then.

Shakie Lil was going to be all right. This was the first hint of compassion I had seen in many months. The fact that she was Chinese made this display of empathy even harder to understand.

Somehow I felt a little better. But I was still too upset and my head hurt too much to eat. I left the bowl on the steps and walked back inside. Al was cleaning up the mess on the floor with an old rag. I kneeled down to help him. We didn't have to say anything to each other, we knew.

Al only lasted a few more days. I was almost glad for him when his time came. He had suffered so long and had seen so much. I couldn't help thinking he was better off somehow. It was over for him now.

CHAPTER 6

Terrible Rumors

Whenever you are in a situation like this with hundreds of people kept at close quarters, with the us against them mentality, you hear many things. It is also difficult in this environment to determine which things are true and which are not. We were lied to so methodically and consistently by our captors that the distinction between fact and fiction had become blurred. We were ripe for any illusion, especially if it held out a glimmer of hope among all this despair.

One of the worst of these illusions seemed to be confirmed to us by a man we called "Farmer Brown" the First Company interpreter.

"We soon will let you students go home to your loved ones. The peace loving peoples of the world, China, Russia, and North Korea, have brought to the attention of the United States (they had a habit of not mentioning the United Nations) that there should be peace here in Korea," he stated.

"The peace loving people of North Korea have convinced the United States that peace will benefit the other people of the world..."

We looked at one another in amazement. This was it. This was the culmination of all the rumors of the past few days. It explained the excitement that we could feel even among our captors. "Farmer Brown" was truly excited as he recited his peace from the usual typewritten sheet of paper. The guards were all smiles.

"The next time we give you beef there will be peace," he said. You could sense from the tone of his voice that he expected this great event to happen in the next few days.

He didn't even attempt to stop the uproar that followed his electrifying statement.

"Did ya hear what he said...peace."

"Jeez, just think, maybe we'll be getting back to the states after all.

"Wow! Steak and eggs coming up."

"I'll bet it won't be long either."

And so went the comments on the 10th of July 1951.

Hopes went soaring. We had been lied to so often in the long months that had past that we tried to force ourselves to take this with a grain of salt, but, we said, there must be something to this one. It has to be more than just a rumor, they can't be giving us the run around.

Some of us couldn't help remembering what we had heard in the past. On the death march they had told us we were being taken home through China. There were stories of men being released after being interrogated. These turned out to be stories just to loosen our tongues. But this had to be real.

The prisoners who were lying in their rooms, too sick to make the lecture, heard the commotion and wondered. They heard the glorious word "peace" being yelled back and forth among the men. They caught enough of the conversations to know what was being talked about...and their hopes soared as well.

The interpreter continued. "And now, students, we will have better food for you. We have learned what you like to eat and we will try and get it for you. We didn't know, we couldn't understand your language well enough to know what you wanted to eat, but now we will try to give you better food. There will be no more cracked corn."

A cheer went up. We weren't stupid enough to believe they understood our language well enough to punish us for what we said during out teachings, but not well enough to understand how much we hated the cracked corn and watered rice. But that didn't matter right now. If this was just a false rumor then it was already having the effect the captors desired.

His voice became insistent. "Don't get yourself in trouble now, students. If you don't follow the rules, you will be sentenced to prison terms. You will serve your sentences. You will not get home if you are sent to prison. Remember that."

There it was, the gimmick. The out for the Commies. We recalled the many stories of prisoners being identified as war criminals and being sent away. Many of them had been gone for months and we didn't know if they were dead or alive.

"Do not worry, students, the Chinese People's Volunteers will take care of you," he concluded. It was the way he usually ended his lectures. We stood up and headed back to our huts jabbering like excited schoolboys.

As I walked into the hut one of the men that was too weak to hear the lecture, spoke up. He was living on borrowed time and we all knew it. The talk of peace had given him the strength to literally lift himself up, both physically and mentally. It was the best medicine he could have received at that point.

"I'll be damned if I'm going to let myself die if there's a chance of getting home from this place," he said.

Within a week he was feeling much better.

There was no stopping this rumor now.

Up to now we had never received any meat. Now we had Farmer Brown speaking of beef and another red hot rumor about some pork.

I don't know how it started, but suddenly everyone was anxiously awaiting a load of pigs supposedly on it's way to our camp.

It caused some wonderful dreams of bacon, roast pork, ham, and pig's knuckles. But we couldn't find the source of the rumor.

By the night of July 12th the rumor had reached the point where the entire camp know that the truckload of pigs had arrived. As it turned out it was not just a rumor.

Early the next morning John from Long Island shoved his head in the door and yelled, "Hey, anybody in here know how to butcher a pig?"

"Who the hell cares," came the reply. "Who's got a pig?"

"No kidding, I mean it, they've got pigs up their right now...one for each company."

"Nuts. Cut the comedy, we're hungry," we answered.

"Take a look for yourself," he called and disappeared.

We jumped to our feet and ran out of the hut. What a sight, there they were, pigs. Some only had three legs and were dragged down the road by the guards, but they were beautiful. They were squealing like hell.

John yelled again, "Now what do you say, anybody here that can butcher a pig?"

"Damned right, buddy, I'll butcher them," one of the men called out.

"Me too," another joined in. The two of them headed for the pigs.

By now half the camp had emptied out into the street to watch this most unusual sight – food on the hoof.

We created a long procession of guards, pigs, and hungry prisoners, headed for the banks of the river.

"Kill them quickly before the bastards change their minds," came a yell from the crowd. We roared in approval.

I had never seen a pig butchered before, but the boys tell me the method the Chinese employ was a little out of the ordinary by American standards. For that matter, so were the pigs on closer inspection. They were skinny, not the usual fat porkers you see in the states.

The Chinese guard that was in charge swung an ax and hit the first pig on the head. Then he deftly stuck a knife in the pig's throat and caught the blood in a pan. Then came the surprise.

He took a long hollow steel rod and inserted it in the left hind leg, up under the skin to the pig's neck. Then he withdrew the rod. One of the other

Chinese soldiers knelt down and blew into the hole, inflating the porker much like a balloon. When the pig was about twice it's normal size, he stopped. Then this process was repeated on the right side of the animal.

They explained that the pig was too thin to properly scrape unless it was blown up first.

After the steps were properly demonstrated on the first pig the two American volunteers were assigned to the butchering process. They let the Chinese do the blowing up, they wanted no part of that operation.

Once the pigs were butchered and cleaned we hung them in a large store room. As this was being done a truckload of flour arrived. One of the interpreters called, "I need a group of volunteers to unload this food. I will need about twenty men. Who will volunteer?"

About twice as many jumped up. He could have easily gotten two hundred volunteers. Hell, just handling rations gave us a chance at getting near something edible.

For the next two days we were licking our chops waiting for those damned pigs. Then came a lecture on food.

Farmer Brown was at his best as he went through the same routine we heard before.

"Now that the Chinese knew what kind of food we liked there would be no more cracked corn," he said. "You will be given pork and dough balls in the future," he continued. "We will give you meals of half sorghum and half rice from time to time." For two hours we listened. We were starving, had been, in fact, for months.

The next morning each company was given a bag of flour and about eight pounds of the long awaited pork. Not much food for a hundred and fifty men, but after waiting three days, and just the fact it was flour and pork we had a feast. And it was good.

I wasn't about to swallow my first mouthful of pork. I just let it sit in my mouth and toyed with it with my tongue. I was determined to get the last possible flavor out of it before I would allow it to enter my stomach. Gosh it was good.

This of course added fuel to the fire as far as the other rumors were concerned. Old ones were resurrected and new ones developed. The best by far was that the peace would be signed on July 20th. When the morning of the 20th did come there was a hell of a dog fight right over the camp. Jets from both sides wheeled in graceful circles through the sky throwing gray streaks of death ahead of them.

"That means peace all right," one of the lads remarked. "They're just dotting that "I" in armistice."

Prison life during this time became anything but monotonous. We were living off a rapid succession of rumors, each better than the one before.

For three or four days in a row the Chinese would read us news that gave the impression that the peace talks were progressing well, that the war was all but over. The sight and sound of yet another dog fight in the skies would tell us that someone was still at war.

Practically every day in the weeks that followed the start of the armistice negotiations, we were brought to the village square for a lecture given by the regimental commander. The thing that bothered us more than the unending talk of peace was the knowledge that these demonstrations were for the benefit of the North Korean civilians. We would be forced to sit for hours on end and listen while he ranted and raved from his typewritten paper, in Chinese. Then we would spend more time waiting for the interpreter to read us the same garbage in English.

Ironically, during this discourse of peace they would inevitable include some information of recent battles. Even though we knew that the information was entirely slanted in favor of the communists we were still happy to hear the war news. It was usually about two weeks old and never gave our side credit for doing anything right, but it was news. Our interest was taken as a positive sign by the regiment commander. After that we started receiving copies of their propaganda paper, the Daily Worker.

We developed a thick skin to their constant tirades against the United States and the aggression during the weeks when peace seemed to be at hand. In our view even if the peace talks did drag on forever, the mere fact the talks were taking place kept many of us alive.

One point they continued to hit on was how our side was holding up the armistice negotiations and bombing the neutral zone. They didn't seem to understand when we told them we didn't care if the peace talks took five years as long as they kept talking.

Upon hearing this one of them asked, "You mean you would be willing to spend the next five years as a prisoner of war?"

We answered, "The peace talks have kept half of us from dying. You have to take care of us now that we may be released at any time. At least we have a fighting chance to survive. And that is all we ask - a fighting chance." We also made it known that we knew the United Nations were doing their best to bring the negotiations to a speedy and successful conclusion and that we felt that only communist obstructionist tactics were preventing this from happening.

They did their best to convince us that the peace talks were not responsible for the improvement in the treatment we received. They still claimed that before the talks they had not known enough about our customs and the kind of food we ate. Then we asked about the shabby medical attention we had been given. "People all over the world are using the same medicine these days, why didn't you have adequate medical treatment available for us - why isn't that treatment available to us now?"

The prisoners knew that they had the peace talks to thank for the better conditions. The talks made the possibility of being responsible to the entire free world and of having to account for each and everyone of us closer to reality. Now every man had to be counted. No longer could men simply turn up "missing". There could be no more uncounted and unidentified bodies taken up to the hill.

Many improvements came as the peace negotiations continued. First there was DDT powder to spare us from the agonizing hours of squashing lice between our fingertips. Sick call was held more often and now at least appeared to provide a semblance of proper medical treatment.

The food still was not great, but it was better. The portions also increased to a point were they were enough to get by on.

Most importantly they allowed us to write home. And they allowed our families to reply to our letters, though they didn't deliver all of them.

In the first letter I received from Ann, my wife, I learned that she had received a letter from the Department of the Army. In it they stated that my name was mentioned over a short wave radio broadcast and that the communist radio had said that she could write to me once a month. The letter was to be addressed to the "Democratic Peoples Republic of Korea, Chinese Peoples Committee for World Peace, Peking, China."

Most of the prisoners would place "POW Camp No.1, North Korea" as our return address. Surprisingly enough, mail addressed to us at this address was delivered in some cases.

We knew that the communists would censor our letters so we tried to develop clandestine ways to get the truth out to our families. In one letter I tried to tip off Ann to the peace petitions the communists were attempting to get the POW families to sign. In my letter I simply said, "Don't worry, honey, tell Sammy I was asking for him and that I haven't let him down. I'm sorry to hear that you have been asked to sign those papers in my absence. Don't worry about it, Ann, but before you sign them be sure you take them to our lawyer, we don't want to get into trouble." She understood the reference to Sammy (Uncle Sam) and those papers. When she was approached to sign a communist peace petition she took it to the veterans' services officer in Brockton, our home town.

Even with all these improvements we were about to find that they were still the enemy.

It didn't occur to us that they had anything out of the ordinary in mind, hell, it was time for a regular formation anyway. When we got the call we fell in and waited, as usual. By the time we did realize what their plans were it was too late. It was a shakedown. The guards rounded up all of the sick who were not able to take part in that days work details along with the kitchen crew. There wasn't anything to do now but hope for the best.

Every last man in the camp were marched into a big open field. We were divided into groups of ten. Each group was assigned two Chinese guards. They lined us up about two yards apart and went to work.

One of the guards kept his rifle ready, the other went over us from top to bottom. Knives that had taken months to make; address books painstakingly documenting our dead; diaries; papers and pencils, anything that might give them some information was gone in an instant. They really caught us by surprise.

To talk meant getting knocked down, so we suffered in silence. We were out there for four hours. When we got back to our huts we realized that their search techniques were even more revealing in our huts.

They had systematically taken our huts apart piece by piece. Our clothes were thrown all over the place. Every book, piece of paper, or anything that might have been written on was gone. Even the pieces of paper we had tacked down to the roof to keep the mud from falling were ripped down. It was a very thorough job.

I laughed. The others searching through the debris looked up.

"What's so funny?" they asked.

"Did you see the look on the guy's face when he put his hands in my pockets?" I answered.

"No, why?"

"He put one hand in each pocket and came out with a fish in each hand."

"A fish?"

"Yeah, I stole them this morning in the kitchen. Boy, you should have seen the surprised look when he grabbed them. He didn't know what to say."

One of the other guys said, "I'm probably in for some trouble, he got my list."

"The one on cigarette paper?" I asked.

"Yeah, he seemed to be specifically looking for writing on cigarette papers. Someone else must have gotten caught, or tipped him off."

We all looked around at each other.

"Now, wait a minute," I said, "Let's don't go imagining anything. They'd love to have us fighting among ourselves. There is no reason for any of us to be suspicious."

After comparing notes on the searches we realized the main thrust of the hunt was to collect our written information. This again sent hopes soaring for the possibilities of the peace talks. Each time there had been positive statements about the talks a frantic hunt for the names of the American dead took place. They knew a full accountability would have to be a part of the negotiations. They also knew that they had killed many without taking notice of their names or nationalities. The best source for this information was with the other prisoners.

"Christ," I said, "I spent the last two months getting my list of names up to date and now I haven't even got any paper left." I complained.

The paper shortage didn't last long. Two days later they provided us with nice new notebooks. This move, even for them, was a bit too obvious. Give us the paper and some time to write some more notes down and then another shakedown for sure.

"I'm gonna fool these bastards," I said. "Let's just write down the daily menus in these things to remind them of the kind of slop they have been feeding us."

"Good idea, and I'll write down the words to some of the songs they won't let us sing just to show them what they are missing."

True to form they conducted another shakedown within two months. This time though they were to get very little information. The handwriting was on the wall however. They were fed up with the sergeants making a mess of their plans. In the past we had given them a hard time on the grapevine, the indoctrination, the entertainment, the food, the medical treatment, and now the shakedowns. What infuriated them the most was the fact that the younger lads were now seeing through their schemes much faster than they had at first. We were, to put it mildly, a bad example for the "students." And we were damned proud of it.

Despite this they were not about to give up in their attempts to gain information from us.

"Well, will you look at this. I wonder just how stupid these jokers think we are?" I said as I turned to the man beside me.

We had just listened to fifteen boring minutes of instructions by our instructor. He had made a very plausible explanation for the forms we now held in our hands. "As students of the People's Democracy," he had said, "we should know more about you so we can adjust our lessons accordingly." We had heard that one before.

We knew what was going on. They had tried torture, guile, and eavesdropping. They had used force in many cases. We had each been through the drill until we knew the questions by heart. Since we were on to the shakedowns they were going to try a different tact. They had passed out these official looking forms with every conceivable question they could think up.

The instructor said that he now "trusted us" to the point that he was going to leave us alone to fill out the forms. Another bad miscalculation on his part.

"Look at this question, 'Who is your best friends?'" I laughed.

I wrote, "The only friends I have want to borrow money from me, so I don't want to embarrass them by giving away their names."

In the space reserved for us to write the name of our Regimental Commander I wrote, "Secret Information cannot be given." Some of the others were more creative and wrote, "Superman", "Captain Marvel", or some other inappropriate statement.

"Hey, Joe, here's a question I've been waiting to answer ever since I joined the Army." It read list your jobs in the Army.

"Hell, I know the answer to that one, KP, guard duty, fatigue, and latrine orderly."

We spent that remainder of our unobserved time making up false answers to their questions and sharing them with one another. It made us feel in control of the situation for a change. We knew the affect our fun would have on our captors, but this was one of those times we couldn't hold back.

We left the forms in the box provided and started back for the hut. We hardly got settled in when the roof caved in. God was he mad. Escorted by two guards he stormed in and tried his best to hold his temper, but it showed through all right.

"Students, you make joke again," he whined. "Now we have to do it all over again. You will please report back to the school and fill out new forms. We must have this information."

We got another lecture, almost identical to the first one, they needed the information to tailor the classes, but this time they read out some of the answers. We thought we had come up with some good ones but the other squads had really been creative. The instructor did his best to quiet the laughter but insisted on reading more of the answers. He didn't know when to leave well enough alone. Not only was he entertaining us but he was giving us some good ideas for the next set of forms they passed out as well.

One of the best responses I saw was done by the guy who put his form in the box ahead of mine. He had drawn a cartoon that covered the entire form along with a brief note. "This will tell you all you need to know about me."

Joe had written, simply, "I'm sorry, but I will have to discuss this matter with my lawyer before I fill out the answers. Will you please arrange to provide me with tickets to New York so I can talk with him."

Another guy wrote this time, "I filled out a form like this once before and I wound up in the Army. God knows that I don't want to end up in the Chinese army this time."

And so it went. And so the instructor got even more upset and put us through it a third time. This time they had all new forms and the instructor was seething. We didn't waste much time on them, we merely filled the blanks with "None.", "Don't Apply," or "I don't know."

Now our instructor was desperate. He didn't know what to do next. We were ordered back to our hut. Later one by one we were summoned to the commanders office to fill out the form separately and under supervision.

Knowing damned well that they had read the only letter I had received up to that time, I mentioned only those names and information that the letter contained. Hell, they already had those answers anyway. We all refused to answer the military information they asked for. We were firm and they knew they had reached a stone wall where this type information was concerned.

As the days rolled on we were driven to the inevitable conclusion that peace, for us, was still in the distant future.

Many who had held on just for the chance at freedom now died. The hope that created a burning determination in them was gone, still no peace.

CHAPTER 7

The Bombings

In every war there seems to be at least one pest who appears to have only one mission in life, to keep you awake. In World War II on Okinawa it had been my sergeant, here in Camp No. 1 it was a B-26 pilot we called "Bed Check Charlie." He had a knack for coming around the camp at midnight looking for trouble.

As an infantryman you developed a natural hatred for pilots and the vehicles of destruction they commanded. On the ground with just your rifle you are pretty defenseless against their onslaught. They were worse than the artillery since they could actively seek out their prey. But after our capture, knowing that the only bombing being done here was by the U.S. Air Force, we fell in love with them. Despite the fact that we were perilously close to their targets it was nice to have some confirmation that our side was still in the fight. Having some of our own flying overhead gave us the feeling that home and civilization wasn't really that far away.

The first of his visits happened one night while I was lying on the hospital floor trying to ignore the terrible aching in my head. Everything seemed so peaceful, the pale moon casting quiet shadows over the hills gave everything a tranquil appearance. The only sounds were the labored breaths of the other sick men stuck in this miserable excuse for a hospital.

Around midnight the low drone of "Bed Check Charlie's" engines could be heard. He was still a long way off but the noise of the piston engines steadily got louder as he approached. Hell, I couldn't sleep anyway so I got up to catch a glimpse of him. As I got to the door I spotted the light shining from the cook's hut. The Chinese cook and several of the guards must be grabbing a midnight snack. The light would provide a perfect target for the B-26 bombardier. I couldn't understand why they didn't kill the lights, surely they heard the incoming bomber as clearly as I had.

The pilot must have been surprised as well, he circled the camp five times before he began his bombing run. Still the cook made no attempt to extinguish the lights. The B-26 was coming in unopposed and I knew that with the accuracy the light was providing them that this could be a bad one. The hospital and the entire prison camp for that matter was not marked in any way, so it was fair game for the bombers. There were no red crosses or any kind of indication that would indicate to U.S. pilots that their countrymen were at risk below. Now the rest of the prisoners and I were the unintentional players in this deadly game.

The first bomb hit, landing near the officers' quarters, killing a few of them, the second fell and the light was gone. This one found it's mark hitting the kitchen. The cook was headed out of the door just as it hit and was thrown against the wall behind him, obviously dead. The remainder of the bomb load landed harmlessly beyond our buildings. By now the camp was in pandemonium with guards, prisoners, and civilians running for cover in confusion.

The B-26 wasn't about to stop yet. With all his bombs expended he now circled around for a strafing run. We knew enough by now to expect this to be a part of the strategy. Most of us headed for the river as the plane came in low and fast. I was sure that in the bright moonlight the pilot could see us scattering across the field. But he didn't strafe. Thank God, he didn't strafe. The plane turned back over the camp, it's pilot probably wondering what he had stirred up.

One of the guys from the hospital ran by me and headed for the ditch. Jumping into the ditch he landed on one of the Chinese guards who also decided to hide rather than fight. Upon realizing he was discovered, the guard jumped up and began yelling orders in Chinese. All to no avail.

By now most of the camp had made it to the relative safety of the river and the cover it afforded. Leading the pack was none other than the Chinese interpreter.

With the plane long since departed for home the Chinese guards commanded, "Let's go," and headed out of the river. They had a hard time rounding all of us up. Of course we did nothing to help the situation, yelling and running around, making the most of the excitement. It was good to see them out in the cold with no protection as we have always been. They had not wasted precious seconds grabbing their overcoats in their scramble for survival.

"Yah, I hope you freeze, you slopehead."

"Look out, dearie, you'll catch cold."

We also couldn't resist letting the valiant Chinese interpreter, who led the stampede to safety, have a piece of our mind.

"Hey, what's the matter with you anyhow, I thought you told us we didn't have any Air Force left that could come north of the 38th parallel."

He informed us that this was just the desperate act of a frustrated pilot and the incident could not happen again.

Well it did happen again a few nights later. Just as a truck entered the camp we heard the roar of jet engines. The truck's driver now hit the gas and was streaking across the main supply route. This supply route passed right through the camp in direct violation of the Geneva Convention, which stated that a tactical route of communication was not to pass through a prisoner of war camp. But the Commies justified it in their own mind by not marking it as a POW camp. Since it wasn't marked as one then they were not in violation of the provision.

This attack was all over before we even hit the ditches. The truck driver thought he could outrun the jet. He didn't even try to stop and take cover, he kept barreling through the road.

The bomb hit between the civilian huts and the POW huts. The jolt forced the truck off the road and into the ditch. The driver scurried away with minor cuts and bruises. The bomb had also injured two of our men, one of whom died shortly thereafter. Two Chinese guards, a cow, and a pig were also killed that night.

The civilians were very happy about the last two casualties. It was their first chance in months at a meal consisting of meat. It appeared as if the entire town congregated at the river to clean the dead animals and ensure it was divided equally.

The reason for their lack of meat was partly do to the fact that the civilians were not allowed to kill their cows and pigs. They first had to get permission from the communist officials and turn over most of the butchered meat to pay the required "tax". This was indeed a holiday for the small village; fresh meat.

For our part we simply buried our dead comrade in a modest ceremony and the remainder of the night went on as usual.

The next morning we were awaken at six o'clock and got orders to fall in for another lecture. We were marched out into the field and huddled around the platform the commissar spoke from.

The subject of this lecture was "The bombing of Prisoner of War camps by the United States aircraft." It was a pitiful half-hour tirade that infuriated all of us.

First on the agenda was to again try to explain how the plane could have made such a strike. We were told that the airplane was lost and it was a mistake that it had gotten this far north, just like the last one. They restated the lie about the Chinese Air Force having air superiority above the 38th parallel. They were stupid enough to think we would buy a pitch like that.

It did nothing but upset us further and we were getting a little hard to handle at this point. Most of us had raised up from our usual crouch position and were becoming rather defiant.

One of the lads had heard enough and decided to speak up.

"If you guys would mark these camps our planes wouldn't bomb them!"

"Oh, so, you are wrong," the instructor said, obviously annoyed by the interruption. "We have tried to mark the camps but still your side bombs them. That is when they can sneak past our glorious air force."

"I can't say as I'd blame them for bombing a prison camp that had a main supply road running right through the middle of it," another prisoner stated.

They were still very patient with us trying to expound the virtues of the communists to us and allowing some discussion. As this discussion continued it was evident that this one was a miserable failure. We kept insisting that they mark the camps and reroute the supply road around the camp. They kept insisting that the U.S. would bomb the camps anyway.

"You just don't understand," the frustrated instructor wound up, feebly, "you are prisoners. It is not just this camp, but all camps that the Americans are bombing. You are of no further use to your country, so they are trying to bomb you and kill you. They are doing it deliberately."

Then the obvious question came from Joe.

"If these were lost pilots making mistakes then why did you say other camps were being bombed? If our pilots can create so much havoc by making mistakes then you are surely finished if they get organized."

Seeing the inevitable outcome of the discussion the instructor attempted to close it off amid continued mutterings in the crowd. Now the main thrust of this days lecture was to come. They wanted us to sign a written protest to the United Nations Command. They had it all written out, all we had to do was sign it. They also said they would have copies of the protests sent to our Senators and Congressmen.

"Now, that's damned nice of them, isn't it," I remarked sarcastically to the man standing next to me. "Yes, I'm sure my Congressman will call up General Vandenberg and raise hell with him when he hears about this."

By this stage of our captivity we had learned that since the peace talks started we could avoid punishment by criticizing ourselves before the rest of the group. This was a small price to pay since we all understood one another enough to ignore the criticism, realizing it was just a part of the game. As long as the Chinese didn't kick, we'd tell them anything - but we wouldn't put it on paper. That's were we drew the line. Statements made on paper would be seen by others on the outside, who didn't understand the game, and could have a devastating affect.

We were all lined up by platoons and the guards passed out the petitions and pencils. There was no need to look to each other for advice, we knew no one was signing. We just let the paper flutter down on the ground and stuck the pencils in our pockets.

The commissars were very patient as long as they felt they had any chance whatsoever at selling their point. This one was convinced that if he sold it just a little harder he could get the papers signed. So we were seated around the platform once again and he started his lecture again from the beginning.

This time he went on for an hour and a half. Nothing in his message was changed - it was just a constant repetition of the same pitch, the Americans were deliberately bombing the POW camps and we should sign a written protest. The guards were a little more tense this time around, knocking the bored and sleepy on the head to keep their attention. Letting your mind wander didn't work either. If a guard turned you in for being inattentive then you could expect some jail time or the loss of your meager tobacco or sugar rations. This time we were literally forced to pay attention.

When he finished he issued his instructions. "We will pass out paper again and you will sign the letters of protest."

Once again we fell in by platoon and stood at attention. The guards walked down the length of our line and not one of us reached out to sign the paper. We had about enough of this and were getting tired of it.

"Take the paper, take the paper. Sign the paper," he screamed. "Guards, make them sign."

We didn't move.

You could tell from the look on his face that he had come up with a new strategy. "I see you are getting stubborn again. All right, we shall see how stubborn you are. Those of you who are stubborn will stand right where you are until you have signed the papers. But those of you who do wish to sign can do so and then go back to your area and take the rest of the morning off."

"Now here is what we will do," he continued. "All of you who do not wish to sign the papers go to the left side of the field and stand at attention."

"Those of you who do want to sign the papers go to the right of the field, sign the paper, and then go back to your area."

One man stepped toward the left side of the field and the entire company followed him. We moved across the field, did an about face, and stood at attention. The right side of the field remained entirely empty.

This visible act of defiance proved to excite the commissar. "Maybe you did not understand. I said only those who did NOT want to sign were to go to the left side of the field. Now, all of you who want to sign come back over to this side."

Nobody moved.

"Very well, then," the commissar said with an icy tone to his voice, "you can all just stand there until you change your mind." With that he jumped down from the platform, gave the guards their orders, and walked away.

"Hell, I might as well be standing here as anywhere else," I whispered.

"Yeah, what difference does it make, we haven't got anywhere important to go," the guy next to me answered.

"And besides, the guards will have to stand right here with us, it'll keep them out of mischief," I chuckled.

The instructor returned around noontime. Standing at attention in the hot field all morning had accomplished nothing but to make us madder by the minute. On several occasions we had tried to relax but the guards stuck by their orders and we stayed at attention. Observing that no one had moved to the right side of the field he retreated back to his office.

By dinner time he returned, a beaten man. If they kept us standing there any longer it would mean that none of the work parties would be performed that day. He finally realized two things, one, we were not going to sign, and two, he was losing more in this deal than we were. He finally relented and let us go eat. When he yelled dismissed I was sure our cheer could be heard for miles.

But they were not about to give up so easily. The following morning they tried a new plan of attack. It was a divide and conquer strategy, figuring we would lose our nerve without the support and watchful eye of our fellow prisoners.

They sent for six of the men, all from different huts, and all at different times. They hoped this would avoid attracting attention to their exploits. Within minutes of the first guys return the word spread through the grapevine.

The first man told us how it worked. He was called in, sat on a chair, given a cigarette and talked to very calmly. The talk ended with a proposition, "You sign the protest of Americans bombing the prison camp and we will give you plenty of good food. We won't tell any of the other men about it. They will never know you have signed."

"Sorry, sir," said the man, looking the camp commander straight in the eye, "I never did learn to write to well, you'd better ask someone else."

"You mean you refuse," asked the commander.

Throughout the day this play was acted out with the same results by each of the other members of our company offered their propaganda that day. Our captors rewarded our stubbornness by cutting our food rations by one third.

They did their best to disguise the fact that we were not getting the same amount of food as the company beside us. Apparently someone in that group had signed their damned petition.

Camp regulations prohibited us from visiting next door, and our system of passing notes across the fence had been discovered and stopped. While the rock throwing method worked well, we developed a number of alternate means of keeping in contact the longer we were there. Soon we were able to know the guards within the camp well enough to determine which knew English and which didn't. If the guards posted along our section of the fence dividing us from the other company knew English we would stick to using notes attached to rocks. If, on the other hand, none of the guards posted on the fence understood English we could use a more direct approach. We would simply yell at one another, even without talking across the fence directly, the word got through. It worked like this.

Carlie and I were in the yard passing the time of day when one of the men on the other side of the fence came within hearing distance.

"Carlie," I said, "Isn't it a shame that Joe over there can't hear us?" I said it loud enough to make sure he caught the meaning. Looking back over to his own hut Joe pretended to be answering to someone inside rather than responding to what I said.

"Yes, I hear you, what do you want?" he yelled.

Someone in his hut picked up on it and yelled out, "What have they got, anything hot?" The signals were established. To the guards it appeared to be two totally separate conversations taking place.

"George, old boy, I think we've been getting the shaft on the rations lately, what do you think," Carlie spoke loudly.

"I think that the boys across the fence are getting more than we are to eat, what about it," I replied.

Joe yelled to his accomplice inside the hut, "They've got a food problem, I guess." To which the voice inside responded, "Give us the pitch, we'll swap notes."

The four way conversation still had not aroused suspicion on the part of the guards. During this exchange we were to learn that while we got one can of beef for six men they received a can for every two. It was the first beef we had in months and were sure to do without for the next six months so every can was cherished.

Carlie and I headed for the instructor.

"How are we suppose to feed six men with a single can of beef," Carlie asked him.

"Oh, so, that is all the beef we have to issue. It is full ration. Everybody get same amount." he said.

"Oh, now look, buddy, don't give us that stuff, some of the boys are getting more than that." I said.

No, no, everybody get same amount," he insisted. "There is only little beef to go around."

"Well, then here, take this back," Carlie said handing him our can of beef. "If you're so short of food you'd better keep it for yourselves." We turned and walked away.

He stood there completely dumbfounded holding the can in his hand. He couldn't understand why we would pass up a chance to have meat. What he did seem to understand was the fact that we knew the game he was playing with some of our compatriots and this could upset his plans to gain further propaganda out of them. He came running up to us about five minutes later, full of apologies.

"So sorry," he stammered, "I just find out. The quartermaster make mistake. You suppose to get one can for each two men. It is all a mistake."

"Some mistake," charged Carlie. "He didn't make the same mistake in the other company over there, did he? He gave them a can for each two men the first time, didn't he?"

We had him on that one. "How did you know," he said, then realizing his admission, quickly shut up. "What makes you think the other company had more meat," he asked.

"A little birdie told us," I said, and again we walked away, leaving him with a puzzled look on his face. The next time we got our meat, all of it.

After a few weeks they tried again to get the propaganda mill started out of the bombing raids. This time they did it in true Hollywood fashion.

The night before they moved the motion picture camera crews into position, then they lit fires in some of the old bomb craters to loosen up the frozen dirt. The next morning they marched us away from the scene. Next they placed dynamite into the holes to make them deeper. Then they rounded up a crew of "actors".

Only a few of the performers were Americans who decided to play along, the majority of the actors were Chinese. There was not much we could do about the American movie stars except hurl curses at them.

I spotted one of the Americans covering himself with mercurochrome to fake the appearance of blood on his body. Joe called to him, "Hey, did you ever hear of the Articles of War?" He just stared.

There were more than a few of us seeing this spectacle that would have gladly taken the opportunity to replace this guy's mercurochrome with the real thing.

I called out, "You dirty bastard, you..," and was interrupted by "Detective Looie". He thought I was yelling at him and brought me up in front of the interpreter. I had to explain that I wasn't swearing at the Chinese but at the Americans who were playing along with this farce. "You guys can't even stick to the facts on a thing like this, can you?" I added for good measure.

"Of course we have facts," the interpreter said. "You see facts being made."

To add to their idea of realization in the movie they set a few small buildings on fire and then the cameras started to roll. It was a sight to behold. The Chinese came running out of the burning buildings and then ran to a small shack to rescue the American. We could have killed him.

If we couldn't stop their production we were determined to louse it up. A couple of the boys decided to give them the action they were trying to portray. They set a haystack on fire.

It literally became a "Chinese fire drill". They tried to keep the movie going while the Chinese dragged their ancient fire fighting equipment to the scene to put out the blazing haystack. They shoved the hose into the well but couldn't get any water. It looked more like a slap-stick comedy than a bombing raid by the time they were done.

The only down sides to this fiasco were, this film might be believed by some on the outside and the two guys who set the haystack on fire were caught.

They were sent to the hole for a couple of weeks as punishment.

Late in the fall of 1951 came another example of how far the communists would go to stage a picture for propaganda purposes.

We were called out early one morning and sat through a lecture on the upcoming corn harvest and how important it was to the North Korean civilians. We didn't pay any more attention to this one than we had any other we had sat through day in and day out. That was until the instructor hit us with, "You will all have to go out and help with the harvest."

"Nuts to that, brother, we're prisoners of war. We don't have to do any work that will help the enemy." That pretty much summed up the feelings of everyone on the matter.

"You do not understand," he interrupted, "this food is for the civilians. If it is not harvested right away it will rot and the people will starve."

We debated amongst ourselves until the instructor made all further discussion pointless.

"It really does not matter, men," he stated, "You do not have much choice. If you want to eat today, you will go to the fields and harvest. All of the food is being sent out today and only those who work will get any." Well that settled it. Out to the harvest we went.

We were issued tools to cut the stocks and went to work. The civilians may have needed our help but they certainly didn't need much. We worked in two crews, one cutting, one gathering. Before noon the job was nearly finished. Then just when we were reaching the last of few rows in the field out came the photographer. Over the next few months we would get to know him quite well.

Along with him came the banners and signs. By the time they were done it gave the appearance of an old fashioned country fair. Every time he came near us with his camera we would stop working. Not many of the prisoners went along with their scheme. Those few who did probably didn't realize just how effective this propaganda can be or how adept the communists were at making the most from scenes like these. Despite our best efforts he did get some pictures, however.

We could only imagine the reaction these pictures showing the North Koreans and American prisoners working side by side under a banner which read, "Freedom Loving People Helping Each Other Out" would have. Since the banners were written in English and Chinese we were sure they were destined for the states and China.

This powerful tool which was used so masterfully by the Nazis in World War II was also to have a great affect in this struggle.

CHAPTER 8

Indoctrination - Our Facts vs. Their Facts

The endless hours of instruction we endured under the name of indoctrination was really a communist reeducation program. In the years that followed it would be given the more descriptive name of brainwashing. To fully understand the nature and impact of this program you have to understand the basic differences between the American citizen and the communist comrade.

Each of us begins our life not only in complete innocents but also with a total void of past experiences from which to draw upon. There is no stored knowledge base of information. From that first day and throughout the rest of our lives we all learn certain things based upon the environment that we are in and the upbringing our families provide.

As an ordinary American citizen I learned certain beliefs and gained certain knowledge. But the only reason I know something is white is because someone taught me that it was white. And the only reason I know something is black is because someone told me it was black. And the only reason I believe in God is because I have been taught to believe in God. Just like everyone else I knew nothing at my birth, I had to be taught everything I know. Everything I know about my country, about democracy, about family values, about politics, the news, prices, wages, unions, education – all beliefs I developed based on what someone else has told me.

It is no different for our captors. They also were born without a base of knowledge and were developed from a society that taught different values. Having lived in a different environment and developing a totally different history, they naturally were driven to different conclusions about the meaning of life. The value of a single life held a completely different meaning to them than to us. In other words he didn't learn things from the same book as I had. It wasn't a case of the communists being told "this is the truth, but we will tell the POWs something else." They held a firm conviction that the things they told us were the truth and they believed them fervently. And they were the truth, but they were their truth, not my truth.

The communist followers learned their truth from an entirely different set of rules than I did. They learned from a planned, nationwide indoctrination through propaganda. As a communist subject the communist government told him what to read, see, hear and believe. He was allowed absolutely nothing else to use as a basis of comparison. In effect, he might call black, white – because no one ever told him differently.

When the communists said that Rockefeller, Morgan, and Dupont ran Wall Street and that Wall Street runs America, he is basing that information on what he considers to be fact. He has been told that as many times as we have been told who the President is. His belief in his "fact" is just as strong as my belief in who is living in the White House today. They only difference is in how he learned his "fact."

We know who is President because we have seen him on television. We may have read about his campaign in the newspaper that we chose to read. We might have even gone to the inauguration. We have conclusive proof of who is our President.

The communist "Student," on the other hand, learns his "facts" about the world he lives in from an entirely closed system. The press is controlled, the education system is controlled, with the inevitable outcome being, what they believe is controlled as well.

Now having this background from which to start, try to understand what we had to go through in our daily, three hour indoctrination. It would have been much easier to take if they felt they were telling lies. It is hard to reason with someone, to expose their entire belief system as being deficient, especially if that someone considers you the enemy. Their truth was just as real to them as our truth was to us.

During these indoctrination lectures we were told their truths. That we were the slaves of the capitalists, it is the capitalists who own everything in the United States, that it was the capitalists who waged war. They let us know that we were treated so leniently because we were not at fault, we were just duped by the capitalists to come and fight in Korea, to fight this unjust war. We were told how South Korea attacked poor defenseless North Korea. Boy, for being defenseless they sure put up one hell of a fight.

Over and over they drilled into us how the peace loving communist masses will win over the capitalists. We learned of the friendship between the North Koreans and the Chinese. We saw their brand of friendship in action. The North Koreans were not even allowed to walk freely around their own country.

A sample of the friendship the Chinese communists had for the North Korean civilians was vividly demonstrated to us during the winter of 1951. A group of POWs were working on the banks of the Yalu river and there were a number of civilians in the surrounding area.

An old Korean man was crossing the river. He used slow, sure, deliberate steps to cross the ice which now covered that part of the river. Following him was probably the only possession of any value he had left, a cow. On the cow's back was a large bag of corn.

Suddenly the weight of the cow was too much and the ice broke. The cow plunged into the river. The old man made it to the edge still helplessly holding the rope tied to the cow's neck. He looked around, pitifully, for help. The only response from the Chinese soldiers was the cruel laughter of a cruel people as they stood and watched.

Several of the prisoners broke from their work and ran to the aid of the old gentleman. They could have helped had the guards not ordered them back. They backed up that order at the point of their rifles. The American soldiers had no choice, they had to go back.

The poor animal continued to struggle for some time but eventually the current was too strong for her. She finally slid under the ice as the rope was ripped from the old man's grasp. The man stared at his empty hand for a moment and then simply turned and sadly walked away.

We tried to help the civilians when we could. To get caught providing any assistance at all meant sure punishment, not only for us, but also for those we tried to assist. Most of the civilians left us alone fearing this reaction on the part of the Chinese. The shy smiles and carefully guarded looks told us that they would like to talk to us and comfort us if they could. We, too, would like to have comforted them on occasion.

Not all of the Chinese were so gruel though. One day we were helping an old Korean mamasan. She was weak from hunger and barely able to walk. One of the soldiers was also helping her and stood a few feet from her at the time. The soldier took pity on her and removed a few crackers from his pocket and placed them on the ground, carefully gaining the old woman's attention. He pointed to the crackers and signaled by chewing to let her know it was food. She nodded in acknowledgment. Just as she reached the crackers another soldier spotted her. He took the crackers from her grasp and laughed as he ate them himself. The woman flashed a grateful, yet sad, smile to the kindly soldier who tried to provide for her. Then she shrugged her shoulders and went back to work.

Sometimes the civilians were successful in their attempts to help us. Very often we would find an egg or other scrap of food conveniently left in a spot they had just worked, knowing we would soon be there. They were delicious. We were never able to express our thanks on those occasions.

Believe it or not, one time we even lent a hand to one of our captors. One of our guards who looked like he needed a friend at the time. He had just been jailed for complaining about the food. Quite a bit of discussion took place over that incident. It seemed incredible that they would jail one of their own just for a few comments about the quality of the food.

"Man," I said, "can you imagine getting locked up for bitching about the chow? Hell, I guess every soldier in the whole United States Army would be in the guard house if that were the case. I can't think of a single soldier who hasn't had at least one meal that wasn't worth the time it took to eat it."

But there he was for about two days, in the jail located right beside the hospital. During that time he had to pass right by us to reach the latrine. Each time he was escorted by an armed guard.

On the second day of his confinement one of the Turks and I were in the latrine when he came in. His escort remained outside. We were both surprised when the Chinese soldier held his fingers up to his lips, giving us the international hand signal that means, "Have you got a smoke?" The Turk smiled and handed him some tobacco and papers. Then he motioned for a light. I struck a match and held it out to him. He smiled his thanks, took a few puffs and then carefully put the cigarette out and placed the butt in his pocket.

The next day when we saw the Chinese prisoner headed for the latrine we left some tobacco and matches on the shelf. I remember thinking how strange it seemed leaving a smoke for a Chinese soldier, for that matter, giving him anything. But at least for the time being he had more in common with us than with the rest of our captors. We both knew we would have felt like heels if we didn't give this guy a break. To our amazement, it paid off within a few days.

On the third day the Chinese prisoner publicly criticized himself and was released from jail. He went back to guard duty.

He visited us two under the pretense of an inspection. When he assured himself that no one else was present, he held up his finger to signal for silence. A few moments later he returned with a box of matches and a bag of sugar, the first sugar we had in weeks. I don't know where he got it because even the Chinese soldiers were not issued sugar.

He dropped his gifts and departed without saying a word. The next day he left some Korean candy.

For the small price of two cigarettes we had converted this communist. From then on he was on our side and it made us feel good.

There was still a lot about our enemy I couldn't figure out, not the least of which was their sense of humor. One day a Chinese soldier came into the hospital with a badly crushed leg. He was obviously in a great deal of pain, screaming louder with each passing minute. But they let him sit there writhing in pain on the floor in agony while they laughed at him. That taught me why we never got any attention when we complained about how our boys were treated. They even lacked compassion for one another.

We saw these experiences and interpreted them based on the American way of learning, for the most part the North Korean civilians saw the same thing but had to struggle with their way of learning. To admit that the people who taught them this "truth" had lied would bring all their other "truths" into question. Many of them did see through the propaganda and resented the Chinese as much as they did us.

One day our lecture was a history lesson on World War II. We were told how the Russians drove the Germans back and finally defeated them. As far as they were concerned, the war in Europe only existed in an area from Stalingrad to Berlin. In the Pacific the Russians helped the Chinese chase the Japs out of Southeast Asia, liberating that part of the world.

Nothing was said about the Battle of Britain, North Africa, Sicily, Normandy, Pearl Harbor, Wake Island, Midway, the Philippines, Hiroshima or Nagasaki. The United States, Britain and France were never mentioned. Since most of us had also served in that conflict and those that hadn't, more than likely lost a loved one, this little bit of propaganda really hit home. The Brits went so far as to tell them if it hadn't been for the United States, Hitler would have ruled the world, and that world included China and Korea.

Very few of the lectures got to us, some were actually laughable. These lectures were usually about the "warmongers" invading the land of the peace loving people of North Korea. At one point the instructor said, "They told you lies. They told you about the pretty girls in Korea and the apples. The delicious North Korean apples."

I said, "The what?"

The instructor repeated, "The apples. You came to Korea because they told you about the wonderful North Korean apples."

He honestly meant it. You could tell he was saying it with total conviction in his voice.

At that point I stood and said, "Buster, we feed our pigs better ones than you have here in North Korea. And as for the women, we have all passed up better ones than any you have in this whole country."

But he continued to insist we came for the apples and the women.

One time we had been listening to the same old drivel for about two hours when a new instructor took the platform. This one started his lecture with a new pitch.

"I will tell you the truth about America."

"The poor people are forced to live in miserable slums. Do you know that only sixty percent of the homes in America have bathtubs?"

I said, "Sure, we know that."

"Oh, so," he asked, obviously surprised that we were so ready to accept his idea. "You know that?"

I stood up and said, "Sure, everybody knows that. Only sixty percent of the homes in America have bathtubs."

By now he was extremely impressed with the progress he was making.

Then I took him down a few notches when I added, "The other forty percent have showers."

By the time the laughter died down he had decided that there was no use continuing with the lecture today and dismissed the class.

Their two main targets seemed to be our President, Harry Truman, and General Douglas MacArthur who commanded the opposing forces.

The President was blamed with starting the war, playing along with the capitalists, and bringing all this suffering to their people.

But the brunt of their hatred they reserved for MacArthur. If we wanted to make them mad all we needed to say was "Just wait and see, MacArthur will be up here any day to liberate us." We made the most of it by spreading the word through the guards, the civilians, and anyone else who would listen. "Pretty soon now, MacArthur is coming up with his army to take us back." We were even able to get some of the kids to hold their fingers up in the "V" for victory sign and yell "Truman." That really infuriated the camp officials. Some officials got so mad that they began forcing the civilians to walk way up the steep hills to get from one side of their village to the other. This way they avoided the prison camp and the harmful exposure to us prisoners. There were still a few contacts now and then. After hearing of the election we tried to teach them to say "Eisenhower" but they had a tough time pronouncing it.

Most of the indoctrination was centered around and about Russia. How nice the Russians people were living on their high standard of living. How they could afford everything they wanted. How productive the communist worker was.

One of the stories that stirred a response in us was the one about the Russian bricklayer. And how this super human communist was able to lay twenty-eight thousand bricks in a single eight hour shift.

"How many," I asked.

He said, right back, "Twenty-eight thousand."

A few nights later the mystery of the Russian bricklayer was solved. They took us to see a Russian movie. It was a documentary showing the construction taking place in the Soviet Union. Our bricklayer friend did nothing but line up the bricks once they were in place. The cement was spread using a machine and four girls put the bricks down for the heroic bricklayer to line up. What a deal. They couldn't understand it when we burst into laughter upon seeing this spectacle.

Over the next few weeks we saw a few movies made in the Soviet Union. They were always depicting life in Moscow, Stalingrad, or some other large city. We never saw the countryside or the small villages. From what we saw of the communist system here in North Korea we knew it had to be pretty bad behind the Iron Curtain as well.

Along with this, we were of course schooled on Lenin and Stalin. How they freed the Russians from capitalism; the five year plan; collective farming; and a bunch of other garbage.

We were also exposed to their idea of a newspaper. It was called the "Shanghai News." We called it the "Shanghai Liar" and we were punished whenever they heard us refer to it as such. It would tell us how many American planes were downed along with the number of casualties the Americans had experienced. If you were to take the time to add up the numbers provided you would find that after a few weeks every plane and soldier in the U.S. Armed Forces had been lost three times over.

There were glorious stories of how a Chinese soldier wiped out an entire American company. Or how they downed one of our jets with their rifles and hand grenades. We use to remark how the Dodgers would have loved to sign that guy.

One in particular that stood out was an article the guards passed around with a picture of a Chinese soldier wearing a jacket with "U.S." stenciled on it. According to the article this man was a Chinese specially trained by the U.S. Army in Seoul as a spy. They planned to drop him behind the North Korean lines to commit sabotage. The story continued describing how he "remained true to the freedom loving people of North Korea." As he was about to jump out of the plane, they said, he threw a hand grenade back into the plane, the pilot lost control and the plane crashed killing all on board. The spy was played up as a big hero to the Chinese guards. Every one of them believed it.

We tried to tell them how ridiculous it was, but it was no use.

"You lie, you lie," they would say. They believed it and expected us to believe it as well.

We realized that the communist theme worked here because they took a largely illiterate society and spoon fed them the things that we had learned through truthful means. It made it awfully hard on us. We were punished for telling lies or for not pretending to absorb their teachings. On the occasions when we weren't punished they assumed we were stupid and spent more time in lectures to indoctrinate us properly. Either way we lost.

The camp also had a library. I was suffering pretty severely now from the blow on the head I received during the march. I had never been able to do as much manual labor as others more fit than I. A friend of was also in this category having lost his toes. It made us the natural choices to run the library.

We liked the idea for a few reasons - none of which had anything to do with the reading material they offered. First of all, it got us out of the hut every night. Secondly, it gave us a chance to scrounge some materials. The most sought after items were boards. These were used to build crude cots that were not comfortable but at least kept the crawling bugs off of you.

More importantly, the library was located next to the rooms where the commissars maintained their offices. We became a pipeline for the grapevine, picking up several very interesting conversations. Another of our duties was to keep tabs on some of the guys who were starting to read too much propaganda. A very few started to belief some of that stuff.

All of the prisoners were encouraged to make use of the library. One of the requirements they placed upon us was to write a report for each book we read. Since most of us had no desire to read that crap let alone write about it, the library didn't get much use. Especially once we learned that if your report didn't reflect favorably on the ideals the book contained, it had to be rewritten.

The books were innocent looking enough, mostly history, geography, or novels, carefully tailored to the communist way of thinking. There were even a few American novels, these of course were doctored so cleverly that only a very educated person could tell the truth from the propaganda.

A number of the American novels dealt with the subject of racial discrimination, a subject the communists could easily exploit. They gave a completely different account of Uncle Tom's Cabin and Tom Sawyer than I remembered from my childhood.

What did get considerable use were the newspapers. Particularly since there was nothing else to read that gave us current information. They did give us some idea of what was taking place in the outside world, especially if you realized they only contained the communist point of view.

There were a number of newspapers in the library. Most a few weeks to a month old by the time we got them. None of them were papers we were familiar with. Two were instruments of the communist party in the states, the "New York Daily Worker" and the "San

Francisco Daily Worker", and of course the good old "Shanghai News."

We hadn't been in our jobs in the library for very long when we drilled a small hole into the wall adjoining the commissars offices. Meetings were held in this room almost every night. We still didn't know enough about their language to get a lot out of the conversations but we were usually able to tell when they were going to work on us the next day. We also could identify the names of the people they had keen interest in or those they were using to their advantage.

We also could tell the guys when to expect mail. We could see them reading our letters the night before they passed it out to us.

From this vantage point we were also able to tell whether the supply trucks making use of the route through the camp were full of material or empty. The convoys would usually go through the camp at night to avoid the air raids which were becoming more and more frequent. By seeing the way the trucks would hit the ditch just in front of the library we were able to tell if they were loaded with equipment. Since the Koreans did not have many trucks they would load much more on each truck than was prudent. The springs were so overloaded they would lie flat on the axles. When a loaded truck hit the ditch the overloaded springs could provide no cushion and you could hear the fenders as they hit the tires. Unloaded trucks made no such sound.

Everything we learned at the library was passed to the rest of the men through the grapevine. It was interesting to see how uncomfortable the instructors were when they found out we knew their plans for the day. We would also disrupt their propaganda sessions by asking them about military convoys that we weren't suppose to know anything about.

CHAPTER 9

The Turnip Bin

By the spring of 1952 the mud had just about dried up and realizing that the peace talks were just that, all talk, we began to think of escape. Throughout the winter the lectures had given us dreams of freedom that never materialized. So we had also used this time to accumulate enough equipment to make the gamble worth the risk.

The first I heard of it was in early April when two members of Seven Company snuck over from their area to see me.

"Matta, we're bustin out," one of them whispered. "What about you coming along with us?"

"What! You're crazy. They'll shoot you."

"Shhhh! Not so loud," he said, looking around apprehensively.

"No kidding, we've got it all planned. We've been working on this deal all winter and nobody's gonna stop us now. Whatta ya say?"

I looked into their eyes and realized they meant what they said. I debated the key points in my mind. It sure beat rotting in this place. I could get back to my wife. But then the risks are pretty tough. And even the staunchest gambler wouldn't take these odds. My head had been killing me for days now and this discussion sure wasn't doing it any good. I stared at them again, trying to talk myself into going along with it and then asked, "You'll never make it, what will you do for food?"

The question got the desired results. They began to pass on more of the details of their plan to me. "Look, we've got food, rice, matches, clothes, the works. We can get out of the camp any night we want. They'll never see us going."

He was right about that, it would be easy to sneak past the guards, but how far can you go when you don't know the language, don't look like the natives, and don't even know how far the safety of the American lines are?

"You certainly can't carry enough food for the entire journey."

"We're going to trade our extra clothing for food, the natives won't turn us down as bad as they need it. We plan to go straight out towards the coast, not to the American lines to the south. Once we hit the coast, we steal a boat and try to get far enough out so our planes can spot us. If that fails then we will head for one of the islands our troops have taken. We know it's gonna be tough, but hell, it's worth it to get out of this hell hole." He waited for my answer. It all sounded so simple.

I thought about it hard for a while finally declining the offer. I told them, "With my bum head I'd be more of a hindrance than a help, I'd only get all of us killed. I'd better stay put for this one."

Before they left I asked, "Will you take a note to my wife for me?" I scribbled out a short note and pushed it at them and then turned to the door of my hut. I didn't want them to see the look of concern on my face. Please God, give them a chance. Let them make it safely.

They left camp than same night. Through the grapevine I was able to learn that one of them had been caught in a Korean's house just down the road. We heard the Chinese caught him in the house, but we couldn't find out what they did with him. The Korean who owned the house also disappeared. No word of the other escapee.

After a week or so my head still hadn't stopped giving me problems so I went back to the hospital. In a few days I had recovered from that bout but they wouldn't let me go back to my company. Instead I became the cook for the sixteen American prisoners in the hospital.

One day the nurse walked up and told me "You cook for seventeen men."

"But, why?" I asked, "There are only sixteen of us here."

"No questions, you cook for seventeen," she replied. I shrugged and did as she said. As I was preparing the rice I spotted her sneaking two bowls off to one side. I really didn't think too much about it at the time, but when this same act was carried out for a week straight, I got more curious. Every night she took an extra meal outside while we were eating.

Some of the guys from my old squad came by one night to bring in another patient. One of them snuck over to talk to me while they carried him in. There was only time for a few words to be exchanged before the guard was there beside us. From what little he said I could tell that someone was in the turnip bin and they wanted to know who. I caught the words, "We think it is Frank and he's got pneumonia bad."

Good God, I thought, the turnip bin. No one can live in that hole even if they are in great shape. A hole is exactly what it was, a hole in the ground used to keep turnips from freezing during the winter months.

I was the logical choice to discover the identity of the poor victim since the bin was only a few hundred feet behind the hospital kitchen. I began to wonder if that was where the extra food was going.

That night I ate earlier than usual and was stalling for time in the kitchen when the nurse came for the two bowls of rice.

"You like my cooking? I asked. She made a face and said, "Boo How" (no good). Knowing that all the guards were equally unimpressed by my cooking I was almost sure she was taking the food to a prisoner. I watched her as she left the kitchen, she headed in the direction of the turnip bin.

Later that night after the guards checked the room I passed my idea on to a few of the others.

"Look tomorrow night I'll cook up soup to go with the rice. I can get away with it once, I think. That way she will have four dishes to carry instead of just two. I'll just offer to help her. Maybe she won't get wise and the guard never follows her down there."

When she came for the food the next night, I handed her two bowls of rice, grabbed some bread and the bowls of soup and walked out right behind her without saying a word. At first she didn't even notice I was there, thinking that the rice was all the food for that meal just like all the rest. I thought it was going to work.

Just then the head nurse came around the corner of the building and started yelling. I almost dropped the bowls. She stormed up to us and started giving the nurse hell in Chinese and then started in on me. I couldn't tell exactly what she was saying, she was talking so fast, but I got the gist of it from her tone. I turned around and headed back in the kitchen.

"How'd you make out," one of the other guys asked upon my return.

"Awe, hell, I got caught. The head nurse chewed me out and the other nurse too. We'll have to think of another way."

We thought we would try sending a note. But if the food wasn't going to an American after all we would really be in a trick. It would be risky but we couldn't think of anything better.

The next evening I cooked up some steamed bread. This was a concoction that had the appearance of a hot crossed bun, the weight of a bowling ball, and the taste of sponge rubber. I inserted the note inside one of the spongy masses of dough. It read, "Frank are you OK? Get rid of this note, but don't eat the bread. Put your note inside." Along with the note I stuck a small slip of blank paper and a pencil stub. I knew that the bread would get back to me if it wasn't eaten. The guards and nurse were not desperate enough to eat our slop and they never waste food on the prisoners. If it is not eaten in one meal they don't throw it away, it is what you are given for the next meal, or the next, until you ate it. I was sure the uneaten bread would be in the bread box upon its return so it could be fried the next morning in pork grease for the next serving. I left the bowls of food and bread for the nurse and departed the kitchen.

We could hardly wait for the supper to end so we could see if we got a note back. We stalled as long as we could to make sure their was time for the leftovers to be returned before we started our cleanup. While the guys were finishing the last of their meal I snuck out to the kitchen. There it was, the roll of bread. I ripped it open and was glad to see a note inside. Quickly grabbing the note I rejoined the others.

Two of the boys kept an eye out to ensure the guards or nurses wouldn't see us. I slowly rolled the small slip of paper open. It read; "I'm sick. I've got dysentery and fever and they won't give me medicine or let me out until I criticize myself." It was signed, "FRANK."

"That poor bastard. What are we gonna do?"

"Wait until that sonofabitch, the Water Doctor, gets here in the morning. I'm gonna raise hell about this."

I lit a match to destroy the note and scattered the ashes into the dirt. We were sure the Water Doctor would stop by in the morning. He always did, it was part of his normal routine. I don't know why, he never had medicine for us. His visits usually consisted of him reading his morning paper and gloating over the Chinese victories it was sure to contain.

At eleven the next morning in he came, newspaper tucked under his arm.

"Ah, so, you are all awake and feeling well this morning," he began. "Too bad you fellow soldiers are not here with you. The glorious Chinese Army gives them big defeat yesterday..."

"Stow that crap, Doc," I started off, "Tell us about the GI you guys got in the turnip bin."

"Yeah," joined in one of the others, "Tell us all about him. He's got a high fever and dysentery and he's getting no treatment. What about it?"

He was obviously surprised at our inquiry.

He immediately turned and literally ran from the room.

"Gosh, I knew he would be surprised, but he looked terrified," I muttered. "What the hell gives?"

The answer came a few minutes later. The doctor had his entire hospital staff in formation outside the hospital building. We only caught a few words but we could tell that he suspected one of them of telling us about the mysterious guest they had in the turnip bin. He kept at them for about an hour. Finally he convinced himself that they had not been our source of information and dismissed them and returned to us in the room.

"You men, come here." His tone was demanding, yet it had a friendliness to it. We were sure it was a false impression.

"You asked about the soldier in the turnip bin. You are right. He is an American, but he is sick..."

"If he's sick, why isn't he in here with us," I interrupted.

"Wait, now, you not get excited. It will hurt your head..." he continued.

"Wait, hell, why isn't he being taken care of?" He could sense I was angry and not about to let him off so easy.

"You should not excite yourself. Please listen to me. Your soldier buddy has to be kept by himself. He has a very serious disease. It is contagious. You would all get sick."

"Don't feed me that stuff, Doc," I yelled. "That guy on the end of that bed over there has cholera, and that is about as contagious as you can get. What the hell are you trying to pull. What disease has Frank got that's worse than cholera? Tell us! Go on tell us!"

"He's getting everything you are getting," the Doc said. He knew that this was no great comfort to us either, considering how little attention we all received. Realizing he had lost this round also he abruptly departed once again.

We tried our note system again the next day to communicate to Frank. We asked him what he needed. His answer stated that he had no tobacco since being tossed into his isolation. So we wrapped some tobacco in a paper with matches and a little sugar and sent off another note. In this note we advised him not to risk writing us unless we told him to. We took this crude care package to the kitchen, put the matches, tobacco, sugar, and paper on the bottom of his bowl and covered them with rice. Our system was working fine.

That night we caught the doctor just before nightfall and asked him, "Say, Doc, is our buddy in the turnip bin still getting everything we get?"

"Oh, of course, he gets the same as you all the time."

"Has he been getting his tobacco and matches?" I asked.

"Oh, yes, he gets it the same as you do." he smiled.

"You lie, you bastard," one of the others piped up. "All the time you lie. That's all you people can do is lie to us. Why don't you try telling us the truth for a change. Why don't you admit he hasn't had any tobacco since you threw him in that hole."

Once again the doctor looked at us in astonishment. You could tell he also wondered how we got this bit of information.

His face gradually returned to its normally stoic condition and he replied, "Oh, I sorry. There must be a mistake. I was sure he was getting tobacco just like you." I will see quartermaster and see he gets it right away." We could only laugh at his rapid retreat.

The next day, "Mighty Mouse", one of the toughest guards in the camp showed up. His sudden appearance meant only one thing, trouble. And boy did we get it. He stuck his nose into everything. He was the one sent in when they needed information badly, or wanted to find out how much we knew about something. This time I'm sure his mission was to find out how we knew what we did.

He was now around the hospital almost every day, but up to now hadn't become too much of a bother and our note sending program continued. He was dangerous and we knew it, we would have to be very careful.

I spotted him just about the time I was fixing a "special" meal for Frank. I decided that sending a note that night would be an unnecessary risk. It's a good thing I did. While I was preparing the other meals I saw him cutting open the bread and sifting through the rice. Our private postal system would be shut down for a while until things cooled off. After three days we began to feel a little desperate and were sure Frank was also.

On the fourth afternoon we were all pretty upset. We had a death in the hospital, the first one in weeks. It was one of the lieutenants who had been in the hospital for months. We had made many attempts to get the Water Doctor to help him, and did everything we could ourselves. But it just wasn't enough. Mighty Mouse and another guard removed his body.

They threw it into a litter and walked out the door. Once outside Mighty Mouse dropped his end of the litter, making sure we were still watching, he spit into the dead officers face.

That was all we could take. Everyone who could stand headed out the door hurling curses at the rotten sonofabitch. We headed for the huge hulk and the noise brought the doctor and nurses running. We would have killed him if they hadn't summoned armed guards to stop us. We told them what he had done and they laughed. All of them. They thought it was a great big joke.

"That's all, brother, we're getting out of here," I told the doctor. "If you rotten bastards will let something like that happen to a dead man, what will you do to a live one. If that's all the respect you have for the dead, we don't want any part of it. We're going back to the company."

"You can't go back to the company. You are all sick," he said, still smiling.

"The hell we can't. You just watch us. We're leaving now." We turned, and as sick as we were, we started toward the company compound.

"Wait, stop!" Again using the armed guards to impose their will.

"You go back inside. We will take care of the guard for what he has done." They were worried. They knew if anything happened to all of us in the hospital, the camp's leaders would not be happy.

We knew their word meant very little but given the fact that we were now facing rifles and sure death if we continued, and more importantly Frank would be helpless in our absence, we finally went back inside.

"I'll get even with that sonofabitch if it's the last thing I do," I raged. The others nodded in agreement.

God must of heard us that day because our opportunity came shortly thereafter. It was the perfect set up and almost too easy.

One of the English speaking guards was checking some of the new equipment that had just been delivered. The light at that end was dim and he was hard to see from the other end of the building. As soon as we saw Mighty Mouse at the doorway we realized this was our chance.

All of the Chinese in and around the hospital had become very suspicious of one another because of our mysterious source of information about the turnip bin. The guy beside me said, "Here comes that no good bastard now." Mighty Mouse looked over and smiled. Fortunately he didn't understand more than a few words of English. I said, rather loudly, "Yeah, that was a lousy thing he did to the lieutenant, but don't forget, he's been a lot of help to us, too." I could almost feel the guards ears perk up on the other side of the room. I went on, even louder, "He was sure on the ball giving us that information on our buddy down in the hole. If Dr. Haung knew it he sure would be mad."

The English speaking guard couldn't get out of the building fast enough. He returned in less than two minutes, bringing along two other guards. All three had their guns drawn. The great Mighty Mouse, they guy who had the gall to spit at one of our dead, had his hands tied behind his back before he knew what had happened. Despite his surprised and vocal objections, they led him to the door.

"Are you going to shoot him," we asked hopefully.

"No, we take him to jail," our cooperative guard replied.

"Why?" we asked.

"He is no good comrade," the guard answered.

"Well, hell then, why waste time, take the sonofabitch out and shoot him now," we suggested. We could tell from the expression on Mighty Mouse's face that he knew we had done him in. That alone satisfied most of us. As they dragged him away we kept shouting after them, "Shoot the sonofabitch. Shoot the bastard."

Our messages to Frank continued the next morning. Mighty Mouse was never seen again.

Unfortunately the cruel treatment from the guards assigned to the hospital continued even in Mighty Mouse's absence. For example, one day when the pain in my head was giving me so much agony I thought my head was going to split open. The only thing I could feel was the pounding, pounding, pounding sensation, like sharp daggers tearing into my skull.

This continued for a few days, I forget how many, it was one long session of me drifting in and out of consciousness. There would be pain, then relief, only to be followed by more pain. The distress caused by the poor food and neglect were compounded by the fact the guards made no attempt to step over us as they made their checks. Preferring instead to attempt to walk through us, or worst yet, stepping on us to make there way through the hospital. Any sign of pain was responded to by the doctor and his nurses in their usual form, laughter. I tried to lie still, concentrate on anything that would force the pain out of my mind. I couldn't lie here any longer, I had to get up. I had to do something.

I struggled to get to my feet and then started walking doing my best not to disturb any of the others. I knew they were hurting too. I began a methodical pacing, up and down a ten foot section of the floor. Up and down, back and forth, holding my head in my hands. I clenched my teeth in an attempt to stop the unintelligible animal like growls forcing their way from my throat. When I could stand it no longer the growls turned into the loudest scream I had ever heard come from my own lips.

In they came, two larger than average Chinese. Male nurses they called them. I had seen them before, but like Mighty Mouse, only when there was trouble. They came towards me and knocked me to the floor so they could pass. Delirious with pain I rose to my feet and struck out at one, my fist hitting his face just as he reached for me.

I could feel my knuckles give way as they connected with his nose. He was stunned, more from the amount of blood than the force of the impact. The other one grabbed me.

"Lemme go, you sonofabitch, let me go!"

I swung again and then something hit me just behind the ear. This combined with the pain I already had in my head was all it took to bring tears to my eyes. But I swung one more time before they wrestled me to the floor.

The one I had hit grabbed all the fingers on my right hand and started bending them backwards. The other one slapped me across the face. My fingers felt like they would break off my hand. I pulled my legs up until I could get them on the chest of the guy in front of me. Having accomplished that I pushed as hard as I could. He went sailing out the door and down the wooden stairs. That was the last thing I remember because after that I blacked out.

Later when I came to I was still lying on the floor in about the same spot where I had launched the one Chinese male nurse out the door. They were both gone by now and all seemed quiet. My head was feeling much better. The pain seemed to have moved to my now swollen right hand. I could hardly move it.

That did it. I decided that I needed to get out of this hospital before they killed me. I would be no worse off back with my company, I wasn't getting any treatment here anyway. I started packing my things, not noticing that it was almost daylight.

Shakie Lil came in, as usual this time of the morning, to wake me up. She found me sitting on the floor with my few possessions rolled up inside my blanket. She was startled and came running to me, saying, "What you do? Where you go? You must lie down."

"The hell I'll lie down," I told her, "I'm getting out of this place before I die. I'm going back with the rest of my company."

She ran to the door calling for the doctor and one of the instructors. Dr. Haung came in immediately with the instructor right on his heels.

"What are you doing, you can't leave here," the Water Doctor said.

"I'm going back to my hut where your gorillas can't get me," I yelled. "I'm not going to stay here and get killed. The pain was driving me crazy last night and I took a few swings at them. I was surprised to have awaken in the hospital rather than the turnip bin or worse. I know it is not over as far as those two are concerned."

"Why, why, they didn't hurt you," he soothed, "they were just trying to help you. You had better lie down and let us take a look at you."

"Didn't hurt me, your crazy, take a look at my hand." I showed him the swollen stump.

"No, no, you must have hurt it jumping around. Or perhaps, you fell, they didn't touch you, there was no fight," he said.

"There wasn't huh! Well take a look at the big one and ask him how he likes his busted nose. And ask him how he liked being booted out the door. The hell there wasn't a fight. Let me go the men in my hut will take better care of me than you guys here."

They finally allowed me to return to my company. I felt a little guilty about the fact that Frank was still in the hole but the message system had been keeping his spirits up. He was also feeling better with the attention we were able to provide him so I thought the time was right.

Once back in my old spot in the hut I learned that some Marine units had landed on the East coast. Some of them were captured and brought to the camp. The news they brought with them cheered us up considerably. They had drawn a large number of Chinese soldiers toward the beach with the mock landing. Then when they were out in the open our planes hit them with bombs and strafing runs. So much for the communist propaganda lecture on how we were taking a beating south of the 38th parallel.

CHAPTER 10

The Comedians

The 19th of April 1952, is a day I remember well. The day started out just as dull and routine as every other day in the camp. We were all formed up outside the quartermaster's building waiting to get our summer clothing issued to us. Then all of a sudden Bob let out a yell that aroused the guards attention very quickly. "The British Are Coming," he shouted with his distinct London ascent.

His message had the opposite affect on the prisoners, we were all loosened up after that. We stood in line receiving our clothing that consisted of a floppy hat, something like our fatigue cap, a loose fitting jacket and pants that were always too short.

I grabbed my stuff and wandered back to the hut to put them on. We had all been given a warning that these clothes were to remain clean for the upcoming May Day show. As I pulled my pants up my mind wandered back to the lines of a poem I knew, "Twas the 18th of April in '75, Hardly a man is now alive..."

Yeah, I thought to myself bitterly, hardly a man is now alive. Today is a big holiday back in Massachusetts. The 19th of April - Patriot's Day. And here I am putting on a Chinese Communist uniform. How about that. But I am lucky to be alive I suppose. I chuckled under my breath as I thought of how the guards had reacted to Bob's announcement earlier.

Bob and Yung, the cocky little Hawaiian, came wandering in with their bundles of clothes.

"Hey, look at me, I'm just coming back from a posh Piccadilly Circus gentlemen's ready made store with my Easter clothes." Bob joked. Yung added, "Yeah, some Easter, but we keep them clean for May Day maybe, huh?"

"You gotta idea, maybe, Bob?" Yung queried. He had keyed in on the mischievous look on the Brit's face.

"Yeah...yeah, for a matter of fact, I have got an idea. I have a swell idea. Wait until those blokes see my idea." He motioned for Yung and they both ducked outside. Those of us left behind looked at one another and smiled in anticipation. We knew that he wouldn't reveal himself until he was good and ready. We could hardly wait.

We should have gotten a hint when Yung started borrowing things, but we didn't. A small length of chain, a small piece of wood, the stuffing from an old comforter, a discarded copy of the Shanghai Liar.

At around 07:30 on May Day morning, the guard came pounding on the huts demanding that we fall out quickly. We each made final adjustments to our ill fitting blue uniforms and formed into the usual sharp ranks. The first morning formations were a serious event and you didn't fool around at these. The guards had a very low tolerance at this time of the day. We had learned through experience that the best thing to do was to get them over as fast as possible. With this in mind we fell out in formation and did an immediate dress right, dress.

But the calm and order this morning was to be disturbed.

With a whoop and a holler, Bob hit the formation with all of the impact of a hydrogen bomb. The laughter started low at one end of the line and, as he came into sight from one rank to the next, the laughter spread into a solid roar. Men were laughing so hard they had tears in their eyes. I was laughing so hard myself that I nearly fell on the ground. The very sight of him threw the entire formation of 900 sick, hungry, defiant men into a mob beset with helpless hysteria. Never before had we seen the likes of this. The looks on the faces of the Chinese were even funnier than Bob himself. Their eyes popped out and their mouths dropped open. They were trying to figure out what the devil was up.

Without saying a word, Bob stepped smartly into the ranks. There he stood rocking back and forth on his heals in true British fashion. In his left hand he held a wooden camera. In his right, a chain ran to the ground and then circled back up into his pocket. He was swinging the chain around in his hand and he looked all the part of a character who had just stepped into a dance hall and was surveying the gals prior to making his selection for the next dance. And his clothes.

The hat was round and firm, its visor slightly creased and pulled down low over his right eye. The crown, was puffed out and smoothed over the back of his head.

His jacket was held up by one button and had gathers that flared away from his hips. There was a silk handkerchief flowing over his left breast pocket. The shoulders of this extraordinary garment were padded beyond the wildest dreams of the most fanatic zoot suiter. From his neck hung an honest to God necktie, with a yellow beer bottle painted on it.

His pants were held in place by what appeared to be a real fancy set of suspenders. His shoes were given just the right hue using yellow clay. Man he was a sight.

It took some time for the commissar's rage to die down to the point where he could visibly react. Two guards recovered in time to fall in behind him, noticeably worried that his rage might explode on them. His first act was to seize the camera, he was sure it carried a bomb of some type.

He held it, slowly turning it end to end. Still unsatisfied, he began to rip it apart. He was still careful lest it contain TNT. The sight of this was enough to start us all laughing all over again.

Through all this Bob didn't bat an eye. He just continued to rock back and forth on his heels. Catching the eye of one of the guards he winked. The guard recoiled as if a snake had bit him. Bob casually blew on his curled fingers and rubbed them along the lapel of his "sports coat." He was having a great time, and so were we.

The commissar demanded, "Who made this?" You could tell from the tone of his voice that he was not amused. We knew we were in for trouble. Bob paid no attention to him.

The guard went to take hold of Bob, but before he could, Yung stepped forward and confessed that he had made it. Adding "But I didn't think you would get so mad."

The commissar gave Yung a look that froze all of us and ordered, "Take him to jail."

We all began to shout, "No, No! He hasn't done anything, let him alone."

"Take him to jail," was his response.

Yung took one more opportunity to make a joke of the situation in hopes of cooling the commissar off. He soon realized that the fun was over and now it was time to pay for it. The commissar screamed

"You have destroyed the property of the people. You have committed a crime. You must go to jail."

"Awe, come off it, it's only a joke," some of us said.

"It no joke. You destroyed property."

"No, look, I didn't destroy anything. I just put a little padding and took up a few stitches, I can get it out easy. Cool off, your damned clothes ain't spoilt."

The commissar's hesitation at this comment gave us some hope. Seizing upon it we all began the laughter once again. I don't think he actually saw the humor in it, more likely he knew he would be on thin ice if he raised too much of a fuss. Bob was ordered to remove the padding and take out the creative stitching, and get back into ranks.

The main result of this episode was to infuse the camp with a new spirit that had been lacking for many months. Everyone felt it. People were smiling, cocky, and we knew we could take their worst and still come out on top. It was like the rebirth of the American soldier, in our own little way we were fighting men once again and it felt great.

Within minutes that spirit was put to the test. We were waiting for Bob to rejoin our formation after making the alterations to his uniform. He came running out tucking his shirt into his trousers and we got the order to fall in again. As we formed up out came a guard with a red flag. The guard handed the flag to one of the guys in the front rank. No sooner had the man taken the flag then a yell went up from within the group. "Hey look, those bastards think we are going to march behind that Goddamned flag." All at once our entire company dispersed. We took off in every direction. The commissar and guards were yelling, trying to restore order with their guns aimed at us. We continued to run. "Take your crummy flag and shove it," someone hollered, "we ain't gonna carry it." The guard now stood their in the middle of the field holding the flag once again, wondering what to do. The commissar signaled to him to head back to the headquarters building. We were having too much fun to stop now, we continued to scatter. Just as soon as four or five were lined up and marched to another group that they rounded up, the first group would take off again. Then they would round up a large group and before they could catch the last few stragglers, the big group would scatter again.

This cat and mouse game went on for almost an hour. What finally ended it was when the guards spotted the regiment commander up on the hill in his car. Once they noticed his watchful eye they became real serious about the whole business and we knew we better fall in quick, or else. At this point the guns weren't only aimed but cocked as well.

The old man in his car was upset to put it mildly.

"You men should be ashamed. We have a nice show all ready for you down at the square and here you waste all this time," he relayed to us. He had put too much time and trouble into this show to see it ruined like this.

"Tell them we won't carry their flag, then," a voice from the formation sounded. "Tell them we don't have to go anywhere under their flag."

"Ah, so you do not want to march with the flag. Very well, there will be no flag." The regiment commander then turned to the commissar to insure he understood, and said, "Now, march down to the show."

But the commander was not about to give up so easily. Just as we left the barbed wire fence marking the compound, out came the flag once again. They knew we would not break ranks outside the confines of the camp. To do so meant certain death, they would shoot without question. They thought they had us but our spirit was higher than they bargained for. The man in the front rank was handed the flag just as before. In a rare display of courage he calmly walked over to the edge of the road with the flag in hand. He leaned the flag against a telegraph pole and walked back into formation, his hands held high just as though he were still carrying the flag. Again we busted out with laughter.

The commander hesitated and then shrugged his shoulders. We knew the only reason they wanted us to carry that flag was for the effect it would have in their propaganda photos for this May Day celebration. We wanted no part of it.

We had won, and the march continued, without the flag.

Approaching the village square we could see that some of the other companies were already in position. The square was filled with flags. It disturbed us to see that the company just ahead of us had the red flag at the front of their column. We started cursing them as we continued along the dusty street. The curses slowly turned into a low ragged voice singing a familiar song. With each word the voices grew louder and louder.

"God bless America, Land that I LOVE..."

"Stop, stop, guards, make them stop," one of the instructors came yelling.

By now the entire column had broken into tune, the sound rolled across the valley.

"Stand beside her, and guide her..."

Then the beautiful sound of this hymn was disturbed by screams as gun butts started pounding those nearest to the guards. But even that was not going to stop us now.

"Through the night with the light from above..."

Here were 100 desperate men fighting for what little dignity remained in their souls. The column now stood proud, every head erect, every man at attention, everyone alive once again, headed to the square.

"From the mountains, to the prairie." As we neared the square the hundreds of other men already in the square were raised in a solid cheer. Then their voices blended in with ours.

"To the ocean, white with foam..."

The Chinese were in a frenzy, guards screaming and slugging. The officers were scattered in all directions in an attempt to restore order.

"God Bless America, My Home Sweet Home..."

Eighteen hundred Americans, with the Brits, and some Turks joining in, finished it up. Tears welled up in our eyes.

"God Bless American, My Home Sweet Home."

As the cheers continued the guards gave up trying to beat us into submission and now looked on helplessly. We reached our assigned position, sat down, looking at one another with glances that were stronger than handshakes. This was our day, not theirs.

The Chinese knew that this victory was going to make us harder than every to control. The regiment commander, attempted to maintain his composure, but looked pretty worn by the time he climbed the platform. A low boo started but was quickly hushed. We were feeling very defiant but didn't want to push our luck too far.

"I'm surprised at first company," he said, looking around. "Don't let it happen again," he added as he stepped off the stage. He was furious but wasn't about to let it show, not to us at least.

Black Hat went on the platform next. We had given him that name because of the jet black crop of hair on his head. He was the Chinese interpreter. He waited for the murmur to die down and then started in with his same old message.

"This is a glorious day for the workers of the world..."

From the middle of the crowd came, "Forty eight."

He continued his talk, but then from the rear came, "Forty nine."

He looked flustered when he next heard, "Fifty."

Then just about every American, Brit, French and Turkish soldier shouted, "Some shit!"

Black Hat was so shocked I thought his hair would turn gray. He looked as though he was having a heart attack, and he might have.

Bill, another of our British comics, had been coached for weeks by the camp officials on how he should emcee the May Day show. We had been giving him a hard time, razzing him about it, ever since he was selected. He would just give us a knowing wink. We knew it would be good.

We knew they selected Bill because of his popularity among the troops. If they knew that his popularity was based on his sense of humor, they would have chosen someone else I'm sure.

When Black Hat had finally restored order, Bill was formally introduced and we waited for his opening remarks. He held up his hands asking for silence. "Once upon a time there were three men who were in the Army." He looked around and saw Black Hat straining to hear his remarks. We figured he was about take a little deviation from the script the communists had prepared for him. We weren't disappointed.

"These three men were killed in action. Subsequently, they arrived at the Golden Gate and were met by St. Peter. The good mentor of heaven said to the first soldier, Where are you from? He replied, I'm from America. Pass on, said St. Peter. Then he asked the second soldier, Where are you from? The lad replied, proudly, I'm from jolly old England. Pass on St. Peter said. Now the third soldier stepped before St. Peter and was asked, Where are you from? I'm from China, said this proud representative of the peace loving people of China."

Bill was speaking faster now, he could see Black Hat moving in his direction. "St. Peter shook his head sadly and said, You'll have to go back. We're much too busy to cook kimchi and rice for just one soldier."

Again the long repressed laughter rolled from the prisoners, accompanied by great applause.

Black Hat shouted "Be quiet, be quiet!"

But instead of quieting, the laughter and applause only increased in volume.

"Guards, guards, make them be quiet."

The guards started shoving Bill around and the laughter finally subsided. The interpreter charged, "You have insulted the Chinese People's Volunteers."

"Oh, come off it, I was only making a joke!"

"We will teach you respect! Guards, take him to the jail. He is to be put in solitary confinement on half rations."

That stirred us up once again. The crowd started yelling at the guards and stomping our feet. But this time there was no helping Bill. Even before he was off the platform they were beating him. He tried to fight back, but it was of no use. When he came from behind the platform he was limp and unconscious.

The sight of Bill being helplessly beaten to near death turned discontent into a riot. Black Hat again took his place on the platform and yelled through the bedlam. "Be quiet, be quiet." We can not let this regrettable affair interfere with our program. Don't you want to see the rest of the show?"

"Shove it!" we yelled back, beginning to do a little pushing of our own. The guards put a stop to it by placing a round into the chamber of their guns. That was the unmistakable signal that the next man to move would be killed, and we knew it. It took more than a few minutes for the tension to ease up. Again Black Hat asked if we wanted to see the remainder of the show.

"The hell with the show, we're going home." And go home we did. Our company fell into formation at the direction of our own officers and marched back to the compound. Some of the other companies remained in the square, notably the ones carrying the red flags, the rest followed us back.

The funny thing was that two weeks later the regiment commander came into our company area to ask us again if we would like to go down to see the show. He must have gone to a lot of trouble to get this show together.

We told him that we were not interested in anything but getting Bill out of jail. A few days later he was released, but he looked like he'd been through hell.

For us to keep our spirits high laughter was essential. Unfortunately whenever our spirits were lifted someone paid the price.

More often than not it was these courageous comics that willingly suffered so we might smile for a brief moment.

CHAPTER 11

Fighting Boredom

There were many things to fight here in the camp but one of the most persistent was the boredom. While the work details and the effort it took simply trying to survive took a significant amount of our time, there were still days when we got bored. In a place where minutes felt like days, even the short periods of time we got to ourselves seemed like forever.

There are not many kids in the states who hasn't built a model of one type or another. Maybe a car, a boat, or a plane. You would go down to the nearest hardware store and buy the kits. Using all sorts of intricate tools you would carve out the pieces and assemble the parts. When you were finished you would display them proudly as a testament to your handicraft.

Well, here in Camp No. 1 we were no different, except our materials and supplies were a bit more crude. We would steal pieces of stove wood while we were on one of our frequent cutting details. Our carving tools were nails, broken glass, or odd bits of metal we would pick up around the camp. Each of these items were painstakingly honed to razor sharpness with stones. While they were sharp, none were long enough to be a threat to the guards. One of the more inventive guys from Louisville, Kentucky, made woven chains from the bark he stripped from the logs. We had quite a collection of planes at one time, a B-26, P-40, B-36, C-47, a F-81 jet fighter, a few ships and even a helicopter.

Someone was always working on some project. As they completed their models we placed them on high poles that stuck into the roofs of our huts. This was the most prominent place we had to display our talents.

There was also a fine collection of dolls, chess and checker sets, and small statues. Some of the guys became quite adept at wood carving. It was one of the best ways to occupy your time.

The Chinese soon discovered that this diversion was of benefit to our morale and since they couldn't let us have fun they were determined to put an end to our handicraft. One day during an inspection, a routine shakedown, they decided to take more than just our written notes.

Detective Looie was the one who started it by demanding that one of the boys in my squad turn over his knife.

"I ain't got no knife," the soldier said.

"You carve airplane last week, I watch you," Looie insisted. "Give me your knife." We muttered our protest as the soldier surrendered the carving tool which had taken him weeks to make.

Looie proceeded to go through the entire company, collecting scores of instruments used for no more harmful purpose than providing us with a little entertainment. Then he ordered, "Now take down airplanes from roof. Take them down now!"

"Awe, why, Looie," one lad spoke up. "They aren't doing any harm. They're just ornaments."

"Take them down," the pride and joy of the people's police insisted. "You no more signal your airplanes with them."

We knew he had to be kidding and started laughing. But he was deadly serious. He actually thought the airplanes were some type of communications with our pilots. We tried to reason with him that even if a pilot was at tree top level he couldn't see a model plane less than two feet long. We had no choice, the poles were taken down and the planes removed. We spotted a few Korean kids walking down the street just a few yards away and one of the sergeants yelled, "Hey, Kim, Come here."

The sergeant handed the shabbily clothed boy his prize model and the boy's face lit up like a Christmas tree. It was obviously the first real toy the boy had ever had. Once the child realized that the model was his to keep he dashed off in a dead run for another group of boys down the road. The excitement on their faces brought joy to each of us.

An ox cart went slowly by us and Harry took his B-26 model and dropped it into the back of the cart. Looking into the face of this little wide-eyed boy he said, "Here, boysan, you take this." The kid was overjoyed and tumbled over the wooden bench into the back of the cart to grab his new gift.

To Korean kids that usually played with nothing more than a piece of cardboard dragged around by a string these new toys seemed like treasures.

Detective Looie wasn't about to pass up this opportunity to display his authority. He rushed over and took the plane from the little child's hands. You could see the tears well up in the boy's eyes. "Hey, you sonofabitch, give that back to the kid," yelled Harry, running toward Looie.

"No, this is for me," Looie said.

"The hell it is, buster, give it here." He grabbed the plane and deliberately smashed it on the ground, using his foot to crush it into small pieces. Whipping the tears from the boys face Harry continued, "If he can't have it I'll be damned if you're going to." Then he walked away.

Looie was extremely upset at this development. He walked away. Once he was out of sight we called the Korean boys over behind our hut and gave them the rest of the models.

Those models did more to convince the North Korean people in that village that Americans were not beasts than anything the Chinese have been able to do to convince them otherwise. Those simple wooden figures were the nicest gifts those kids have had their entire lives. From then on the sergeants were "Ding Ho". They would stick up their thumbs in the Number One sign and yell "Ding Ho" whenever they passed us. That little scene didn't amuse the Chinese either.

After observing this for two days we were lectured on a new order they were publishing. From now on, we were not to make any more models. There was also to be no conversation with any of the North Korean natives. Any violation of these new orders would result in a jail sentence.

Our contacts with the North Koreans were less frequent after that. That same day an order was published in the camp that added new force to the prohibition of civilians in the camp. They now had no choice, they must go around the prison camp over a tortuous mountain trail rather than using the road through the middle of the camp. This was nothing new, they had been told this in the past. What was new was the fact that instead of just ignoring the violation or chasing them off, now they would be jailed for their disobedience. I am sure the Koreans were very impressed with communism when they learned that not only couldn't they walk through their own village, but their children could not even receive the simplest of gifts to make their miserable lives a little happier.

Taking a bunch of Americans, particularly American soldiers, and giving them absolutely nothing to do for pleasure, add in lots and lots of boredom and you have a very inventive group of characters. The natural outcome, of course, was horseplay at every opportunity.

It was never planned, it just seemed to happen. It started with some little thing and grew into total nonsense quite rapidly. It always drove our guards crazy.

Some of the guys would drive their imaginary motorcycles all over the prison compound. Some would catch the guards attention by jabbing their middle finger in the air in a symbolic, yet defiant gesture. We would also resurrect long forgotten games such as charades, twenty questions, and other kids games which lurked in the recesses of our minds. Any memory in our heads was fair game and usually once acted out by one person was perpetuated by all those in the area. These antics kept us amused for some time.

One game in particular started out just that way. It was called "Billy the Kid." One of the guys strolled over to a box out in the yard and pounded his fist on it demanding that he be given a drink.

Just as sure as if it had been rehearsed for a western melodrama back in Hollywood, it came to life. Three other prisoners galloped up on their imaginary horses yelling "Hi Ho Silver." Another immediately stepped behind the box and became the bartender.

"What'llya have, stranger?"

The three cowboys hitched their horses to the non-existent rail in front of the saloon, walked bowlegged up to the bar and announced their intention to blow the bank wide open.

A small unimposing fellow with particularly long hair slinked up to "Billy" at the bar and said,

"How about buying me a drink, big boy, I can be had, cheap."

And just then in walked the "sheriff."

"Billy the Kid," he boomed, "I'm sheriff of this here county and I ain't aimin to have no trouble. I'll give you until sundown to hit the road, I mean the trail."

By now the Korean kids and their parents were straining to see the production from their huts outside the compound. They all looked puzzled, sure we had all lost our minds.

Like any other good western there was bound to be a good fight scene, and this one was no exception. The sheriff and Billy went at it very convincingly. They kicked and punched. They swung imaginary chairs and lamps. They broke non-existent bottles and used the jagged edges to carve up their opponents faces. All this eventually led to the gun fight. They drew from the hip and fired. Like any other group of ten year olds they were arguing about who outdrew who.

They were playing it to the hilt. The bartender sprawled across the box protecting the mirror behind the bar. The piano player continued to belt out his tune, having seen this happen many times before in this rowdy bar. The gambler calmly dealt out the next hand, ignoring the commotion. The town drunk was at the other end of the bar downing another double scotch.

We were laughing so hard our sides hurt. Every possible scenario that was ever in a good old fashioned western was tried, and a few that they wouldn't dare put on the screen.

The ending wasn't your typical ride into the sunset. It included a communist commissar, four Chinese guards, and the regiment commander. This unlikely group entered the set and proceeded to give us hell.

"Awe lay off, will ya, we're only trying to have a little fun," one of the actors said just before he was brutally pushed aside by two of the Chinese bad men.

"You men make joke again. I told you to stop making joke," the instructor ranted and raved. They were mad because they didn't have the slightest idea of what we were up to. It was anything but fun to them and they saw no humor in the situation at all. I guess to someone who had never seen a western movie the whole idea was beyond explanation. We just stood there and took our verbal reprimand in silence. The instructor summed it up by saying, "The next time you want to play a joke you write it on paper and get permission first."

The main reason something like this was so much fun was because it was totally spontaneous. Without that element of the unexpected it would have just been silly, not funny. So, the next time the opportunity arose we had just as much fun, without writing it down. Guard or no guard, we were going to have our fun. The more they tried to maintain our purely monotonous existence, the more we tried to do anything to have fun. There was a direct, and opposite, correlation between our inner feelings and the way we acted. It seems the lower we felt the more we tried to convince our captors, and ourselves, that we were having fun. It was pretty sad to think so much enjoyment could come out of a simple act of deception such as this.

Occasionally singing would also bring a pleasant diversion to the monotony of prison life. All it took was a hot night, a bright noon, and someone was sure to start whistling.

A usual we were sprawled out on the floor. Carlie was whistling "My Buddy" and from the looks on every ones face I could tell it stirred the same thoughts in their mind as it had in mine. I was wondering what had happened to some of my buddies. I wonder how many of them are still alive. I thought of my family, did they know I was still alive? It was a night for remembering the quiet times at home shared with those we love.

Our thoughts soon turned to music. What were they playing on the radios back in our hometown? Songs were a special part of life in the military. There was some music you never wanted to hear again, like Taps. There were the old Army songs that kept you in cadence during a long march. There were the loud boisterous songs heard during time off in the beer halls. But on a quiet night such as this it was the old soothing, sentimental songs that came to mind.

I said, "Gee, I remember back on the Islands when Gracie Fields came over with a USO show and sang 'Now is the Hour.' That was back in '44. Boy, what a wonderful woman she is..." We started singing.

Like all other good things in a communist prison camp it wouldn't last very long. Six guards came storming into the hut yelling for us to stop singing. The sight of their machine guns broke the peaceful atmosphere.

"Stop that singing. You are keeping the other men awake," the interpreter demanded.

"We haven't heard them complaining," I said. "What's the matter, we having too much fun again?" But it was no use, we stopped singing.

As he left the interpreter added for emphasis, "There will be no more singing. Don't forget no more singing."

About a week later this same interpreter finished his lecture on the evils of life in America and passed out sheets of paper with the words and music to a communist song written on them.

"You must learn how to sing this song," we were told. "You must learn all the words."

"Wait a minute," I piped up. "We can't sing this song."

"What do you mean," he asked.

"Sorry, but remember last week you made us stop singing, you said there will be no more singing. We don't want to break your regulations." The guys started to laugh.

"This is different. This is different," he screamed.

"Different, hell, if we can't sing American songs, we're not going to sing communist songs, are we fellows?" I looked around.

"No, no," they all yelled. "We ain't allowed to sing. So sorry."

They thought we were kidding. But we passed the word to the other companies, "No singing."

The song they wanted us to learn was an oriental tune. They explained that it was a song about their leader, Mao Tse Tung.

We destroyed our sheets of oriental music, rejecting their compromise that they would let us sing American songs if we would also sing one of theirs.

That night we had another singing session in our hut, this time a little softer. Their attempts to keep us from singing were never successful.

I also remember one time when Bill wasn't his usual cheerful self. He was tired and sweaty from a long mornings work. He entered the hut, ducking his head through the doorway, and slumped on his blanket. He let out a long, comfortable sigh as he stretched out on the floor.

He used one hand to fumble with the makeshift shoes off of his feet. Then, sitting up, he reached into his pocket for the makings of a cigarette. "Well, whatta you know, I'm all out of papers. Whose got a piece of paper I can use for this smoke?" He looked over at Chuck.

"Never mind, I'll use this." Reaching back into his pocket he pulled out one of his military payment certificates. Initially we were amazed that he still had one of these after so many shake downs.

"Hey, fellows, I'm better than Morgan or Rockefeller now, I've got money to burn." He rolled some tobacco into the $10 certificate, and then, in an eye catching motion struck a match. He blew a long column of smoke towards the ceiling and laid back on his blanket. We smiled.

Out of habit Bill then reached behind his head for his mess kit spoon. His hand shifted back and forth wildly trying to find the precious instrument. He muttered to himself "damned," and then rolled over to make a proper search for the missing spoon. Looking slowly around the hut he stared at us and then questioned, "Ok, which one of you jokers got my spoon?"

Those of us in the hut looked at each other with a puzzled expression. Chuck shrugged his shoulders. I said, "Hell, don't look at me, I don't have it."

"Gentlemen," Bill said, with a stern smile on his face. "I'll give the sonofabitch that took my spoon about two seconds to return it or I'll beat the hell out of the hole lot of you."

"Honest, Bill, we haven't seen it," Chuck replied.

Bill seemed convinced that we didn't know what he was talking about after sweeping the room with his eyes. He got a puzzled expression on his face and observed, "I hope one of the guards didn't steal it, I'll never get it back."

"Were any of them in here?" he asked.

"Nope."

Chuck added, "The only ones in here besides us were a couple of guys from the squad across the street."

"What the hell did they want?"

"Nothing, they just came in to talk for a while. Come to think of it, though, they were both sitting on your sack. Maybe..."

"That does it. If Alabama thinks he can raid my squad and get away with it, he's got another think coming." Bill could see the chance to have some fun in addition to recovering his property.

He searched the pocket of his fatigue jacket for the stub of a pencil. "Now, give me some paper," he said. I handed him a sheet out of my notebook. He wrote;

"Sgt. Alabama

I have been robbed of one spoon, mess kit, GI, M-1. Unless that spoon has been returned to me by 2 P.M. this date, I am about to fall in my squad and beat the hell out of your squad."

"Chuck, take this to Alabama."

Five minutes later Chuck returned with the reply. It read;

"We can see no reason for your squad to get aggressive in this matter. However, we are willing to discuss the subject at a peace conference in the middle of the street at 2 P.M."

This was better than we hoped for. Immediately both squads went into action. A messenger was dispatched to inform Alabama that our squad accepted his invitation to attend the peace conference. We fashioned some briefcases from some cardboard and used some extra cloth to make white arm bands. Alabama's squad constructed the negotiation table from a door that had been discarded behind the kitchen. They surrounded the table with stools made up of an assortment of available material.

Shortly before the appointed hour we saw Alabama's group forming up into two ranks on the far side of the truce table. They comprised our Honor Guard. We took our cue and marched sharply into position, faced one another and stood rigidly at attention. The two squad leaders then proceeded through their respective ranks, I called, "Attention - Present Arms!" We held that position until the delegates and their interpreters were seated.

"Order Arms - Parade Rest," I commanded. Out of the corner of my eye I saw a Chinese guard approaching. This guard knew a little English, just enough to get him in trouble. And so the fun began.

The preliminary negotiations had just started when Bill jumped to his feet and shattered the afternoon calm with, "So help me, if I don't get my spoon back I'll blow this whole Goddamned place right off the map!" His acting was so good that the guard thought he meant it and took off in a dead run to get the instructor.

Soon the instructor arrived, along with four guards, just in time to catch Bill pounding on the makeshift table again. With a startled look on his face the instructor began shouting, "Stop it, stop it!"

The more we laughed the more the instructor flew into a rage. "What are you doing?" he demanded.

"Nothing," Bill said, "don't get so excited, we're just having a little fun."

"You lie, you lie! he screamed. "You make plot." Bill laughed very loudly, loudly enough to get all of us marched off to the camp headquarters.

We spent the next few hours going over, and over the same statements. "No, sir we were not plotting the overthrow of the camp. Yes, sir, we will not get caught doing it again. No, sir, he didn't mean he would blow up the camp. Yes, sir, we realize we could go to jail. No, sir, we don't want to go to jail. Yes, sir. No, sir..." I don't know who grew more tired of this mindless chatter, us or our captors.

After a while this current stream of stupidity was not funny any longer. Rather than endure any more of it we decided it was easier to just criticize ourselves and get it over with. At least that shuts them up.

Thoroughly disgusted, we headed back for our hut. After such a long grilling our tempers were rather short. Bill was the first one back in the hut and remarked as he entered, "You know, they were really getting serious about this whole thing. I figured we were headed for jail. I hope that self criticism garbage and our promise not to hold any more meetings keeps them happy." He then looked around the hut and cursed under his breath.

"Will you look at what those flat faced bastards did." While we were being interrogated about our "capitalist plot" the guards had ripped the hut apart. No doubt looking for evidence of our insidious plot.

We never could get them to appreciate our sense of humor.

About a month later the need for any further negotiations between our squad and Alabama's squad ended. During one of the public self criticisms some amazing information was provided by one of our fellow prisoners. This took place immediately after the morning lecture. None of us were ready for what he relayed during his confession.

At first I thought he was just kidding, as we so often do during these ridiculous sessions. Then I began to realize that he meant every word. The more he talked the more interested we became.

His confession went on and on. He had been caught stealing and first listed about 25 or 30 things he had taken. He went into minute detail about how he pilfered each item on the list. When we began to laugh at some of the ways he was able to gain access to these items, he took a breath. But it didn't stop there. He continued, "That was the first time..."

We were shocked to hear him say, "Now, the next time I stole...," listing off another couple of dozen things he had taken. They ranged all the way from a toothbrush to a 25 pound bag of sugar. This guy must have been a kleptomaniac. His confession cleared up a number of disappearances that had occurred throughout the camp, including Bill's mess kit spoon.

MAP LEGEND

#	= Capture Site		12 Feb 1951	
	= Bean Camp		17 Apr 1951	
1	= Camp No. 1	Changsong	17 May 1951	
2	= Camp No. 2	Changsong		
3	= Camp No. 3	Changsong		
4	= Camp No. 4	Pyoktong	Nov 1952	
5	= Camp No. 5	Pyoktong	Oct 1952	Short hospital stay
6	= Camp No. 6	Pyongyang		
7	= Camp No. 7	Pyoktong		
8	= Camp No. 8	Kangdong		
9	= Camp No. 9	Pyongyang		
10	= Camp No. 10	Between Sinuiju and Kusong		
11	= Camp No. 11	Pukchin		
*	= Repatriation Site		25 Apr 1953	

CHAPTER 12

The Fourth of July

One day in June Ray came into the hut all excited. We couldn't help smiling just at the sight of him. He had this expression on his face before, it usually meant that something was up. We hoped it wouldn't get us into trouble this time.

"Hey, guys, I got him worried. Yes sir, I really got him worried."

"Who?" I asked.

"Doc Haung," he responded, "Who else? The Doc just stopped me outside and asked how I was feeling. I said to him, "Doc how do you think I feel running out of here every five minutes for the latrine." Then he really got confidential trying to get some information out of me but I spotted it right away. The Doc asked, "What do you men talk about in there?" I said, "Hell, Doc, we talk about almost anything, why?" And he said, "I hope you do not get into any more trouble, I hope you do not do something foolish."

I told him, "We ain't gonna get into no more trouble than we already have, we like it here." He looked surprised and added, "Well, I hope so, but after all the trouble that happened on our holiday, May Day, I not so sure you not trying to cause trouble."

"Christ, are they still yapping about May Day. I figured they'd forgotten all about that," I said.

"Forgot it, hell," Ray said, "We musta scared the hell out of them that day."

"But anyway," he continued his story, "I told the Doc, that's only because you people don't know how to run a holiday." Doc's eyes opened wide, "What?" Then I honestly don't know what made me say this to him, but it was a stroke of genius, "Hell, Doc, if you want to see a holiday, watch us go to town on the Fourth of July."

You should have seen his face. He seemed to know the significance of the Fourth of July because he got awfully worried all of a sudden. When he asked me, "What's going to happen on the Fourth of July?" I knew I had him. I leaned over to him in a very confidential manner and whispered to him, "Wait till you see the fireworks on the Fourth of July."

"Oh, God, you shoulda seen his face, he got all excited. And he said, "What do you mean, fireworks? Where you get fireworks?" I told him, "Never mind Doc, wait till you see the fireworks on the Fourth of July." Then I walked away. "Come on now fellows," he ended, "Don't let in that it's really a gag. Let's have some fun."

Nothing more came of it that day, but the seed was planted and it would be fun for a while. I must admit that some of the guys wished Ray had never thought of it. From past experience they realized that every time we had fun at the Chinese expense we paid dearly for it in the end.

We used the remainder of that day to pass the word throughout the company area. We even started using it as a password. "Wait'llya see the fireworks on the Fourth of July." We began driving the guards crazy. We said it in the morning and after the propaganda lectures. We would shout it across the room and even on the way to the latrine now and then you would hear someone shout, "Wait'llya see the fireworks on the Fourth of July."

Whenever they quizzed us about it, we would look around and whisper, "Shhhhh, It's a military secret." Yeah, they were going nuts all right.

As Independence Day approached, however, they began to tighten the screws. The secret surprise inspections became more frequent. They established special squads of guards to search all the huts looking for our fireworks. To us it was just a big joke. Now we realized how seriously they were taking it and we began to have faint twinges of worry and regret.

Their questioning began to take on a different tone. We realized how concerned they were when one man returned from his session. At the time they called for him we were all preoccupied in a desperate attempt to save one of our buddies from succumbing to dysentery. Most of us didn't even see him leave. A half hour later he returned and clued us in.

"Boy, has Ray got them worried," he said slumping onto the floor. "They don't know what the hell to do. The surprising thing, though, is that as worried as they seem, they didn't try to beat the answers out of me. They just asked questions. They actually tried to be nice."

I was the next one selected for questioning that day. Flanked by two machine gun carrying guards, I marched into the interrogation room. In the room were the commissar, Detective Looie, and Dr. Haung. They waved the guards outside and I stood rigidly at attention. All kinds of thoughts were running through my mind as I tried to hide the fact my head was killing me with pain once again. Even after hearing the other guy's account of his questioning, their attitude surprised me.

"Sit down, sergeant, sit over here and have a cigarette."

Well, I thought, this is a new pitch. We really do have them worried.

The only time we got cigarettes was during one of their holidays when they tried to butter us up. Even at that we would only get about 10 butts that tasted very flat for the entire hut. I am not a smoker but the boys tell me the ready made cigarettes are much better than the loose tobacco they normally smoked if they could find the papers to roll one.

I reached for the cigarette and placed it in my pocket for one of the other guys. You don't turn down anything here, everything has some value, either in trade or as a favor.

The commissar started it. "What are you going to do on the Fourth of July?"

"The Fourth of July - why I'm not going to do anything," I said.

"You know what I mean, what is going to happen on the Fourth of July?" he demanded, getting a little angry and trying not to show it.

"Oh, have they told you?" I asked innocently.

All three of them leaned forward in their chairs expecting to finally hear something.

"Yes, they have told us," Detective Looie said, "we know all about it."

"Well, what are you asking me for then," I smiled.

"Do not make jokes, sergeant, or you will pay the consequences. Now tell us, what is going to happen on the Fourth of July."

I thought I had them going now so I said, "I'm sorry, but that's a military secret."

I felt pretty sure that they didn't intend to use any rough stuff or the guards would have remained in the room. This bit of knowledge allowed me to get a little braver and push my luck a bit further.

Dr. Haung said excitedly, "This man knows where they are." He looked me straight in the eye and asked, "Where are the fireworks?"

"The fireworks, what fireworks," I replied, trying not to smile.

"You know what fireworks, where are they?"

"Oh, I'm sorry, I didn't know which fireworks you meant." Again they leaned forward in great anticipation. "No, you'll have to wait for the Fourth."

"We want to see these fireworks right now," Detective Looie insisted.

I couldn't resist pushing just a bit further. "Wait'llya see the fireworks on the Fourth of July," doing my best to match Ray's Bronx accent. Then I laughed out loud.

I kept up this cloak and dagger type exchange with them for another half hour or so. They were still trying to use friendly persuasion. My head was really beginning to give me a lot of trouble. The pain made the teasing no longer worth the effort and I began to respond to their questions with strict yes and no answers. This finally convinced them to let me go.

They kept up the secret, middle of the night, searches of our huts in a desperate attempt to find the allusive fireworks. They also cut our food rations. We never imagined they would take it so seriously. Hell, everyone in the camp except them knew it was a big joke.

Finally the fateful date was near. The night before the Fourth everything was uneventful. There was a little action over by the headquarters but not really much more than usual. Someone it seems was getting balled out. We found out it was Detective Looie catching hell for not finding the fireworks. We ate our supper and settled down for the night. As far as we were concerned, it was just another night.

Suddenly into our hut came twelve guards positioning themselves in a circle around us. We thought for sure this was it. Then one of them announced that they would be there all night.

"Let em stew," I said, "Just go to sleep and let em stew. No reason we should stay awake just because they have to."

"Just wait'llya see the fireworks on the Fourth of July," came the muffled voice from the other end of the hut, Ray's bunk. We fell asleep chuckling into our sacks.

The next day we heard from some of the others that they doubled the guard around our company that night. They also confined all men in the compound to their huts. If you needed to use the latrine you had to secure permission, had an armed escort, and went straight to and back from the latrine.

While the Fourth of July came and went, the guards remained. Some of the men from the other companies were getting rattled. One of them sent a message to us saying, "For Gods sake, call off the dogs, will you guys. They have all of us pinned down tight in our areas. We can't make a move without them. Tell them the Fourth of July stuff was just a gag or this company will come up there and knock your blocks off. They're getting mad down here."

Four days later and the camp officials still couldn't figure out it was just a joke. Ray decided to tell them. He very patiently explained that it was all a joke, we never had any fireworks, no demonstration was planned, and we were not going to blow up the camp. Even after his admission they did not believe it wasn't for real. Even when he made his self criticism in front of all of us and we laughed it up like the was the greatest hoax in the world, they didn't believe it. They thought it was all just an attempt to get them to take the heat off so we could blow up our fireworks.

Finally they decided to let the regimental interpreter have a shot at our story. This guy was very shrewd, and knew his business. He asked a few questions and then laughed.

"And just how did you men enjoy spending the Fourth of July under heavy guard?" he jokingly said as he departed. That ended it, the heat was off. All but one of the guards were relieved. They let it be known that it would still be some time before we would be back on full rations however.

The following day another note from the company we heard from earlier reached us through the grapevine. It simply stated, "Have your fun fellows, but Goddammit, no more jokes that keep us locked up too, please."

With the events of the Fourth now behind us our attention this time of the year naturally turned to football. It took some doing and a great deal of groveling, but we finally got the Chinese to allow us to play some football. They even provided the football. I am sure they dug it out of one of the many packages they pilfered from our relatives back home. This was the only form of recreation we had.

The games were a blessing to most of the men. Many were lonesome, homesick and so damned tired of sitting there staring at four mud walls.

It also helped some of the younger men who were weakening under the constant barrage of communist propaganda. The younger seemed to have a more difficult time with this misinformation that the rest of us. Their faith was shallow, their despair deep.

The games were able to give all of us something else to focus on. It was something typically American, something we would probably be doing even if we were back in the states right now. It was also something that all of the American prisoners could relate to, it helped bring us together.

The First Company had a very good team by camp standards. They use to have a lot of fun. The play was rough and everyone knew that to get hurt in this place would only bring laughter, not assistance, from our captors. But the physical nature of the sport was also a benefit. It was a marvelous way to work off the stress we were all under. Each man did his best to keep physically fit. It was only physical stamina that kept most of us alive this long. We also saw it as part of our duties as a soldier to be as ready as we could possible be to fight the enemy. Those of us in Camp No. 1 had seen enough of the communists to have fought through sheer will, with or without, physical fitness.

Whenever I got the chance I would watch the football games that fall. The guards would pretty much ignore us as we concentrated on the competition taking place on the field.

Watching the games I would think of many things. I thought of how I would watch the Waltham-Brockton High School games many years ago. Boy, those use to be great games. My thoughts also drifted to a little over year ago when I was fighting like hell and we were sure the war would be over in a matter of weeks. But that was before the Chinese got into the act, crossing the river and driving the U.N. forces back towards the south.

One of the games got very intense. My company was playing Third Company. Over the past this game had developed into quite a rivalry. When these two played the scores were always close. They also had quite a draw, always turning out a large number of spectators. Today was no different.

Boy, Boston College never had such enthusiastic fans. The sides of the field were filled with members of the opposing companies. It was a lot of fun and very confusing to the few guards who looked on. They couldn't understand the reason behind all the yelling and screaming. I must admit that the sight of our improvised cheerleaders had me a bit bewildered as well. The guards figured we were just plain crazy, and maybe they were right.

These games were very important to us, I didn't really understand just how important until I was hassled at this particular game.

I stood on the sideline having a great time, rooting good old First Company on to another touchdown. Then I caught the eye of Detective Looie. He came over and stood in front of me.

He was still upset about the hell he got for the Fourth of July incident. He was even more upset now that he knew the whole thing was a joke. Needless to say he was not amused. I soon found out just how upset he was.

Why he chose me out of the large gathering of prisoners I don't know. Or why the hell he chose this particular moment to vent his frustrations, I don't know. Maybe, it was the fact that I was the last person they questioned and the fact that I was obviously enjoying myself for once.

He said, "You go back to your hut."

"I will like hell, buster," I replied, "I have as much right to watch this game as everyone else. Neither you or anyone else is going to make me miss it. Scram."

He took me by the shoulder and began to steer me through the crowd. I pulled out of his grasp and said, "Leave me alone, you big ape, I'm not going back. I'm not hurting anyone. Get the hell out of here."

That one got him mad and he started to reach for me again. This time bringing the bayonet of his gun up, pointing it at me.

"Shove that thing up you butt, boy, I'm staying right here," I said, getting a little angry myself. The idea of missing the game didn't bother me as much as the fact that he was doing this just because he knew it was one of the rare occasions when I was having a good time. I didn't like him having that much control, manipulating my emotions, as well as my thoughts. A group of people started to gather around us. Trying to save face he grabbed me again and began to shove me away from the scene.

Cries of "Leave him alone," came from my buddies who now encircled us. Looie wasn't about to give up at this point. He took the tip of the bayonet and put it square into my chest and then ordered me back.

"Go ahead, you big bastard," I said, "push it in. Go ahead, shove it in me. I ain't going back. You have no reason to make me leave." I grabbed the bare end of the long blade and held it against my chest.

"Look out, Matta," one of the guys yelled, "Take it easy, he'd love to run you through."

Another shouted, "You better go back, Matta, he's looking for trouble."

I don't give a damn if he's looking for trouble. I'm just watching a football game I don't have to take this guy's crap. I'm staying right here."

A crowd began to gather a short distance from the field. It was about that time that one of the

English speaking instructors heard the yelling, and came on the double.

"What is the matter here," he questioned.

I got the meaning of Looie's version of the affair and then said, "I have permission to see this game just like everyone else. Now this guy wants to send me back. I don't want to go."

The instructor said something in Chinese to Looie and he lowered his rifle from my chest. Our eyes were still glaring at one another when the instructor left. A cheer went up from the gang.

"Matta, what would you have done if he had pushed that bayonet into you," somebody asked.

"Man, I would have crapped my pants, believe me," I yelled back. "But I did put their lenient treatment policy to the test, didn't I?"

They all laughed.

"Come on, let's get this game on the road," I called, "I've got eight sugar rations, and seven tobacco rations that says First Company takes this game. Any takers?" While I lined up the bets, the game continued. The game was a good one and we did win. A perfect ending.

In a way it had been a test. Recently they had stepped up the education on Communist Theory. They were doing their very best to keep things running smoothly as a means to strengthen their propaganda pitch. Most of us were quick to see right through it. We always pushed to see how far we could get without getting hurt.

I wasn't the first of the prisoners to put this policy to the test. Many were afraid to be the first guinea pig in this experiment. After all there were too many bodies buried up on the hill already.

This policy was first explained to us shortly after the peace talks started. It was the reprieve we had been looking for and so desperately needed at that time. The longer this policy continued the more serious the Chinese soldiers took it. By late fall the guards knew that a violation of this policy didn't sit well with the commandant. The commandant seemed to know what the consequences of being tried as a war criminal would be. The trails at Nuremberg still fresh in his mind.

It was one of the Turks who pulled the first successful test. He was fixing up his hut and was searching for something to keep the cold from coming through the windowless door. What could be better than glass? So he stole some. He walked up to one of the buildings and carefully removed two of the panes of glass. He wasn't caught until he was in the process of installing the glass in the opening of his door.

The guard took him out into the middle of the field and made him stand at attention. He was ordered to look directly into the sun, a mild form of torture used now to punish minor offenses.

The Turk stood out in the field for a very short time then he decided to take a chance. He slowly slumped to the ground, pretending to faint, appearing like he had collapsed. The guard prodded him with his rifle but became very frightened when the Turk didn't move an inch.

The guard looked at him laying unconscious on the ground, looked around him to see who was watching, then carried the Turk into his hut. Not only that but when he revived the Turk from his fake condition the guard gave him a duty excuse for the next three days. These duty excuses were usually reserved for the most seriously ill patients only.

Every few hours he would stick his head into the hut to check on the poor man's condition. The Turk played that guard for all he was worth. The guard confessed that he was scared the commandant would find out he had broken the lenient treatment policy.

It seems strange but there were times when we actually felt sorry for some of the guards. Whenever they did do something that displeased their brass they were given six straight hours of guard duty and then they would be sent out on a wood chopping detail. They really had to battle fatigue when they were on guard duty. The commandant had the right to shoot anyone found asleep on duty immediately, on the spot, no questions asked.

So in some cases this policy afforded us better treatment than the guards themselves could expect. The guards for our camp lived directly across the river from our hut. Some of them had never left the compound since I arrived in the camp. They had no stores from which to get the niceties of live. They were issued one bar of soap and one package of tobacco each month. They got no sugar, very little meat, and little else.

The Chinese soldiers were issued one pair of pants in the summer, one shirt, and one set of underwear. This issue had to last until winter when they received their padded uniforms, provided they turn in their summer uniforms.

The guards got up at five o'clock in the morning and were still hard at work at nightfall. They worked seven days a week, with no relief. During limited periods of rest they were permitted to go to the river to wash their clothes.

Through all of this they were also subjected to lectures. Almost as many as we were. From what I was able to find out, their version painted the American people and way of life in even a worse light than our lectures did, if that was possible.

Most of them were downright lonesome as well. Those that could speak English often stood and listened to our stories about wives and children. The few times we were lucky enough to get pictures they would beg us for a chance to look at the photos.

That caused us trouble one night when one of the nurses, a strict party member, became upset at one of the pictures. One of the guys had received a nice picture from home in which the kids were sitting in front of the fireplace looking at their daddy's picture. In the background`you could see the table filled with all kinds of food. It was a simple, innocent, homey picture that made all of us homesick.

The nurse insisted that he hide the picture from view. She didn't want it to influence the younger men. She was sure that it was a staged picture. We had quite an argument with her, telling her that it was a normal everyday home in the United States, owned jointly by the soldier and the mortgage company. She was sure it was a form of propaganda and nothing we could say would convince her otherwise.

To be honest though people like her were the rule rather than the exception. While the Chinese did have it rough by anyone's standards, it still didn't excuse the fact that very few of them displayed any type of human emotion at all.

We would survive this fall though, just like the last. The football games kept us thinking of better times and better people.

CHAPTER 13

The VERY Red Cross

More than a few of us in the camp had fought in the last war either in Europe or in the Pacific. Because of that we were familiar with the Red Cross and all the good work they did for the guys in World War II. We also knew that back at home the Red Cross was something you could count on in times of trouble. Because of this we expected to see or hear from them shortly after our capture. Of course, this was not the case in Korea. The communists were not about to let the International Red Cross anywhere near their prison camps or their prisoners.

Even the little things that would have been provided to us like, playing cards, writing paper, cigarettes, candy, razor blades, and socks, would have been great. These things were made even more important simply because we couldn't have them. No Red Cross packages were allowed to reach us.

Once the mail started getting through we would receive writing paper and envelopes from home. This was of little consequence since the Chinese would not let us use them. If our letters were not placed in one of their envelopes with the dove of peace embossed on it they didn't stand a chance of getting through. The Chinese went out of their way to prove to the world that they were treating us better than the Red Cross could. They had as hard a job convincing their own people as they did convincing us. Since my capture I had received only one package. In the last sixteen months our hut had received 10 packages of cigarettes, one half pound of hard candy, some sweet cookies, one pair of socks, one razor, and three blades. All this for the thirteen men now in our hut.

A few of us were able to get a few items in from home. But to do this we had to devise a covert system. We knew they would not allow a letter asking for these things to be mailed to our relatives. To get by the camp sensors we would write our families thanking them for the things we needed. The sensors allowed it to go through to show that the packages they sent were getting to us. Our relatives generally got the message and sent the items they could. Using this system I was able to let my wife know that I wanted her to send playing cards, song sheets, and on one occasion, Kool-Aid.

Many rumors circulated the camp from time to time about the Red Cross. August 5, 1952, was such a time.

"Okay, outside. Outside you guys. Come on, shake it. They're gonna take us for a walk. Outside, come on, hop to it!" Our platoon sergeant yelled disturbing the morning silence.

We tumbled into formation and quickly formed into a column. We were pointed in the direction of the hills and off we went.

"Hey, what gives? What's all the rush?" the guy beside me asked.

"Hell, I don't know. It is another wood detail, I guess."

"Christ, since when do they empty the kitchen and hospital assistants to come along in a wood detail. Something's up," he observed. It was out of the ordinary for them to relieve the men working the kitchen and hospital from their duties for any kind of work detail. It appeared they wanted the camp emptied out for some reason.

Sure enough the entire camp was on the move. Every man that was able to stand, including some of the sick, were included in the formation.

"Yeah," I agreed, "Something must be up."

We continued to trudge up the side of the hill for an hour and once we were over the crest of the hill the guards motioned for us to sit down. And there we remained, hour after hour, just sitting. No work detail, no wood to be cut, just sit there and listen to lectures that seemed improvised at the spur of the moment. A sharp contrast to the usual well thought out, typewritten, and well delivered lectures we were use to. The lectures didn't have the same old monotonous pattern, this had to be a sign that they were trying to hide something. The very nature of the lectures fed the fires of our curiosity and stir up the rumor mill in the semi-circle of massed troops.

When the topic of the next lecture was announced we knew for sure something was up.

"I will talk to you today about sanitation," the instructor announced.

"At least that is better than the crap they usually feed us," I whispered. "What do you suppose is going on?"

"I bet the Red Cross is coming into the camp and they don't want us to see them," my neighbor offered. It was as good as any of the other explanations that were floating around the company, traveling from one group to another. "Maybe they are pulling another shakedown inspection." The rumors kept flowing from one man to the next until almost everyone had ventured a guess. The instructor still droned on and on and on, his message was boring and had a hard time competing with the gossip among the men.

One of the many rumors that was making the rounds that afternoon was that they were moving troops through the camp and didn't want us to see them. After all they knew we could get good information on the convoys they moved through camp. But this one wasn't given much serious consideration. After all they had moved columns of troops and supplies through the camp before and never went to all this trouble to avoid arousing our interest.

We got our lunch right there on the side of the hill, the usual rice portion served by a Chinese cook. Now it was about five o'clock and the instructor was beginning to loose his voice and he had long since lost the attention of his audience. Then he received a signal, abruptly stopped his lecture and said, "All right, now we go back to camp," he announced. We got up from our positions and stretched the kinks out of our bodies. We were all very anxious to return to the camp and see what was going on.

Once back in camp we were even more startled to learn that the men in the hospital who were too sick to join our little excursion had been herded into a small room and left behind a locked door for most of the day. They said that they heard trucks, a lot of trucks, but didn't have any idea what their cargo was. Every prisoner in that camp had been taken out of sight for the entire day. What on earth were they up to?

We had just about resigned ourselves to the fact that they finally were able to keep a secret from us when we got our break. Two of our boys were halfway between the hospital and their secluded room when the activity started.

In only a half hour the news spread through the hundreds of us who were impatiently awaiting the scoop.

"Yeah, did ya hear, it was a convoy of twenty trucks and they had Russian soldiers."

"It was the Ruskies, I saw them."

"There were twenty trucks all carrying blond soldiers in Russian uniforms."

And so the story went, from company to company, hut to hut, man to man, through the whole camp.

One of the instructors was in our company area and one of the guys yelled at him, "Hell, you didn't have to take us all the way up in the hills just to run a convoy of Russians through here, we don't mind." He laughed.

The instructor's next actions confirmed our information. He got to the closest telephone and really raised hell up at the hospital.

The following day they tried to tell us that we were all mistaken, there had been no convoy, and got two of their "favorite students" to make self-confessions to the camp for making false rumors. It was a waste of time, we all knew their secret convoy had taken place and took great pleasure in telling them all about it. Of course like any other rumor it did get exaggerated a bit as it went along. By the time we were through the guards were learning that a complete Russian Armored Division had gone through the camp in their absence, complete with Stalin's personal bodyguard.

Soon it became a relatively common sight to see Russian pilots walking through the village accompanied by Chinese airmen. Usually this occurred after a MIG-15 had been shot down in the vicinity of the camp.

A few days later I was back in the hospital with my headaches and without any assistance from the hospital staff or guards, we did our best to make the place livable. The peace talks must be progressing well because now we had beds to sleep on in the hospital. After sleeping on the ground or straw pallets for over a year the beds felt great. Even though the mattresses were only about an inch thick it felt like heaven.

Other than the beds, the only furniture in the hospital was a bare table and four chairs that we placed in the middle of the room.

On August 13th, about a week after the last Red Cross rumors had proven to be false they started once again. We were lying on the beds just shooting the breeze when in walked two nurses.

"Hey, will you look at the nice white uniforms," I said. Sure enough, the usually drab nurses were all decked out in pretty white nurses' uniforms. These were the first clean white uniforms we had seen since our capture. And better yet they wore big Red Cross arm bands, also the first we had seen.

They were a little self conscious about the looks they received from us as they started to clean up the joint. Normally it was left to us to perform such routine tasks as sweeping the floor and straightening out the beds.

"Fellows, this is it. Somebody's coming to see us," they guy on the end bed said.

We were dumbfounded. This had never happened before. We almost fell out of our beds when they brought a bright white tablecloth into the room and placed it over the small table.

"Brothhhher, look at that. The world must be coming to an end. They have a reason for all this, and don't for a minute think they don't."

A vase of flowers came in next and the flood of rumors began. "It's the Red Cross." "It's the end of the war." "Mao Tse Tung is gonna visit us." These were just a few that had sprung up. "Somebody must of complained to the management." "They finally are beginning to feel sorry for us." And so it went.

Just when we thought it couldn't get any better, another pleasant surprise, two new decks of cards. "Now this is what we expect from the Red Cross. Great, now that we have 52 cards we can play bridge." A sense of excitement and joy was in the air.

We smoothed the covers out on one of the beds and began dealing the cards. "Oh, no, this is too much," I laughed at the next move the nurses made. In they came with one tray full of apples and another with tobacco.

"Now I know something's wrong, we just got a tobacco ration yesterday," I said.

One of the nurses finally spoke up, "Gee, why we treat you so good." It was the same thing we heard whenever they gave us something, no matter how small and insignificant if might be. "Gee, why you treat us so good," we all mimicked.

Then the Doc walked in, all smiles, and said, "Why don't you play cards at the table, it is all right."

"Whooee, did ya hear that," one of the guys exclaimed, "That's the first time he's let us anywhere near that table since they brought it in months ago."

"Well," I said, "I don't care what it's all about. I know there is a catch in it somewhere, but right now it looks like a good deal so far. Let's live it up while we can. Come on, let's move over to the table." These new cards were a welcome replacement for the pinochle deck we made out of old tobacco boxes. "Okay, you guys, get out your sugar," I said, "Same bet. Two spoonfuls of sugar each, winner take all."

Then the trap was sprung. In came two Chinese with cameras at the ready.

"Oh, oh, here comes the catch. That does it. Let's get the hell out of here," I said as I stood up from the table. I walked out as the cameramen were still setting up to take the shots. Most of the other men followed me, only two remained behind.

"Awe, come on back," one of them yelled at us, "This isn't going to hurt anyone. Come on back in and play cards. What the hell do we care if they take a few pictures."

Looking into the doorway we could see the two willing subjects seated at the table. One of the Chinese guards sat in one of the chairs we just vacated. The doctor took his position at the other empty chair on the opposite side of the table. It was quite a scene as one of our young fools was being fed by one Chinese nurse while the other received a fake shot form his Chinese guardian. It made for a very cute set of pictures as the cameraman clicked away for all he was worth. They had the boys pose in many different ways that would have given the viewer the impression that these two were in a Las Vegas casino rather than a POW camp. The communists were great at propaganda, and they used these two idiots like experts.

Those of us smart enough to see through the smoke screen and see their true intentions remained outside the hospital until the Chinese had their fill of pictures.

When we reentered the room the two misguided souls could tell we were not happy with the performances they gave.

"They made you two look stupid," I announced upon my entry.

"Awe, come on Sarge, they just took a few pictures," one of them said. "At least now we have some fruit, cards, and a table to play on."

"Do you honestly think that this stuff is going to stay now that they have gotten what they want out of you?" I asked.

"Sure they will stay. They have no reason to take them away now," the other spoke up.

Even as I continued talking to these two, trying to get them to see the light, their new friend's true intentions came out. The two nurses came back in very sheepishly, knowing exactly how most of us felt, and removed the tablecloth, the tobacco, the flowers and even the apples, some of which were only half eaten.

As they left I said to the now enlightened soldiers. "Now do you get it. It wasn't just a simple game of bridge. It wasn't just a harmless picture or two. It was a cleverly planned game of deceit. A marvelous attempt at propaganda. It was a slap in the face of every man we have buried up on that hill. And you two made it a great success. Congratulations!"

I was a little hard on them but I had to make sure they were ashamed of what they had done. Maybe the next time the memory of the shame they felt today would help them remain true to their ideals.

We use to wonder what happened to pictures like those they took that day. The pictures always showed the communists at their best. Some of the guys just couldn't understand how they could be used to benefit the Chinese.

Those of us that had been in the camp a while knew how their rotten minds could distort the most innocent of pictures. Most of the time they used guile to get their photos. Sometimes they used pressure. Usually the settings were so harmless that the participants had no problem with them at the time. Sometimes of course, we thought we were smart enough to make the pictures come out more to our advantage than theirs.

I saw one of these cases in action. I was there as the pictures were being taken by the Yalu river. A group of soldiers let them be taken thinking the Chinese would not dare use them. In reality the picture was of the soldiers taking the rotten fish they were given for the evening meal to the river. At the river they did their best to clean these stinking fish in hopes of getting them clean enough so they could be eaten safely. The soldiers were sure they would never show shots of the rotten fish the prisoners were given as their meal.

The Chinese had an annoying little habit of sending a copy of their propaganda magazine to the families of some of the captured men. A while after this photo was taken one of the participants received a letter from his mother. In the letter she described the picture of the boys with a big pile of fish beside them. The caption on the picture read, "Prisoners of War Fishing." His mother went on to remark, "It was nice of them to let you go fishing." The Chinese won that round, gaining big propaganda points. The picture presented just the message our captors wanted to get across.

What the magazine didn't contain, I'm sure, was the sight of about fifty Korean kids fighting one another to get the rotten, stinking fish heads that we refused to try to eat. I know, I was one of them cutting the heads off the fish. I had to be very careful not to cut the hands of some of those children off as they reached frantically go get a handful of food.

Words can not describe how I felt for those poor kids. Starving to the point where they would treasure the taste from the heads of these rotten fish. We were hungry, God knows, but at least we had something to eat, especially after the peace talks started. The Korean civilians had nothing.

This wasn't an isolated occurrence. A few times we received fish so rotten that we wouldn't even try to salvage any of them. We took the whole box and just dumped it. Within minutes there was a mass of Koreans, young and old, fighting over what we had just discarded.

I said to the guy standing next to me, "Take a look at that, it makes me sick. These poor people. I wish we could get a picture of that."

He replied, "Do you think anybody will believe it when we get home and tell them about this?"

The memory of the stories we heard about the German concentration camps and the horrors that they inflicted upon those people came to my mind. I remember how many in the states did not believe that such things could be true. Not until the photographers started sending the pictures home that is.

"Right now they don't have any reason to believe it, at least not until we get home and tell them about it," I answered.

"If anybody tries to tell me that communism isn't all that bad when I get home I'll blow my stack," he said, then added, "No, I got a better idea. I'll invite them to the house and cook them up a mess of rotten fish and some rice loaded with gravel...that'll teach em."

Even through all this the rumors about the impending visits by the International Red Cross never stopped. I am sure they persisted more because we needed to <u>think</u> it was possible, than we actually <u>believed</u> it was possible.

CHAPTER 14

Face of a Traitor

There were a number of things that we, as Americans, had problems dealing with during our long ordeal. The fact that some of our compatriots were so easily swayed away from the ideals, morals, and values we were fighting for, was perhaps the hardest thing to come to grips with. The term that was used to describe the process some of our men went through was "Progressiveness." Descriptive because it turned these good men away a little at a time. One indiscretion at a time, until they had nothing left to fight for, and no one to fight against. None of us pretended to understand just what drove these few men to do the things they did. Perhaps it was the easy thing to do, others probably didn't understand the true implications of their action until they were in too deep to back out. Regardless of why they did these things all of us lost a little bit when one man set aside his principles. Thank God they were but a few.

In Camp No. 1 the first sign that a soldier from our company was having progressive tendencies came as quite a surprise to all of us. We were totally unprepared for it. It was a speech made at one of the regular sessions during our indoctrination lectures. John F. stood up and began talking. It was obvious from the words he used that the instructor knew his intentions and had briefed the soldier on what to say.

In his first few sentences he stated that he was duped into coming to Korea by the warmongers, (a typical communist phrase). He tried to convince us that we should all write to our congressmen and complain. "We are only the tools of the capitalists," he charged.

His statements hit us like a ton of bricks. A dead silence settled over the company. When the shock of his words finally wore off we realized that he wasn't joking, every man in the group started yelling at him.

"Sit down you foolish sonofabitch..."

"You'll hang for this..."

"Come off it Mac, you'll get your butt in a sling for this one..."

These condemnations were followed by a round of boos and cat calls. Everyone was stirred into a rage.

The statements he had used in his declaration that day appeared again in the camp newspaper under the headline, "Towards Truth and Peace." The word circulated around camp faster than the papers, "John F. had turned progressive."

"Boy, he'll get ten years in Leavenworth for this..."

"Ten years in Leavenworth..." That phrase became the code word used around the camp when an unreliable was within hearing distance.

Two other men allowed themselves to be used. They wrote articles for the camp newspaper. These turncoats made those of us that had learned how to say no and mean it, even when threatened, the most upset. It made life tougher on everyone. Now because of the actions of a few men an attitude of fear, suspicion, and distrust sprang up in the camp. We began to worry about who we could talk to without the Chinese finding out about it. These three men were completely ignored by the rest of the camp. No one wanted to take the chance that they would be accused of being buddy-buddy with them.

We also learned that it wasn't a good idea to try to make these progressives pay for their crimes. If any of these men were punished their Chinese friends would take it out on the rest of us.

The Chinese were smart. Prizes were offered to those who would contribute articles to the paper. Of course the articles had to be about subjects that the communists had chosen.

One day a tall private first class from Pennsylvania came walking in gloating over the prize he had just won for his article. He carried in extra cigarettes, cookies, sweet soap, and a towel. One of the guys asked him where he had gotten his riches.

"I got them for writing the truth," he replied.

"What do you mean, writing the truth? What did you write?"

"I just wrote that we had no right to come over here and fight the peace loving Chinese," he said innocently. That was all we needed to hear.

The offender was picked up, presents and all, kicking and screaming as we departed the hut. We took him over to the latrine pit and just threw him in.

But the lesson we tried to teach him did no good. As quickly as we had put him into the latrine the Chinese were there to get him out. He was washed up, given a new set of clothes, and his prizes were replaced. Luckily for us he didn't have the nerve to tell the Chinese who had tossed him into the pit. He knew what the consequences would have been had he ratted on his fellow soldiers. To make a general statement about the war was one thing, to turn in a bunk mate was something else entirely. Even he was smart enough to realize that.

He wasn't the only one led astray. Another lad had gotten himself in too deep with the manipulators and couldn't get himself out of it. He was a skilled artist and had drawn some relatively innocent pictures for the camp paper. Gradually the photos they wanted became more and more slanted to their point of view. He should have known better, but obviously didn't.

In return for a few extra luxuries he started drawing some cartoons about Truman and MacArthur. One of the cartoons depicted Truman and MacArthur with money sticking out from all of their pockets. The caption, written in both English and Chinese, read, "They are the only two who get rich out of the war." These portraits were attached to a monument post and the Chinese cameramen made great sport of them. The propaganda magazine went to great lengths to ensure the readers knew that an American serviceman was the proud artist.

This guy quickly realized that he was taking a chance if he was caught outside his hut at night. For some reason every time he tried it someone bounced a rock off of his head.

Another of the men, who was from Arkansas wrote to his father. In the letter he asked his father to start a peace petition. That it would be the only way he would every get home to his family again. We didn't argue that the man had the right to start the petition, hell, no one wanted this conflict to come to an end more than us. What did cause us a problem was the fact that the letter also specified what should be said in the petition. It of course asked for peace on communist terms. We wanted peace, but an honorable one, not a communist one.

One of the POWs tried a little too diligently to get his family to sign the peace petitions. His stubbornness was rewarded by letters from both his wife and mother disowning him. They wanted no part of his schemes.

After receiving these letters the broken hearted soldier kept pretty much to himself. At the time we didn't know what had happened, but knew it was a relief not to hear his stupid arguments and excuses for the communists any longer.

We stayed away from him as much as we could, as we had since we learned that he had signed the petition. Each day he became more and more bitter and it was hard to not belt him in the mouth now and then. It was hard enough fighting the enemy, I had no desire to fight one of my own as well. I guess I felt more pity for him than I actual disliked him. I also felt sorry for his poor First Sergeant. This guy was always complaining about something, always ready to throw in the towel when things got rough. I wouldn't put it past this guy to have signed the petition just to spite the rest of us that disagreed with his gloom and doom. He was that kind of a character.

Naturally the word got around. The Chinese had tried to get all of us to sign similar petitions, and ask our relatives to sign them. Their many attempts were not well received by the majority of us.

When the idea of having most of us ask our families sign their petitions failed they began sending the petitions straight to our families using the addresses off our letters. During the censorship process our mail went though they began to place a petition in the envelope along with the letter. You can't imagine how afraid some of us were that our mothers or wives would sign that damned piece of paper. It would have been hard to explain to our superiors later.

To be safe I continued to try to get a surreptitious message to my wife not to sign anything that the communists presented to her. I couldn't just say it in my letters or it would have surely been cut out before delivery. The only thing I could think of was to constantly tell her to take any papers that "she didn't understand" to a lawyer. She got the message. She took every petition she received to the local veteran's services officer.

Luckily before another of our comrades had a chance to get caught in this trap we caught wind of what was going on.

The victim walked over to us, looked over his shoulder, and began to whisper.

"Hey fells they just asked me about writing an article asking the United Nations to hurry up and sign the truce papers so we can get the hell out of here. What do you think? Should I do it?"

"Hell no."

"But what harm could it do? They said they would give me some extra cigarettes and soap and God knows we could all use it."

"But, hell, you aren't going to do it!"

"Why? What the hell harm can there be? The paper stays right here in camp and everyone will know that it's for the birds. The guys won't believe it, but it will give us some extra rations."

"Look, buddy, don't kid yourself. And quit trying to talk yourself into it. You know damned well that it is out and out propaganda. You know you shouldn't do it or we wouldn't be having this conversation. You would have accepted it right off if you really thought it was so harmless. We may understand that it is a crock, but don't believe for one minute that they won't make the most of it. They will send it all over the damned world. People outside the camp won't understand that it is a crock.

Besides, the main point is you have absolutely no right to cooperate with the enemy in anything, big or small, harmless or not, it's called collusion. You'll get home someday and I don't thing the Army will be too receptive to the idea that you didn't mean it, you just wanted a few cigarettes."

"How are you going to feel when you get a letter from your relatives disowning you just like the last guy did? Do you think he has much to look forward to when he gets home now? You don't think they are going to kiss him and welcome him back with open arms, do you? He is headed straight for Leavenworth, and after getting out of this hole I don't ever want to get stuck in another prison, no matter who is running it."

"No, if this is something you feel you need to do then you do it without our approval. Don't do it with some glorious idea in mind that your helping all of us by your sacrifice. I tell you here and now, we want none of your extra cigarettes or anything else you get by selling out."

Our constant arguments with the progressives and those they tried to enlist led to further segregation between us and those they thought they could reach. While the Chinese could punish us for bothering their prized students they could not watch us all the time and the students knew this as well. They knew when it was no longer safe for them to be out in the general prison population they could seek help from their teachers. Then they would be placed in a safe area with other sympathizers.

It wasn't always necessary to get into an argument with them, at least openly. Sometimes a simple anonymous note tacked to the bulletin board that read, "Tom...Warning...This is your last chance," was all it took to get them to see the light.

Seven Company had a unique way of dealing with the progressives who went a little too far. They established a system of kangaroo courts. The court would determine the guilt or innocence of the man.

If guilty, someone would follow the guilty party into the latrine one night, belt him on the head, and escape. The individual selected to carry out the sentence needed to be extremely careful. If he was caught they would really work him over.

One of the camp cartoonists was caught in Black Hat's office one day. We had our suspicions and wanted to know for sure if the artist was really the one we thought. Two of the boys walked in without the traditional knock and found him sitting there very comfortable chatting about his next piece of work. Soon afterward Black Hat moved his office and reiterated his policy of knocking before entering.

On October 31, 1952, Woody Woodhouse from Norfolk, Virginia, and I were sent to the hospital in Camp No. 5. The trip was meant for us to receive medical treatment, but we didn't get any. The fact that we didn't accept the "MENTAL" treatment that went along with the medical treatment had something to do with that.

Woody was a great guy. He was suffering from more than a few machine gun slugs in his right arm that the Chinese never had the time to remove. But this guy was tough and had a lot of guts. For months he had been getting by with what little first aid he and his buddies were able to render. I remember once when his arm was so clogged up with puss he got a length of wire, heated it red hot, and then stuck it into the hole in his arm to let it drain. It must have hurt like hell, but he hardly flinched.

They had tried their best to break Woody, but he never did crack. They even tried sending him out on a wood detail. He always returned with one of the largest logs without a whimper. Since Woody was a black soldier he always received their "special" treatment.

We arrived at Camp No. 5 hospital which was a little better equipped than the one in our camp. After all Camp No. 5 was the headquarters for all the other prison camps. We were immediately assigned to a large room. In fact we were the only two in this big room.

Before we had a chance to relax two nurses entered.

They began to systematically go through everything we had brought with us. They searched everything looking for the usual things the Chinese hunted for, knives, food, and diaries. Since Woody and I knew that this would happen either when we left our camp or upon our arrival here we had already removed everything of possible interest. They found nothing.

It wasn't before long that we got the first bad taste in our mouths for Camp No. 5. The nurses weren't gone for more than a few minutes when some of our soldiers walked in.

We had seen a few men in our camp that were on the verge of accepting communism. But they were small time Reds compared to some of these guys in Camp No. 5. Our sergeants could usually keep most of our men from making complete fools of themselves. It could be a hard fight at times. The communists were so skilled at this indoctrination that few civilians would understand the pressure. I'm not sure I ever understood the entire process. All I knew was that I had put an end to several of their attempts to "adapt" some of the men in my company. So much so that I was classified as a "Reactionary." I wore this title proudly, it meant more to me that being called sergeant. It was a title I was not about to relinquish just because I was at a new camp.

Woody and I were putting our things back in order when one of the patients came over to us with a few books under his arm.

"Hi fellows," he said, "How are you feeling?"

"Pretty good," I replied, standing up. "My name is George Matta. This is Woody." Names were always one of the first things you exchanged with new prisoners you met. Not to be sociable but to get your name known by as many prisoners as possible in case they escaped or were released. Then they would be able to take word of your whereabouts back to your loved ones.

"They call me Doc," he said. "Where are you from?"

"I'm from Massachusetts and Woody here is from Virginia. How about you?" I asked.

"I'm from Michigan," he replied.

"What's the scoop on this joint," I asked. It was usually the second question asked of new acquaintances. The answer I got almost floored me.

"Oh, this is a swell place," he answered. "They are treating us wonderfully. That's what I wanted to talk to you about."

"What do you mean swell." I growled. If it was so great then it is the first place I'd seen in North Korea that was. I didn't like the tone in his voice.

"Well, here everything runs smoothly, if you don't fight it. We get just about anything we ask for. That is, most of us do. Now here's a couple of books you can read if you want. They expect you to study while you're here..."

"Now look, buddy, I don't know what your game is, but you can just take those books and stuff them, I ain't about to study communism..."

"Me neither," Woody added.

"Who said anything about communism," he said, "I just said they expect you to study."

"Look, I worked the library back in Camp No. 1," I told him. "I've seen those books before. They're just about as Red as they can get. I ain't about to read them."

"What's the matter, are you afraid to learn the truth," he taunted.

"The truth! Listen, buster, don't you hand me any of that crap. I don't have to read the truth, I've been living it for a year and a half now. What's the matter with you anyway? What the hell, have you made friends with these guys? I wouldn't read those damned books for all the tea in China. I still haven't forgotten all the boys we buried up on the hill outside our camp. Your friends tried to teach them their truth too. Get those books the hell out of here and get them out fast before I bust you one..." It was getting hard to control my temper and I started for him. Woody moved right along with me.

This member of the local book of the month club looked at both of us, shrugged his shoulders, and started out of the room.

"We'll see," he said over his shoulder.

"Go on, scram. And don't come back."

"Well, whatta ya know about that," I said to Woody. "That guy's really gone. Can you imagine him coming in here and trying to get us to read that stuff? What the hell does he think we are?"

"I wonder what makes a man do things like that," Woody reflected. "I wonder."

The next day Woody and I decided to check out the other ward to see if there were any familiar faces.

"George!" I yelled, "George, how the hell are you? Boy, it's good to see you. How have you been?"

"Matta! Well, I'll be damned. What the hell are you doing here?"

"They're suppose to patch up my head for me, I guess."

"When did you get in?" he asked.

"Just last night. How are you feeling?" I asked.

"Not too bad. I've been here for quite a while now. But they haven't done much for me."

Somebody called from across the room, "Hey, George, What did ya find another Boston Bean?"

"Yeah," he yelled. "Practically a neighbor. He lives in Brockton and I live in Stoneham."

"Does he pahk his cah in the Hafvuhd yahd?" his friend asked using his best imitation of a Boston accent.

"Damned right I do," I called back, "And I'd like to be back there right now."

"Where the hell is Boston?" another voice rang out.

"Where's Boston," I kidded back, "Hell, if you don't live in Boston, you're only camping out. You know...the seat of culture, the hub of the universe..."

"That's probably where they're making the cultures they're dropping over here." That remark changed the tone of the entire conversation. It hit like a bombshell in the mist of the laughter. I recognized the voice, it was our old friend Doc.

"What do you mean by that crack," I challenged.

"You know. The culture. The germ culture they've been dropping over here," he replied.

"Germ culture. What are you nuts? Who says they're dropping germs?" I asked.

"Awe, come off it. Everybody knows they're dropping germs. Don't you read the papers?" he said.

"Yeah," I said, now quite interested, "I read the newspapers. When I get them. But I haven't seen anything in the papers around this joint worth reading."

"Oh, there are some papers here, all right. And there are some magazine articles, and films, and confessions from the guys who dropped them. Now I suppose you are going to say they're not dropping them."

"Buddy, I don't know what is wrong with you, but you better quit with that stuff. I didn't come in here to listen to a lot of junk about germ warfare. Why don't you be a good little boy and go outside and drop dead." I turned back to George.

But he just couldn't let well enough alone. He went over to his bunk and grabbed a handful of magazines, came over, and shoved them in my face.

"Take a look, wise guy," he said, "Go ahead. Tell us those pictures don't show germs. And tell us those aren't our planes." He thumbed through a few pages. "And now tell me these Koreans aren't dead and that those aren't germs all over her. Go ahead, tell us."

The pictures did look genuine. All of them. I am no expert so I can't say how they had been retouched and faked. I also am not a scientist so I couldn't tell him whether or not there were germs in the pictures. Being an infantry sergeant I naturally didn't have access to all the information on bacteriological warfare. It was obvious they had done a good job on Doc. He was filled with this garbage up to his ears.

"Listen soldier, who are you trying to kid. You know as well as I do that our country has never dropped germs in warfare. You know that we don't have to drop germs to beat these Chinks. We have enough power at our disposal without any of that crap."

"And just how do you know we haven't dropped any germs?" he queried.

"Because they said so," I shot back.

"Because they said so," he mimicked. "Isn't that nice. They said so. And what do you suppose they say about these pictures? And the radio broadcasts by the pilots who dropped the germ bombs?"

"Wait a minute, you stupid jerk. Wait just a minute. What kind of a soldier are you, anyway. What kind of an American are you? Since when do you figure it's okay to listen to these stinking Commies when they tell you lies. Is it so much easier to believe what your enemy says rather than what you own country says." I was getting really steamed.

"Who said they are lies?" he asked.

"I say they are lies. Look, when the day comes that I can't believe what my country tells me then I don't want to go home. When the United States said they were not using germ warfare they meant it. And no damned fool like you is going to make be believe anything different."

"Where's the proof," he rebuffed.

"Proof!" I exploded. "Who in the hell needs any proof. For Christ sake, look, I personally don't see any damned reason in the world why they can't use germs if they want to. What the hell, this is a war we're fighting, not a ping pong game. I can't see why they don't use the atom bomb. But they said they are not using germ warfare and that's good enough for me."

I was ready to introduce my fist to this guys ugly puss. George realized this and grabbed me by the arm, urging me, "Matta, Matta, don't hit him. Come on outside. Come outside, I want to tell you something." I relented and we stepped outside.

Out on the steps George pleaded, "Look, Matta, for goodness sake don't fight with that sonofabitch. It'll get you nothing but trouble. He's in with the Chinks."

"Boy, I guess he must be. That's twice he's crossed me in two days. I'm going to knock his head off the next time."

"No! Don't fight with him. It will only get you into trouble. Everybody that comes here has been hurt bad if they touch him. Just leave him alone. Let him rave. We're getting use to it. Just ignore him."

"Okay," I said. "I'll try."

"Look pal, we don't go for his bull either. But the only way he can hurt any of us is if we hurt him. We know what he is. He figures he will get a better break if he plays along with their game. But he also knows we'll kill him if we ever get the chance."

That summed the situation up pretty well. Doc had gone so far helping the Chinese that he had too much invested at this point to stop. If he did stop now the Chinese would get him. If he didn't stop the Americans would get him. At this point in time the Chinese were more of a real threat to him than we were, they had opportunity, we didn't. He had also convinced himself that the Reds had the upper hand and would come out of this thing on top. He simply took the path of least resistance.

A few days later George and I were sitting on the edge of his straw mat talking about our plans once this war ended. I had just finished saying, "I would like to open a little mail order outfit, maybe handle a few vending machines, and build a few small houses I could sell."

Doc interrupted the conversation with, "There you go, always trying to think up some way to exploit the people."

All my good intentions of trying to avoid this guy and stay out of trouble went out the window.

"Yes, you dirty rotten bastard, I'm thinking of schemes to exploit the people. And it's guys like you that make me willing to exploit them. I would exploit my own mother and father to get a buck, if I could use it to hang you. And I'm going to keep right on reaching for every crummy buck I can get my hands on. I won't be a Rockefeller, but I just might be able to buy a new Ford to drive you to Leavenworth in."

"That is where you are going when this is over after all the things you have pulled. Someday you're going to have to go home. When you do I'll be waiting for you. And when I find you I'll knock the living crap right out of you. And don't you forget it. Let me give you something else to think about. What do you think your communist friends are going to think of you once this thing is over. They won't need you any more, you will have lost your value to them. When your not the favorite student any longer, then what will you do? You have already sold out your country for a few lousy packs of cigarettes, some candy, and cookies. Do you honestly think they are going to hold their arms out wide to welcome a traitor. You won't have anywhere to call home, except Leavenworth."

"Well," he said, "somebody has to suffer to learn and to teach the truth..."

"I'll teach you some truth, I'll use my fists for emphasis," I said, and started for him. Once again George stepped in between us and stopped me before I could take a swing.

"Don't be a damned fool, Matta," he grunted. "Hit the dog and you'll land up in the hole with the rest of them. Stop it...Come on, let's get out of here. We need some fresh air."

It was hard to leave, it would have felt great to deck that guy just once. It may have even been worth a few weeks in the hole. Quite a statement knowing that the sick seldom survive long in the confines of the hole.

I decided to go back to my room and cool off. Suddenly Woody came in. You could see in his face that he was furious about something.

"What's the matter with you," I asked.

"I've been catching it from the blacks sympathizers in this crazy camp," he said in anger. "They say I'm just being used by the government in the United States, fighting for a country that won't let me live free in it's confines. I'm not saying that everything is great for me in the states, but I am free to control my own life and make my own decisions. That is a hell of a lot more freedom than I see the Chinese giving the Koreans. I hope they never let those guys back into the states. Then they'll see whose free."

The communists targeted the blacks, Hispanics, Catholics, Jews, Protestants, the young, any minority group. They would work them over pretty good. Using them together in a very systematic way. Pitting them as the oppressed peoples of the capitalist American society. Then when it pleased them they would pit each of these groups against one another to cause discontent. All the time they tried to get us to fight amongst ourselves. Usually most of us were able to see right through their plans.

The next day we got a little more of the fine treatment here in Camp No. 5. Woody and I were cleaning up the room when the chief doctor came in. He came to the point very quickly. Woody and I were to remain in our room. Under the pretense that we had a contagious disease we were confined to solitary. We both laughed in his face.

"Why don't you come right out and admit it, Doc," I said. "You just don't think we are a good influence on your other students out there. Isn't that the real disease we have?"

We were both glad when they came in the following day and told us we were being transferred back to our old camp.

We never did receive any of the special medical treatment we were sent here to receive. Frankly, I was more than glad. Camp No. 5 had no X-Ray equipment and the thought of them tinkering with my head under these circumstances scared me.

What they were able to accomplish with some of the Americans in Camp No. 5 made us sick.

It felt awfully good to get back with some of the old guys back in Camp No. 1. The only Red characteristics these guys had came from the blood in their veins. These were in fact true red-blooded Americans.

Upon our return one of the new prisoners, captured the previous day, started asking Woody and I a number of questions. One of them really threw us for a loop.

"What does a traitor look like?" the young naive soldier asked.

After successfully holding back a laugh, I could tell his interest was sincere, so I answered. "They look just like we do, the face of a traitor is your face, my face, it's seed is in each of us. They didn't enter the war with thoughts of turning against their country. Their faith was too weak, they took the easy way rather than the right way. They thought of themselves; not of the cause; not of their country; their fellow soldiers; or their families. That's the only difference."

CHAPTER 15

Quality of Life?

Shortly after returning to good old Camp No. 1 I was placed into the hospital since I was no better off now than before my special medical attention in Camp No. 5. I was lying on the floor of the hospital when all of a sudden we heard a roar in the distance. It got louder and louder, and soon the sound roared right overhead. A great cheer was heard in the field so those of us in the hospital rushed out to see what the commotion was all about. There they were, what a beautiful sight, about eighty American planes. We all just stood there waving. Dr. Haung came out at that time.

"Take a look at that, Doc," one of the men yelled, "That's what's going to knock you guys out of this war."

The doctor didn't look well as he took in the sight of the precise formations above, so I joined in, "Those ain't our planes, boys."

"Whatta ya mean, not our planes, take a look at those stars and bars, chum, there from the good old U.S.A."

"Now wait a minute. They can't be our planes, can they Doc? How could our planes get this far north when the Chinese have been telling us for months that our planes can't get any further than Pyongyang. Hell, the Chinese and North Korean Air Forces have knocked all of our planes out of the skies, haven't they, Doc?" I yelled snugly.

The Doc looked worse and worse with every minute and with each plane that passed. The other guys caught on to my pitch nicely. What a great time we had working him over like that. The hoots and hollers were mixed with remarks about the nice looking Chinese and North Korean B-29s.

"When did your outfit get such nice looking bombers, Doc," one of the men jeered. "Boy, no wonder the United States Air Force can't fly up here if you guys can put that many planes in the air."

About that time the big planes began their bomb runs. We could tell that their target that day was the hydro-electric plant up on the river. The jet escorts were playfully streaking through the hills and mountain passes. There wasn't any sign of opposition whatsoever. No interceptor aircraft, no anti-aircraft fire, nothing. The attackers had clear sailing all the way. The target area must be taking a real pounding.

"Hell of a sight, Doc," I yelled. "They must be lost. Why do you suppose they're bombing their own power plants. Kind of silly, isn't it?" The crowd cheered again as a massive explosion was seen and heard over the hills.

Finally having his fill of our comments, the doctor began screaming, "Stop making jokes. Guards, guards, make them stop making the jokes. Make them go inside."

That put an end to our party as we were forced back indoors until the planes had left.

The raid occurred at about 2 o'clock in the afternoon and that night no lights could be seen in the entire area. The bombers must have done their job well.

"Hey, guards, what's with the lights? How come no lights," we yelled, and then laughed like hell at their discomfort. The official version, of course, was that the lights were out because of an accident.

It must have been one hell of an accident, the lights were out for quite a while.

A few days later still no lights. We decided to bring the subject up at our next propaganda lecture. The interpreter admitted that our planes had "caused a little damage" to the power plant but assured us that it was fixed right away.

"Where are the lights then." someone asked.

"Oh, the lights are all right now, we are putting the lights out now to save electricity. It is a new policy. We are saving it for the winter time."

That got a good chuckle out of the group and he didn't have the slightest idea why we were laughing.

A couple of days later we were hit with a new protest stunt. It seemed that the oppressed peoples of the freedom loving country of North Korea would be without lights for quite some time because of the activities of the warmongering United States Air Force.

"I want you to write a protest about your Air Force blowing up peaceful power plants," he explained.

"Who wants lights," we yelled, "Give us more bombings." Now that they had the camps marked, we weren't too concerned about them dropping a load on top of us.

The jerk still passed out the paper and pencils and told us to write the protests. We turned them in without divulging our names.

One of the protests we wrote read; "We were glad to see you fly boys, nice job of putting the power plant out of action...how about Peking next?"

Another read; "Nice job, keep up the good work, only more often."

On mine I drew a crude map of our camp and marked each building that housed Chinese soldiers and wrote a note that said, "Please put the buildings marked on the enclosed map out of order as soon as possible. Try not to hit the adjacent huts occupied by prisoners, however."

They spent a week trying to find out who wrote it. Fortunately for me they never did.

As I have stated already on a few occasions the Korean civilians were in a terrible situation. They had a very bleak existence and in most cases they had as bad a time of it as we did. They certainly were treated about the same as us by the Chinese. The civilians knew that they would receive no compassion from their allies, so often they would turn to us, their enemy.

"Outside in five minutes, fellas," the voice came from the doorway, "we're heading for the river for a wood detail."

These wood details would either take place up in the hills or on rare occasions down by the river. We enjoyed the rare occasions mostly because it meant a chance to do some clandestine trading. Whenever we approached the river the North Korean civilians would conveniently happen to have some of the things we needed. They would make spoons, pipes, buckets, and pans out of the fuel tanks dropped by our planes during their raids.

The item they sought the most from us was the rubber-soled tennis shoes we wore. We would normally have a few old worn out pairs that we would bring along with us. Even though they were usually worn to the point they had holes in them, they were better than what the civilians could get. They were as valuable as cash.

We quickly scurried around the hut picking up anything we thought would help us during our bartering exchange and then fell out. This particular detail involved the entire camp. That was a good sign for us. It meant that there would be too many prisoners for the guards to keep a close eye on our activities.

Within a matter of minutes a small highly mobile, very secretive department store had set up down by the river. They must have had as effective a grapevine as we did. Usually the guards turned a disinterested eye towards the transactions. It was only if they spotted an item that they desired that they interfered. The item was then given to the guard, otherwise all trading would come to an immediate and unhappy end.

"So help me," I said, "If you had enough stuff to trade with these guys you could arrange passage all the way back to the states." They were very skilled at their trade.

"I think your right, at least they would be willing to haggle about it for a while." replied one of my buddies.

An old papasan came over to where we were. He cast a frightful glance in all directions, looking like a fugitive on the run, and said, "You have watch to trade, no?"

"Uh, uh, have no watch, papasan," I answered.

He glanced at my wrist and tried once again, "You have watch to trade. You come with me home. My daughter very pretty."

The bluntness of his offer stunned me. A father pimping off his daughter. I walked away in disgust and wondered what could have brought a man to do such a thing. I know that it wasn't the watch. The only use he had for the watch was the leverage it would give him in his next transaction. Usually it would take a series of trades before they would get the real object of their attention. Usually this was food, it was hunger, the deep burning hunger of his entire family, that brought him to the point he was at now. With the watch in trade for a few hours with his daughter he would be able to promote that watch, through a series of negotiations, into enough food for his family for at least a week.

I realized that the presence of the communists had not just affected some of our soldiers it had also transformed the civilians. Their instincts were now more realistic than paternal. Food is always a commodity in short supply during a war but it seemed even more terrible in North Korea. These people had been reduced to the level of animals, daily scrounging for enough food to sustain them for one more day.

On our way back to the camp, laboring under the heavy load of wood, we passed many small children who reflected the worst aspects of this miserable war. They were destitute, unclothed, and disease ridden. They pleaded with us to trade with them. Unfortunately we had nothing left, everything was traded to those at the river or taken by the guards.

I passed a little boy, I guess he was about nine, and got the inspiration of a lifetime. There were no guards around at the time and the boy started singing.

The fact that he felt there was something to sing about was incredible enough, but not as incredible as what he sang, or how he sang it. With crystal clear, melodious tones he sang, "Jesus loves me, This I know..." It was in English, I wondered who taught this song to him. His voice reflected his pitiful existence but also contained a note of hope.

I stopped dead in my tracks and stared. For an instant the pain in my head and the weight of my load could not be felt. It completely left my mind.

He stopped singing, a startled look came to his face. I smiled. He began to sing again, "Jesus Loves Me, This I Know..."

Tears came to my eyes as I joined in with him, "Because the bible tells me so..."

Together we sang through the beautiful hymn. The little boy was happy to find someone who knew the song. And I was even more elated to find this symbol of Christianity here in a world clouded with communism. We continued on with the column of other prisoners. As we approached the camp we knew it would have to come to an end. I looked back at the boy and saw a big grin on his face and we waved a lonesome good-bye to one another.

From then on whenever I wondered if this stinging country was worth the effort I would think back to this moment and I knew we were doing the right thing.

The communists use to preach to us about how the capitalists in the United States would exploit the masses. This was nothing compared to how the Chinese exploited and corrupted the North Koreans. The situation made it easy for them. The civilians had nothing and the Chinese controlled everything in their lives. In many cases having as much power over life or death over them as they did us. The North Koreans had to succumb to their will to survive in many cases. The women were especially susceptible.

"Sleep tight, fellow," I called. As I began to doze off I caught the glimpse of a skirt on the front steps. It was a young Korean girl going into the doctor's office. I had seen her around the camp before.

"Hey, there goes that girl into the doctor's room again," I said, "I wonder what gives."

"No kidding," one of the other guys said, "I saw her around here yesterday. Maybe the sonofabitch is making out."

"He wouldn't know how to," another man called out.

"I don't know about that, he looks like the lover type," I said.

"Let's take a peek and see," someone suggested. We did. The three of us snuck outside and around to the window in the doctor's office.

"Wow, will you look at that!"

"He's having a great time with that little lady!"

"Look out! He heard us!" We ran like hell back inside. The doctor must have hated like hell to have us break up his party, but he came out and looked around. Not seeing anyone, he went back inside. A few minutes later the girl came out, looked in both directions, and lit out for the village.

Dr. Haung came in the next day and looked carefully at us, but didn't say a thing about what had occurred the evening before. You could tell he had his suspicions. He asked to borrow one of the prisoner's watches so he "could keep track of the sleeping time" as he put it. He was given one and then he left.

We jumped to the window to see in which direction he would head. "Look at that, will ya, he's headed straight for her house," I said.

"Yeah, he is afraid he might get caught if he messes around in his office."

"We must have really scared him yesterday," one of the others said.

"Oh, how I'd love to give him the shaft by telling one of the instructors."

It wasn't that what he did was so against the low standards of our captors, it was the fact that he was caught by us that would have meant his doom.

"Boy, they would kill him if they found out we knew."

"Good, I'd like that."

"Take it easy, bud, think about it. He isn't just another guard or instructor. He is the head man in this hospital. Doctors are in short supply. Yeah, he would get into trouble but they can't afford to get rid of him. He would still be here, and knowing a prisoner squealed on him, he is in a perfect position to really make life hard on us. We'd be the ones to wind up on the short end of the stick."

A couple of days later we had our chance to really put it to him. The doctor had once again borrowed the watch and headed for the girl's house. We weren't sure if the watch was his way of ensuring he was back in his office in time or used as a proof of some future payment.

While he was out one of the big wheels from the regiment came in and asked for him. It was with a great deal of pleasure that we pointed out the doctor's whereabouts.

We wanted to give this guy enough information to make the good Doc squirm a little, but not enough to hang him. Our information could only be useful to us if the doctor knew we had it and thought we would use it.

"Why, yes, we've seen him," I said, "He just went up to the road and into that house there on the right." I pointed the house out to him.

"Thank you," he said and left. He headed straight for the house, but he was back in a matter of minutes.

"They tell me the doctor left there an hour ago," he informed us upon his return. "Tell him I was looking for him if you see him."

As he departed, we saw the doctor sneaking into the back door to his office. He came in to see us a few moments later with a very guilty look on his face.

"Hey, Doc," I said, "That guy from the regiment was just looking for you. He went that way."

"Ah, so," the Doc replied, "I'll see him later, thank you. Did he say what he wanted?"

"No, Doc, he didn't," I said.

My buddy from New York piped up, saying, "We told him you'd gone visiting, but we didn't tell him where."

"What do you mean, visiting?" the doctor inquired.

"You know, we saw you going up to see your girl friend."

A look of sudden, deep and lasting depression hit the doctor. He choked, sputtered, and then turned gray. Now he knew we were well aware of his little rendezvous and in our hands this knowledge was a very serious threat to him. The last person the prisoners informed the camp officials of was given a five year jail sentence. He simply turned and walked out. We had the upper hand, at least for the moment, and he knew it.

From then on Dr. Haung couldn't do enough to keep us happy. We loved it. We knew that in reality this amounted to blackmail so we were very cautious. We also knew that we were walking a tightrope with this guy. Pushed too far he could reach such a deep despair that he would sell us all down the tubes, himself included.

The first peace offering was a bottle of port wine. It was delicious, so we asked for more. He hedged, but with a gentle nudge, "Doc, I'll bet this is better wine than your girlfriend gives you," we got the next bottle.

It was eating at him and we knew it. He was desperately trying to put an end to this hold we had on him. Finally when he could stand it no longer, he made his move. He came in the next morning and said, "Men, I have a favor I would like to do for you."

"What is it, Doc," I asked.

"I know you men have been here a long time without having any fun. I would like to see you men happy. I know that you would like some girls and the guards will not let you near the girls. How would you like to have me send my little Korean friend in to see you some day, huh?"

"Oh, boy," one of the guys yelled. "That's for me. Send her in, Doc, and I'll show her how a real man spends his time."

Another of the guys added, "Yeah, Doc, send her down. Hey, fellows, we'll draw lots to see who gets her first."

The doctor was glowing just at the thought his scheme was about to pay off. He was convinced that he had a way to get himself off the hook. It was a great temptation for all of us.

Coming back to reality I spoiled his fun by saying, "Yeah, and then we'll draw lots to see who gets shot first."

Thinking about it the boys realized the huge gamble it would be to trust the doctor's kind hearted gesture.

"No, Doc," I said, "You keep her. We'll wait until we get home. We ain't about to get shot for shacking up with a Korean dame."

"Oh, no," he protested, "It will be all right. They will not do anything to you even if you should get caught. I can fix."

"Look, Doc, they've been reading us regulations for over a year now that give a minimum of five years for a prisoner even making a pass at a Korean girl. I can just imagine what would happen if she came in here. No, Doc, we'd rather keep you worried. We're not interested. Isn't that right, fellows?"

Some of the guys answered a little reluctantly, but they did answer correctly. It was unanimous. The doctor could have his girl and we would keep him in line with our information.

There was little the Koreans could look forward to. The exploitation and manipulation of their minds and souls had gone on since the end of the Second World War. It had truly become their way of life. For even if the peace talks were successful they would remain under communist control.

While those in the United States and most civilized countries were busy with thoughts of increasing the quality of life at wars end, the people of North Korea were simply hoping for life. Quality was a luxury they could no longer afford.

CHAPTER 16

On the Move Again

The normal routine we had fallen into during our stay at Camp No. 1 was shattered early one morning. All of the sergeants were instructed to gather whatever possessions we had and fall out into the field. At first it appeared like another one of the many shakedown inspections we have had in the past. This time though no one started searching through the huts or our bundles.

A large number of trucks were lined up along the road. It could only mean one thing, they were moving us out. There didn't appear to be any logical reason for the move. And as usual since no explanation was provided we dreamed up a few of our own. Most of us wanted to believe that we were being sent back to freedom. It was just as likely that we were headed for extermination. We had caused the officials at Camp No. 1 enough trouble that I'm sure they wanted to kill us.

The thought of leaving was disturbing. While this wasn't home by any means, we were beginning to feel settled. We had just completed the latest round of repair work on our huts. We were also about to complete work on a make shift basketball court. The news of another move was truly disappointing to us.

While this trip would be considerable better than the one that brought us to Camp No. 1 so many months ago, it still would not be fun.

The rain started as soon as we pulled out of the camp and headed for the unknown. Any soldier that has ever been in the back of an open truck in the pouring rain knows it is a miserable experience. We were packed in, thirty men to a truck, it was impossible to get comfortable.

Our mood changed many times during the long hours on those trucks. Someone would reflect, solemnly, "This sure beats walking." That remark got all of us thinking back to the terrible days of the Death March.

Then someone else added, "Yeah, but it depends on where we're going." That got us thinking of those miserable days at the Bean Camp when the men were dying by the dozens.

In an attempt to drive those remembrances from our minds we strayed back into talk of repatriation. "Perhaps we're going home," a voice sounded from the back of the truck. It went that way through most of the night. We would think and think and think. Our minds were a mix of terrible memories and some hopeful thoughts for the future.

The only thing that interrupted these thoughts were the times when our overloaded trucks hit a ditch. The jolt brought us back to the realities of the present very quickly.

Around midnight the convoy stopped. By now we were all soaking wet, hungry, and dead tired. This was it, our destination, at least for the time being.

They ordered us off of the trucks and we brought our rain soaked equipment into a large building.

They assigned a detail to get some food for us but most of us just collapsed and went to sleep huddled on the damp floor, wrapped in wet blankets. We were both mentally and physically exhausted from the journey.

Once again the communists had succeed in their attempt to wear us down. By keeping us on the edge like this, always awaiting the unknown, they were able to keep the upper hand. The procedures used to keep us guessing were well planned and very systematically executed. The one constant throughout this process was the single all important question, "What happens next?" Today was no exception.

Surprisingly enough it was well after daylight when they finally awoke us. They used a welcoming announcement stating that breakfast would be ready in a half hour to get us up. We used the time until then to clean up a little and stroll around outside to relax our overtired muscles. We also began to hear the first indications from the rumor mill. Even more surprising than the extra sleep, or any of the rumors, was the fact that the breakfast was pretty good.

After we ate we were instructed to pick up our gear and fall in outside the building. "Let's go fellows, they're going to assign us to our huts," somebody yelled. We had been through it before, we knew the drill. We picked up all our gear and headed for the door, not the least bit suspicious.

Even when we got out into the field it didn't dawn on us what they were up to. It wasn't until they ordered us to separate five feet from one another that we realized this was another shakedown. We should have expected it, but we didn't. After all they were sure to want to know what we were bringing into the new camp. I guess we thought it would come after the hut assignment. But now they had us, we didn't have any time or any where to hide anything.

When we arrived in the middle of the night we were too tired and too wet to worry about it.

"Give me your attention," a big guard ordered. "All of you will spread out your bedding and place all your equipment on top of them. You will take everything out of your pockets and put it on the comforter. Then you will move to this side of the field. When the guard reaches your belongings you will march up and stand beside them. When he is finished you will go over there to the other side of the field. Do you understand?"

We understood all right. They weren't about to give us a chance to hide anything. We knew we were about to loose some valuable property. It had been two months since the last inspection in Camp No 1. Most of us brought our notes and lists of names up to date during those two months. It was terrible to think of starting all over again.

I dumped everything from my pockets, placed all my gear on top of the comforter and walked to the line of men along the edge of the field. One of the guards walked down the piles of equipment and started sifting though the material. Another guard preceded him unbuttoning all pockets and untying all bundles.

As they continued down the line they approached my stuff and I stood beside it. I looked down and a paralyzing shock hit me, there in plain sight was my diary. It took a lot of self control to keep myself from reaching down and snatching it up. I felt sick. If he opened it and found the names I had listed I would be headed for jail. We all tried to maintain lists of those we knew were dead or those that had not been seen for a period of time. For obvious reasons the communists did not want that information to ever make it back to the U.S. officials until they had a chance to go over the list. Even if he simply took the diary I would be out over two months of work. I prayed that he would just leave it there on the pile of my equipment.

The guard stood over my equipment for what seemed like an eternity before he reached down and started going through my things. He picked up every single item in that pile, felt it, then dropped it. As he reached for the diary with the list of names he also spotted the notebook that the Camp No. 1 officials had given us months ago. He picked them both up together.

"What is this," he asked.

"Nothing," was my only reply. I fought to keep the anxiety I felt in my heart from being reflected in my voice.

"What do you have in this notebook," he asked, obviously not satisfied with my response.

"Nothing," I answered once again. He opened it. Luckily I only had written the words to a few American songs in it, along with an account of the daily meals we had been served. This information wasn't too damaging so I wasn't overly concerned. He glanced at a few pages, closed the notebook, and then tapped it idly against his hand.

"What is your name?"

"Sgt. George Matta."

He then pulled out a pencil and wrote my name on the outside of the diary and notebook. Then he tossed them into a box that held all the confiscated items from their search and said, "You will get them back."

Next he picked up the comforter and felt through it for any hidden objects. While he continued with my equipment his partner had me hold my hands over my head and frisked me.

I was instructed to remove my shoes and socks and he searched them carefully. I let out a sigh of relief as they finally moved on to the next man in line.

I knew that this was only a temporary reprieve since my name was now on my diary. There was still the chance that they would just throw away that stuff and not find my list. I hoped I wouldn't hear anything more about it.

This search had been a lot more thorough than any of the ones conducted in our last camp. This started the rumors flowing once again. "We're going home and they want to be sure we're not taking anything with us," was the word passed up and down the line.

When they finished the inspection we were formed into a large group. Then they began to read out names from the list they had of the prisoners transferred from Camp No. 1.

The very manner in which they called the names out added credibility to the going home theory. The first group called were all British. The second group called out were all black sergeants. The last group were all white sergeants. The excitement went through us like an electric current. "That's it. We're going home. We're finally going home!"

Each of the companies of sergeants were marched off in a different direction. What they now called Third Company, mostly black soldiers, headed off across the small river off the road that ran to Paktong. My company, First Company, along with the Second Company went to the other end of Wiwon into a cluster of buildings surrounded by barbed wire. My group was herded into what once had been a school. It was pretty well demolished.

"Hell," I said, "Even they won't keep us in a joint like this for very long, this is a mess."

"Yeah," someone replied, "They must be sending us home. This has got to be a transfer point."

After waiting for a few weeks we realized that the misery was going to continue for a while and we started trying to get the school in shape. We worked like dogs trying to close up the open walls of the school. We carried mud and rocks for hours to plug up the many holes and build some stoves. It was beginning to get colder in the evenings and we knew that this work could mean our very survival. Next we built bunks to get us off of the cold floor. This place wasn't like the Korean homes we had been in before. They at least used radiant heat to keep the floors warm, this schoolhouse had nothing.

To complete the now familiar segregation of the prisoners they had erected a barbed wire fence between us and Second Company. They didn't realize that they were wasting their time. We had plenty of experience with setting up our own lines of communications, separation or not. The techniques we learned in Camp No. 1 would serve us well here. We knew as much about Second Company as if we were living in the same building with them.

The guards here pulled the same old tricks of ordering us to keep away from the fence and adding to the guard detail along the fence. When these failed they announced that we would build a stone wall to separate the two companies.

This got us mad and we really raised hell. They had an official explanation, of course, the wall would be built to keep the cold wind from blowing into the building during the winter. That was simple enough, real simple.

We let the instructor know we weren't buying this bit of propaganda. "Why are you so worried about putting up a wall to keep the wind from getting to us when you weren't concerned at all about placing us in a building with holes in the few walls that do exist?"

The outcome didn't change but we felt better just making our point. We knew that the wall would be built but they also knew that we understood the real reason for it.

We slaved away for two weeks putting up that wall. For hour after hour each day we did nothing but carry rocks. Even though our hands were very use to physical labor, they still blistered and became sore. They had given us a couple of small shovels and a pick to do the job, they were about as useless as sunglasses in a subway.

This activity demoralized us in more ways than one. Not only did it place a noticeable physical barrier between us but it drove home that we would be in this place for a long time to come. Depression set in hard and each day became a struggle.

Of course our thoughts turned once again to our loved ones at home and the freedom we desperately yearned for. I was thinking of my wife and daughter and felt very alone. It had been so long since they last heard from me, or I from them. Did they even know I was still alive? What were the papers saying about us, if anything? Have they all given up on us? I reached in my pocket and pulled out my Rosary beads.

As I walked along I softly recited prayers to myself. Out of the corner of my eyes I noticed one of the guards standing near the corner of one of the buildings, but I ignored him. My thoughts were thousands of miles away from this place right now. I continued reciting my Hail Marys when he came over and stood in front of me. Suddenly I became aware of his presence and shoved the Rosary back into my pocket.

"Give me!" he demanded.

"Me? Oh, no" I replied.

He reached out for my pocket and I grabbed his arm. We wrestled around for a short time as he tried to get loose from my grip. Finally his anger gave him the strength he needed to free himself. He took a few steps back, then pointed his rifle at me and again demanded, "Give me!"

"No, I won't give you," I said. "These are mine."

It is hard to explain the emotions that lead a man to be so defiant at the point of a gun, but I had reached a point where they had taken all I had to give. My freedom, my family, my happiness, even my future, all of these things were at their mercy. I could not let them take my faith as well. It was all that I had left. To take my faith would end what little hope I had left. In my mind they were one in the same, in my mind I was not being defiant, I was fighting for my survival. It was a fight that would be lost just as surely if I surrendered those beads as if he pulled the trigger. One way I retained my dignity, the other left me just a shell of a man, existing but not alive.

He started giving me hell in Chinese, motioning to my pocket, but I made no moves to give him my beads. Now I was mad too. I grabbed the end of his rifle and placed the bayonet on my chest.

"The only way you get these beads is to shove it in. Right here."

By now the commotion had aroused a number of people, including the instructor who came running out of his hut.

"What is the matter?" he asked.

"This guy wants to take away my Rosary beads," I answered, "And I ain't going to give them to him."

"If he wants them, you give them to him," the instructor stated.

"No sir, I won't"

"It is only some beads. Give them to the guard," he insisted.

"Only beads? That's all they are to you, but they mean a lot more than that to me," I replied.

His eyes narrowed as he asked, "What do you mean? What do they mean more than just beads to you?"

"These beads represent the fact that Jesus Christ died for people like me and you on the cross. And by God, you'll have to kill me to get them away from me. Go ahead, I'm not afraid of you."

He realized that I meant what I said and saw the crowd reacting to the situation so he called off the guard and ordered me into his office. I knew that meant another long interrogation session but I still felt vindicated.

He sat behind his large table and ordered me to stand in front of it. As usual he had the bright light glaring into my eyes. I'd been through this routine before and I knew how tough it could get standing there. He began speaking softly.

"You said that you were willing to die for those beads. What did you mean? Why did you say that?"

"You wouldn't understand," I answered a little sullenly.

"I think if you tell me I can understand," he continued, "Tell me what you meant."

"You wouldn't understand," I repeated, "You don't even believe in God."

He laughed, "God! There is no God. Why should I believe in God? What has he got to do with the beads?"

I tried to explain. It is difficult to find the right words to convey meaning to a man about a subject totally foreign to him. I talked for a few minutes about Jesus Christ, the crucifixion, the Holy Trinity, of the Blessed Virgin. I soon realized that I was wasting my breath. It didn't even register and never would. I continued not so much to persuade him as to reaffirm my own beliefs to myself.

He finally interrupted, "Do all you people believe in God?"

"Most of us, I guess," I replied.

"But that is so foolish," he said, "There is no such person. Why do you believe in this God?"

"Well, I guess we believe in God for the same reason you believe that it is light during the day and dark at night. We know that it is true."

Again he laughed, "That is so silly."

"Look," I said, "Why don't you leave me alone. You believe in communism. I don't. I believe in God. You don't. Someday you will find out how wrong you are."

"And just when will that be," he asked, smiling.

"When you roast in Hell," I answered.

For the first time during our discussion something I said seemed to have an affect. "What is this Hell? What do you mean when you say when I roast in Hell?"

I once again attempted to explain the concept to him.

"I'll put it in simple words for you. And it's just as true as I'm standing here. If you are a good boy you go to Heaven when you die. If you are a little good and a little bad you go to a place called Purgatory and serve some time there. But if you are bad, and stay bad like you are, then when you die you go to Hell and roast in the eternal fire forever. See?"

He had heard enough and proceeded to explode at me. "Sergeant, you go back to your room. And don't let me catch you playing with those beads in front of the other men. Understand? If I catch you using those beads again you will go to jail!"

"Well, take me to jail now, then, because I intend to keep right on saying my prayers whether you like it or not."

"Get out! Get out of here!" he screamed.

When the other guys heard about my run in they advised me to take it easy. With the shape my head was in these days another trip to jail might just finish me off. I took their advise.

From then on I continued to say my Rosary, never missing a day, the only difference was that now I kept my beads in my pocket.

The communists did not believe in religion and did not like the fact that we did. But they also realized that they could not prevent us from conducting religious worship.

It wasn't only during the tough times that we looked to our religious beliefs to give us strength. I can remember a few times when we said prayers for our pilots as they flew overhead on the way to their targets. Unfortunately the largest turn outs were on the all too frequent occasions when we buried our fallen comrades.

Each person would join in according to his own faith and ask God for help. And we got it.

As time went on we began to conduct formal religious services. These were always conducted in secrecy for fear of getting caught. Some of the men stopped attending these formal gatherings as the peace talks dragged on but most of us kept right on saying our prayers. The prayers always had a common theme no matter which religion you believed, they all asked God to bring us back safely.

One night in our new camp about a half dozen guys were reading their bibles behind one of the huts when a guard spotted them. He suspected they were conducting a secret meeting of some type, plotting against the guards. He ran for the headquarters building and turned them in. Within minutes they were surrounded by a number of guards and forced to scatter. They were each warned that the next time they held a group meeting their bibles would be confiscated.

One of the most religious men in this group was Beatty. He had a unique ability to rally the men for religious ceremonies in the camp. Beatty and a man named Ernest Jenkins usually arranged the Protestant services. The time and place of the service would be established and some guys were posted to sound the alarm if the Chinese started getting curious.

After these clandestine meetings were going on for some time the communist officials in the camp realized they could not prevent all such gatherings and decided it would be best to allow them. It wasn't that they felt particularly generous, they knew they had very little control over the situation. They felt that by allowing the services to take place, with some restrictions, they could gain some control and monitor the our activities a little closer. Besides it was a good boost for their on-going propaganda efforts.

They now allowed the services, even to the extent of allowing Jenkins to broadcast a sermon over the public address system, after it passed through the censors of course. The Catholics in the camp now began to run regular recitations of the Rosary led by a guy named Alan from Michigan.

As Thanksgiving approached we got the boost we so desperately needed. Here we sat November 1952, just like November 1951, in captivity. Little progress being shown at the peace table and our spirits as low as I've seen them in many a day. Surprisingly enough it was the camp officials that provided this infusion of spirit. They decided to allow Alan to read the whole mass from the Missal each Sunday. There was always a Chinese instructor present to ensure he didn't depart from the text. This was more for show than effect. While the instructors could speak fairly good English, I'm sure they couldn't understand one word of Latin and Alan would often use Latin phrases and we would respond in kind.

I can still remember the look on the instructor's face the first time he said, "Dominus Vobiscum."

And we responded with, "Et cum spiritu tuo."

Alan was usually a quiet person to be around until he took to the pulpit. Then he became an imposing figure, tall, thin, swaying back and forth as he read the mass. The swaying was not to add emphasis to his words but to provide relief to his feet which constantly burned and were sore due to a vitamin deficiency.

We now became settled in our third home under communist domination. This was Camp No. 4. Different name, different people, but the treatment was still the same. We use to wonder what our fate would be in Camp No. 1. Would we be driven to our allies in the south? Would we see American tanks approaching the fences? Or would we take the long final trip to the hill and become a name on someone's hidden list of fallen soldiers. None of us expected to end up in yet another in a series of Chinese prison camps. How would we leave this one, dead or alive, none of us knew but all of us hoped that one way or another this would be our last camp.

CHAPTER 17

Beware of Germs

The instructors in our new camp were very similar to those we had in the previous camp. The methods they used were well known to most of us by now and had become a little tiresome. The constant barrage of misinformation which they used in their attempt to reeducate us to the communist philosophy had become monotonous.

While their techniques were very transparent to a majority of us there were some of those who fell for their tricks and believed their lies. At the beginning of this process we spent a lot of time with those most susceptible to them. Our goal was to try to get them to see what the instructors were really up to. If we could expose our captors for what they were then we could save a fellow prisoner.

"Did you ever try to convince your high school teacher that you knew more about history than he did?" I asked. "What do you mean?" the man beside me questioned.

"That's what I feel like in this place. The instructors come with a lot of writing on a piece of paper and don't give us credit for having any common sense. We should believe it simply because someone else says it is so. They don't even imagine that we can think for ourselves, as individuals, without needing a higher authority do make decisions for us. I'm so disgusted with it all."

"Yeah," he replied, "I know what you mean."

It was the same way in this camp. Mental torture, pure and simple. From early morning until late at night, every day of the week, with the only breaks coming during chow and details. Hour after hour, day after day, it had become more than just monotonous, it was a sadistic and cruel form of torture. The only weapon we had to fight back with was our faith. Faith in our God, our country, our family, and sometimes most importantly, faith in one another.

They had many terms for it, the communist's favorite was enforced study. Just as in the other camps we read, we listened to lectures, and took tests. They hit us with the same old garbage over and over. They left no room for argument, cutting off any discussion that turned into a debate. Since the techniques were the same as we had seen for well over a year now, I can only suppose that it was the duration of such measures that was eating away at us so badly. After so many lectures over such a long period of time your ability to shake off little insignificant things deteriorates rapidly.

Their favorite subject lately has been germ warfare, something I hadn't heard about since my short visit to Camp No. 5.

This subject became as much a part of their war information as the bullets, guns, tanks, and planes. This subject was also more difficult to fight off. We knew very little about germ warfare. We knew it was used in World War I but it hadn't been a part of our military training. We never learned how they could be used to spread fear, confusion, and frustration during a fire fight. Or how this new mental warfare could be just as deadly as any other we had encountered. We decided to use that as part of our key elements to battle this subject. While we didn't know about germ warfare we did know the democratic principles we grew up with, the sense of right and wrong, and the American's dogged determination to play by the rules. We were sure that if such capabilities were ever envisioned by our military leaders they surely would have drilled that into us, as much as any other battlefield tactic, yet we knew nothing of it.

They harped on this subject so much that we knew the material by heart. That was just how they wanted it. It is just like when you hear a foreign song. Even if you don't know the language, if you hear it often enough you will soon learn the words. That was the fix we were in.

It started being mentioned during a few lectures. The instructor "deplored the outrageous actions perpetrated by the United States in dropping bacteria into North Korea to kill innocent civilians."

This was followed up by doctors who provided us with more technical information in their lectures. They told us which germs were being dropped and how the population was being affected. You would have to be a doctor to be able to call him a liar, but we all knew he was in fact just that.

Next we were shown films which they claimed showed "United States planes bombing a North Korean city with germ bombs." They even gave us eye witness accounts of the incident.

While this would appear to have demoralized even the most staunch supporter of American values, the communists staging of the event left a lot to be desired. This film and others like it backfired on them. The communists position was that the U.S. planes were dropping insects infected with contagious diseases on the helpless civilians. They showed us pictures of the "germ infected bugs" being dropped on the populace. They claimed the effect was evident by the presence of dead mosquitoes laying on the ground. There were dead insects in the photos that did resemble mosquitoes. They wanted us to believe the germs induced into their system finally resulted in their death.

One of the guys from Louisiana spoke up, "Hey, anybody here from New Jersey?"

A boy in the back called out, "Yeah, I am, why?"

The first yelled back, "Brother, let me tell you that I know we don't have any mosquitoes like that in Louisiana, how about up in New Jersey?"

The answer came back, "No, we don't have any mosquitoes that could survive living at a 40 below wind chill on three feet of snow."

"Maybe they flew over from Texas," someone else offered.

"Hell no," a Texan called out, "We got em big and mean, but I don't ever recollect seeing any as tough as those must be."

"They must be good communist mosquitoes."

The instructor didn't have the faintest idea of what all the horseplay was about. I don't think that he even realized that the picture showed nothing but frozen mosquitoes. He undoubtedly was convinced that these poor creatures died as a result of some kind of germ they were exposed to. Hell, why shouldn't he believe it, the script he was reading from said it happened that way, so it must have.

He must have reported the discrepancy to his superiors because we never saw mosquitoes in any pictures from there on. In their place we started getting unintelligible views through a microscope. They still didn't realize that we would not have recognized a germ through a microscope any more than they could tell a Dodge from a Chevy. Besides that even if they were germs sitting in a test tube, that still doesn't prove the United States was dropping them.

Whenever they pointed out the unusually high number of North Korean civilians sick with disease, we reminded them that the failure of the communists to provide the food needed to maintain proper diets, and the lack of even the most basic of medical care had caused numerous deaths. People were dying from the communists total lack of compassion, not from germs dropped by American planes.

Once they realized that their efforts were a dismal failure they took another unfortunate step, further segregation. We were divided into groups based on how receptive they thought we were to the message they were trying to drill into our heads. I felt sorry for some of the susceptible ones. They were all pretty good kids, but for the most part they had little or no education and that made the pressure on them even more extreme. God knows it was hard on most of us, even those with high school education.

The camp officials began to question us about how the Americans planned to use germs in battle. Disbursement techniques, proposed targets, and anything they thought would be of use. We knew nothing about it and had trouble dreaming up answers to their foolish inquiries.

They were beginning to learn from their earlier mistakes. The information they provided us was of better quality and increasingly more realistic. A verbal defense in the face of the almost overwhelming "evidence" they kept throwing at us was almost impossible under these conditions.

On and on it went. More movies and now tape recordings with American prisoners "confessing" to having dropped the germs. We were sure they were coerced statements, but it was still hard to argue the point. We had no proof, they would say. We sure didn't think much of their proof but there also wasn't much we could do about it, except listen.

All of the material, the lectures, the technical discourses of the medical men, the pictures, the tape recordings, had the same pitch. We were dropping germs and the prisoners had the duty to write protests to their families, to the Army, to the Congress, and even to the President.

A few of the boys swallowed that tripe. It is a real tribute to the vast majority of prisoners that they were able to withstand the tremendous barrage of propaganda. Even more it is a tribute to how we as Americans are taught to believe in our country.

We did our best to convince those few who were falling for their crap that it was all wrong. For the most part a good long talk was all many of them needed. A simple reassurance that the fight was still on, we were still on the right side, striving for the right purpose. Only a few took the bait the communists provided. Luckily no one in my group appeared to be wavering at this point.

"What are we going to do about those guys?" I muttered, pounding my fist into my hand as I paced the floor.

"Which guys?" asked Carlie.

"The poor slobs that are buying that germ warfare garbage. It gets worse every day. Some of them don't even know which way is up anymore."

"Yeah, I know," he replied. "It's pretty rough...you know that guy we had today makes it awful easy to believe."

"That's not the hardest part," I said, "The hardest part is that even though you know it is a bunch of bull, what can we tell our own guys when they start to argue with you."

"I dunno. It's hell to have to spend all day listening to that crap and then spend half the night telling some punk kid that it's all a bunch of lies," he said.

"Especially when you don't have any proof to back you up," I added. "We are asking them to ignore what they see and hear and believe what we feel."

One of the other men in the hut joined in on the conversation. "What really gets you is you can't even knock some sense into them or the Commies will whip the hell out of you."

"I'll knock em all right," I threatened. "I'll knock their damned block of if I catch one of our guys peddling that trash around here. We have enough trouble with the Commies without worrying about our own men."

"But what more can we really do," Carlie asked. "We've told them it's crock. We can tell them it's lies from now till hell freezes over, but it ain't gonna do no good the way it's going now."

The other guy said, "Hell, did you see that poor kid out in the field with this afternoon when the Chink doctor was putting bugs in the jar. That poor kid was so scared he wouldn't get near those bugs."

"Yeah," I said, "And the sonofabitch was just picking up very common, very healthy, very common bugs, and dipping them in alcohol. What the hell is that suppose to prove."

Carlie said thoughtfully, "I'd say that kids reaction proves how much headway they are making. Even though the guys figure that it is a lot of rubbish they still react to it. Look fellows, let's face it, they have us on this one, they hold all the cards. There isn't anything we can do to prove otherwise."

That was the how it stood. We knew it was a bunch of lies. We also knew that most of the prisoners agreed with us. We simply had to ride it out as best we could and wait for an opportunity to provide our own proof to the few who didn't.

Luckily that opportunity provided itself in a magnificent stroke of luck only a few days later. We were listening to the same old message on germ warfare when the wonderful drone of high flying aircraft busted up the lecture.

"Hey, look, it's one of ours," came a yell from the crowd. "Yeah, look, look, one of our guys. Yipee...one of our guys."

"Look, he's dropping something," came another voice. "He's dropping something."

We could see it drifting to the ground. I had seen it before. It was tinfoil. I remembered that the Air Force dropped it in an attempt to send false signals to the enemy radar during bombing raids.

Our main instructor sure capitalized on the situation in a hurry.

He yelled, "Germs! Germs! Clear the field! Everyone inside! Hurry! Germs! Germs! American germs!"

It worked. Most of the guys went running for shelter. A look of great satisfaction came over the instructors face. He had done more in the last few seconds to sway the prisoners than had been accomplished in months.

"Wait! Wait! It's only tinfoil," I yelled. A few stopped to watch. "Look it's only tinfoil."

"Don't touch! Get inside! Don't touch it! It's germs!" the instructor kept screaming. People were running in all directions.

The doctors and nurses in the hospital picked up on the instructor's cue without missing a beat.

Armed with tweezers, rubber gloves, and bottles of alcohol, they came rushing into the field. Very carefully they began picking up the strips of tinfoil with their tweezers and placed them into the bottles.

The instructor kept right on yelling as our guys watched in awe as the medical staff put on their performance.

Oh, hell, I've had enough of this. I said to myself and started toward the nearest piece of tinfoil.

"Get away! Get away! Don't touch!" We were ordered.

"What for," I asked. "They're harmless. It's just tinfoil."

"You lie!" he screamed. "It is American germs. All over the camp. You see, I told you. The Americans are dropping germs. Like I've been telling you..."

"You're nuts!" I yelled, "Those are just strips of tinfoil to mess up the radar and you know it..."

"Get away, while we pick them up," he ordered again. He put on a most convincing act.

Before they could stop me I reached down and grabbed one of the strips holding it out to the instructor.

"Put it down," he screamed. "Germs!"

One of the doctors came over and grabbed me. Before I knew what he was up to, he grabbed the tinfoil from me and swabbed my hand with alcohol.

"Now you safe," he said.

"Safe, damned," I yelled. "These things won't hurt you!" I immediately got hold of another one.

"Look, look at me. Watch what I do." I rolled the tinfoil up into a little ball, saying, "Watch me, now, I'm going to take this pile of germs and..." I threw it into my mouth and swallowed it.

"Let's see how many germs I get now," I challenged.

"You crazy,...crazy.." one of the guards cried out in horror.

I figured that would put an end to it but the instructor wasn't about to give up this golden opportunity that easily. Seeing the chance of success in his propaganda effort literally swallowed up in front of his eyes, he was furious. But he didn't let his anger cloud his thinking.

"Doctor," he shouted. "Quick! Take this man to the hospital. Hurry, or he will die from the germs."

"Don't worry about that," I taunted, "I'm not about to die from any germs today."

Three of them grabbed me and dragged me toward the hospital.

The instructor followed along scolding me. "That was a very stupid thing you did, sergeant. Endangering the life of every man in camp."

"Endangering their lives, hell," I replied. "I'm okay and you know it." They continued to drag me away.

One of the American soldiers, a kid about 19 years old, shouted in awe, "Why did you do it, Matta? You might die."

I looked at him coldly. "Look, kid, if I die it will be worth it. But you stick around and watch. If I don't die, these guys got a hellofa lot of explaining to do."

As they dragged me off I could hear the instructor telling a group of prisoners, "...impregnated with a virulent type of disease producing micro-organism..."

"Bullshit," I yelled back over my shoulder.

I was taken into the hospital and placed in isolation in one of the small rooms. The patients in the next room knew what had taken place. They heard every word of what transpired outside. The doctor ensured he spoke loud enough for them to hear also. I did the same.

The instructor and doctor were in a fix and they knew it. Their own propaganda was now coming back to haunt them. In each of the recent lectures they went into great detail about how quickly and brutally a man dies from the effects of the germs being dropped by the American planes. They knew that they didn't have the ability to induce those symptoms on me in the camp, yet they had to do something and fast.

"Here take this medicine," the doctor urged.

"No, sir, I won't take any medicine." I insisted.

"Now look, sergeant, you are a very sick man. Luckily we have perfected an antidote. You must take this medicine and..."

"Oh no, not me Doc," I replied. "I told you, I won't take any of your medicine."

"But you must, sergeant," he said. "This antidote will save your life. First you take this medicine, and then we can inject you with this antidote..."

"Look, Doc, knock it off, will ya. I know the gag. Once you get that stuff in me you can claim your medicine killed the germs. You get a perfect out. Well not from me. You know damned well I ain't gonna get sick. That tinfoil was dropped to jam the radar, not to kill anyone, we have plenty of bombs for that."

"Sergeant, you must take this injection." His anger was increasing.

"You haven't got enough guards in this whole damned camp to make me take it. I won't do it. Look, why don't you just leave me alone. If I get sick, okay. You win. You have perfect evidence of germ warfare. You'll have all the proof you need if I die. But I ain't gonna die. And if I don't die, Doc, you better start dreaming up a whole new collection of lies about germ warfare...you're gonna need them."

"You'll die," he stated, the insistent tone now leaving his voice.

"If I die, I'll die laughing. Now get the hell out of here and leave me alone."

The gang in the other room started cheering. They heard it all. I'm sure that it was only because of those guys that they didn't claim I had taken the medicine, or given me the injection by force.

They kept up their little charade for three days during which my buddies were sure to keep someone outside my room listening. They couldn't pull any rough stuff without the entire camp knowing about it within minutes. The first day ended in a stalemate. No medicine.

The second day was pretty much the same as the previous. The doctor attempting to convince me that my life depended on their antidote, and me insisting that I wasn't about to give them the out they so desperately needed.

At the start of the third day they came in with a whole flock of propaganda leaflets. They contained photos of American flyers and statements they signed stating that the United States had been using germ warfare in North Korea.

"Look, I've seen those things a million times. I don't believe it any more now than I did then. Now take that stuff out of here, I'm not interested in reading that baloney."

"Then if you get sick," the doctor said, "You will get no treatments, no medicine."

"Hell, Doc I told you yesterday that was fine with me. I've lived this long without any treatments. Just go away and leave me alone."

I finally got my point across. They gave up in their attempt to provide treatment for my ailment. They continued to watch me for almost a week and then let me go without any fanfare. It proved to be the turning point we needed to keep some of the men from straying from the truth into the propaganda pit. It also seemed to have an affect on some of the Chinese soldiers who now figured the "evidence" they had seen might now be a bit flimsy.

It wasn't only the American prisoners that gave the Chinese a hard time. We also weren't the only ones infused with a spirit of honor and duty to our country. For my money it was the Turks that gave the Chinese the most trouble as prisoners of war. Not only was there a language barrier, damned few Chinese could figure out what the Turks were trying to say, but the Turks stuck together despite all hell. They were a tough and courageous group of soldier.

Luckily for most of them the peace talks dampened the Chinese inclinations towards outright murder. That was one of the main reasons we didn't care so much how long the talks resumed, as long as they continued, they were keeping us alive.

On this particular day three of the Turks were jailed for playing poker for money. It was another example of, "It's not what you do, but what you get caught doing that gets you in trouble." All of us were doing the same thing, they just had the misfortune of being caught at it.

Shortly after the three Turks were taken away they announced that we were going on a wood detail. As the column moved off headed for the hills, the company of Turks stood fast. Not one of them moved.

The Chinese halted the column and tried to make them march. They continued to hold their ground. Finally the rest of the prisoners were instructed to go ahead while they tried to convince the Turks to join us. We kept an eye on the situation below as we headed up the hills. The senior Turkish noncom stated that they had no intention of moving an inch until there three buddies were released from jail.

And true to their word they didn't make a move. The guards refused to back down and became more insistent that the Turks were going after some wood. The Turks even more insistently refused. The Chinese answered with more guards in an attempt to prod the Turks into moving. It soon became quite obvious that someone was going to get hurt. If this had taken place before the peace talks all of the Turks would have been jailed - or killed. It was only because of the talks and the fact they were still trying to win us over to communism that kept them from using more forceful measures.

For two and a half hours the two groups faced one another, neither side willing to give an inch. The Turks had won the battle, if not the war. Upon our return from the detail the Chinese ordered them into their huts.

That night at chow the Turks were conspicuous by their absence. They were now on a sit-down strike in their huts. Not a one of then would eat a bite. They calmly announced that they couldn't possibly eat without their three comrades in the jail. There was not doubt in our minds or in the minds of the Chinese that they meant it. This threw the Chinese on the defensive and they began to plead with them. They would have no way to explain how over one hundred fifty Turks starved to death.

The Chinese knew they had lost and released the three Turks from the jail. The entire camp, Americans, Brits, Aussies, and Canadians, broke into a thunderous applause.

This was the most heartening display of solidarity and camaraderie that I had witnessed in my life. The fact that it occurred in a place such as this made it all the more miraculous. Once again an event had taken place that infused the camp with a new spirit of defiance that benefited us all, no matter what our nationality, beliefs, or philosophies.

CHAPTER 18

Another Korean Christmas

In most parts of the United States you could tell when Christmas was approaching. There were trees for sale on almost every vacant lot, families made plans to be together, stores were full of shoppers, and turkeys and hams were on sale constantly. Here in Camp No. 4 the only things that gave the impression of another Yule tide were the bitter cold and deep snow and ice.

About two weeks before Christmas the Chinese offered one of their Yule tide gestures. In reality it was another thinly veiled attempt to get us to talk. They distributed some of their so ju, a strong Korean whisky, it was as strong as pure alcohol and tasted much worse than the worst moonshine.

As usual those men who did drink made deals with those who didn't for their portion. As a result there were a few hearty drinkers that had enough to feel more than a little tipsy.

Three of these stout hearted souls decided it would be a good idea to visit the British company and help them celebrate the holiday season. On their way they were stopped by one of the guards who soon learned he had made a mistake. The drunken trio, full of bravery provided by the so ju, jumped him, took his rifle and beat the hell out of him. Then they continued with their visit as planned.

However their visit was abruptly cut short once the guards located them. They were headed off to jail. We knew they were in for it. Even under the Geneva Convention, which the communists never worried about anyway, this was a serious offense.

The Chinese surprised us a bit by announcing that they were going to be really lenient this time and let the Americans conduct the trial of these three individuals. They wanted the top sergeants from the companies to sentence them. A nice piece of propaganda.

The top sergeants talked over the situation looking for the angle. There had to be an angle, there always was. After some concerted effort we finally realized what they were up to.

One of them summed it up nicely by saying, "Hell, no, we won't try them. We know just what you guys have in mind. If we find them not guilty then you will sentence them anyway and blame it on us. On the other hand if we find them guilty and you don't like the sentence we impose, you will double it. Either way we can't win. If you want them tried, do it yourselves. Besides, it was the so ju that made them do it in the first place, and it was you who gave them the so ju. So why don't you really demonstrate your policy of lenient treatment and let them go. You know as well as we do that the only reason we were given the liquor was to see if it would loosen our tongues.

It worked. The Chinese formed us all up into the field, gave us a long winded speech about their leniency, pointed out that they could legally hang these men for their actions. They also gave us the usual speech about how all of us were the victims of the warmongers, who had been duped into coming to Korea to fight for the capitalists. Then the three men were released. I think this experience cured all three of them of any desire for alcohol for a long time.

This incident also had another side affect. It proved to these three former progressives that the communists had a treacherous nature. After all who else would dare try men for actions that they themselves instigated. These three changed their political beliefs as well as their drinking habits.

They weren't the only men jailed as a result of the so ju binge that occurred that day. Another man was caught in the kitchen with some Korean civilians. The camp officials accused him of negotiating a trade in violation of the rules, but they couldn't prove it. So next they tried to prove that he had stolen the so ju but that wasn't convincing either. He too was released. It was a stupid form of justice we practiced here in Camp No. 4.

There were to be a number of highs and lows this holiday season.

"Did you hear that guy this morning? I wonder if he really meant it?" I remarked.

"You mean about the Christmas dinner?" my buddy replied.

"Yeah. Sounded good, didn't it?"

"Hell, anything would sound good after the crap we've been eating. I won't believe any of it until it is right here on a plate in front of me."

"I don't think I'll believe it until after I've eaten it. They way these bastards work, they might take the plate right out from in front of you."

"I guess you're right at that. Boy, I can almost see it now. What was it he said, we were going to have...turkey, and coffee, ahhh, delicious coffee, and pudding, butter, jam, even peanut butter. Gee, can you imagine getting excited about the thought of getting peanut butter."

I answered, "Boy, I'm so damned sick of kimchi, rice, and turnip soup, that peanut butter will taste as good as a steak. Well almost as good as a steak."

And so we dreamed of our Christmas dinner. Christmas 1952, the second one most of us were to spend behind the barbed wire. Our homes and families were so far away. The only reason we looked forward to it was the hope that it could break the monotony of life in this camp.

On Christmas day we awaited our dinner just like kids back home were eagerly awaited the arrival of Santa Claus. We conducted a special religious service this morning, the Catholics in one group, the Protestants in another. The remainder of the morning was spent talking about food. It helped keep our thoughts off of the loved ones we left behind.

It was an hour before meal time when a congregation began to gather by the kitchen. It was heaven just to smell the delicious aromas emanating from the many pots on the stoves.

There certainly was a variety of food. There was pork, fish, beef, and chicken for the main course. For desert there was sugar bread with extra sugar. Yes, there certainly was a variety. But then the blow came. We were to get just a teaspoon of each item.

"Will you look at what these bastards call a Christmas feast," somebody yelled after receiving his meager portion.

"Be quiet," yelled the guard, "or you will not eat."

Our cooks didn't even have the heart to make the coffee. When we complained they showed us why. For the two hundred sixty five of us eating in this kitchen the generous communists had provided a single pound of coffee.

"Take it back and tell them to shove it," somebody shouted from the crowd.

"The hell with that, that stuff is to precious to waste on them. Let's have a raffle instead. The lucky squad goes home with the coffee." The crowd roared its approval.

This was the first honest to goodness coffee we had seen in more than a year. One of the guys held up his hand for silence.

"The generous peace loving people of North Korea should be told what they can do with this overwhelming gift of precious coffee, but we can find better use for it. Now let's have all the squad leaders down here in the middle. We'll cut cards. The high card gets the coffee. Is that okay?"

"Yes!" We hollered.

The first squad leader grabbed a king. No one else was lucky enough to tie his feat so the first squad felt like the rich kids on the block, and they were.

We had planned a Christmas party for some time and now it was in full swing. The Chinese actually helped us for a change. They gave us permission to organize a camp band.

It wasn't the best band in the land, but it had it's moments. The idea actually came from a Texan named Barney and a guy from Chicago we called Aaron. They had put a foundry into operation.

In our wanderings around the camp we began to collect some scrap medal. From these scraps they were able to construct a bellow, some molds and other gadgets that made up the menagerie that was their foundry.

Most of their time was spent making smoking pipes. This was better than using the tobacco with papers, which were becoming harder and harder to find. They also made some bowls to eat out of. They were doing a great business and the Chinese didn't bother them too much.

It was through their efforts that we were able to create the instruments needed for our band. Small horns were made from old tin cans that were cut, flattened, and then rolled into crude horns.

We shaped our bull horns after those I had seen some enterprising soldiers use on the Pacific Islands during World War II.

They consisted of a 55 gallon drum, cut in half length wise, and fastened to a two by four. The strings for the base and a guitar were donated by the Chinese. They also provided a trumpet just before Christmas day.

Using goat skins stretched over a plywood frame, or over large tin cans, we were able to make our drums.

A Marine sergeant played the trumpet and boy was he good. We started practicing before Christmas and held a concert the Saturday before the holiday arrived. By now we were as good as we were ever going to be.

We also had a special attraction. It was Yung, our Hawaiian friend, doing female impersonations and another guy who performed old vaudeville songs his father had taught him.

Well, anyway, this little group of performers provided the entertainment for this holiday. They spent long hours rehearsing the songs, the Christmas Carols, and a skit in which Yung played the part of a violated girl. One of the Brits we called Nocker was ready to perform some of his artistry as well.

We finished our lavish holiday dinner and then stayed behind to listen to the band and sing Christmas Carols. Everything was fine until a group of visitors arrived from Camp No. 5 to hear our performance. This group of so called prisoners were obviously "progressives". The guards became very firm in their warnings when one of the performers began a song he called "Uncle Sammy." It was a parody that opened with the line "Don't bite the hand that feeds you." Our progressive friends got the message. And our opening night just about ended before it began.

Just then the toastmaster for the evening announced, "Ladies and gentlemen. As an added feature attraction to our show this evening, I am about to introduce that outstanding cartoonist, that brilliant young British soldier, who will perform outstanding feats with his clever pencil. Just call out your initials and this master of the pen and pencil will write them on the blackboard, and then, believe it or not, construct a picture from the initials. Ladies, and I wish we had some, and gentlemen, I give you, Nocker.

We all cheered dutifully and Nocker took his place on the stage. "All right," he announced, "who's first?"

One of the men stepped out from the crowd and placed his initials on the blackboard himself. Nocker laughed, "That's easy," and immediately began to sketch a landscape scene. We cheered once again.

The next man made his initials so large that they took up most of the blackboard. From them Nocker drew a picture of three men talking to one another.

One of the Chinese guards seemed quite amused at the artist's skill and was smiling broadly. After about another five or six took their turns at the board, seeing their initials cleverly transformed into cartoons, the Chinese stepped up to the board.

A dead silence fell over the group as he scrawled out "C.P.V.", the initials of the Chinese People's Volunteers. We booed. Nocker took charge of the situation, holding up his hands and asking for silence so he may complete his work. Studying the initials very carefully he began his drawing.

The more he drew the more we knew we would like the final results. As the picture unfolded it depicted a Chinese soldier hanging by the neck from a scaffold. Above the scaffolding was an American and British flag. The cheers were deafening. The guard was not amused.

Pulling out his pistol, he ordered Nocker off the stage. We yelled, "Leave him alone. Leave him alone." But he marched Nocker away. That was all that was needed to break up the party and the guards chased us back to our huts.

A delegation of the squad leaders went to the camp commander to find out Nocker's fate.

On our way back to our hut I told Carlie, "Let's go pay the first squad a visit, we have a few friends over there."

"Matta," he replied, "That sounds like a right bright idea. Let's go. Come on, Joe, you come with us."

The three of us went and paid our friends in the first squad a very sociable visit. We were very lucky, we got there before a mob of other friends that happened to stop by for a chance at some coffee. The three of us were given a few swallows. The prize did indeed go to the correct squad. They were masters at cooking coffee. They boiled it so many times it nearly boiled away.

"It sure tastes like more," I commented.

"More, my foot," the first squad leader answered, "Scram, buddy, you've had all your getting."

Realizing we had overstayed our welcome we thanked them and departed.

From then on we were back to our usual way of getting coffee. Take rice, burn it until it turns brown, then boil it until the water changed color. We had convinced ourselves that it tasted something like coffee.

It wasn't until the next morning that we learned of what had happened to Nocker. He had been sentenced to jail. But he was not in jail for drawing the picture the previous night. That would have made them look bad. They jailed him for drawing what they called escape plans six months earlier. The evidence of his crime were the plans he had drawn for two guys from Pennsylvania for a night club they planned to open once the war ended.

These drawings had been found many months ago. We thought the incident was long since closed. The two Pennsylvania boys had thoughts of opening a night club. They knew Nocker's reputation for drawing and naturally asked his assistance to draw up designs for their new club. It was more to pass the time than anything else.

Nocker agreed and whipped out his pencil and began making deft strokes across the paper. He explained as he went along.

"I'd place the bar right about here...and there must be booths arranged in this area so the patrons can see the entertainment."

The other two nodded in agreement. It certainly was a strange conversation for a prison camp.

I guess it wasn't any stranger than many of the dreams we all had for the time when our incarceration would come to an end. There was little else to do with our time.

The trio continued making plans for the nightclub. I don't know if they seriously expected their plans would materialize after the war or not, that didn't matter at the moment. All of us began to join in the endeavor making suggestions and recommendations to the sketches. The drawings were great, clear enough for anyone to understand, anyone except the Chinese that is.

It was such a harmless business that none of us gave it a second thought when the guard came in. Hell we had nothing to hide. But when the guard saw the innocent drawing he must have thought they were the floor plans to the Kremlin.

Nocker and the two would be nightclub owners were taken before the camp commandant to explain the meaning of the dastardly drawings. Of course there was no talking common sense to these guys. For over two hours they tried to reassure the commandant that they had no evil intentions. But when the Commies smelled a plot nothing was going to prove them wrong. The idea of drawing plans for a night club while imprisoned in this camp seemed so ridiculous to them that they were sure our guys were lying.

Finally the three of them were released on the condition that Nocker would do no more drawing without their permission. None of us expected they would use this against him months later.

Something even more ridiculous would soon to prove to us that we would pay dearly for our enjoyment during the holiday season.

The other valuable commodity besides coffee, was sugar. We were able to save up enough once a week to make up a batch of fried bread sticks. Two days after Christmas we reported to the quartermaster for our regular allotment.

"Sorry," he said, "You had your sugar on Christmas."

"Oh, no," we protested, "That was special."

"No more sugar," he insisted.

That was another of the many curve balls they threw us. Many more were to come. They began to starve us. Camp officials insisted they had used up all the regular supplies, and any extra they could find, to provide us the fine Christmas dinner. I don't know who got to eat all the food that was kept from us. But I do know that the little cup full of food we were given, a teaspoon full at a time, was far less than the amount they kept from us.

CHAPTER 19

Escape Plans

Another year, 1953, and still we sit here behind these barbed wire fences while they continue to talk at the peace table. Many men have died since the talks began and many are still alive simply because they continue. Most prisoners are glad to hear they are still discussing things at Panmunjom, but there are times when you wish they would just stop all the talking and fight this infernal battle out to the finish. At least that way it would have an ending. That is what we yearned for more than anything else now, an ending.

"What will you do if the peace talks stop and the fighting starts up again, George," Don asked thoughtfully.

There we were lying on our mats contemplating our dismal future while the others in the hut passed the time by blowing smoke from their cigarettes up to the ceiling. Would 1953 bring our release or would we be celebrating another Christmas in this, or some other, stinking camp in this God forsaken country?

I thought for a minute and said, "Don, you know something. If they start the fighting again, I've got it all figured out. I'll escape."

"Yeah," he jeered, "You and about 1800 other guys."

"No kiddin Don, I've got it all planned."

"Well by the way they have been treating us lately you better firm up those plans. They have given us hell since Christmas, next to nothing to eat, and they are getting rough with us again. It doesn't seem that they think there is too much of a chance at the peace table."

"Awe, hell, there has to be a chance. They have too much invested, they can't stop now. I'm sure they are in enough trouble as it is without starting an all out war again," I said.

"I know damned well I ain't gonna stay around here if the war gears up again. We wouldn't live for a week."

"You're right. Unless they can use us as pawns at the peace talks we are a liability to them. We would have no value any longer and they must expend food, men, and material to keep us here. Remember the days back in the Bean Camp and how we saw dozens of men left to die each day. That's how it would be again if the talks stopped. At best they would move us into China and that would mean the end of us."

By now most of the others in the hut had become interested in our conversation. Whenever a discussion turned to the subject of escape it caught everyone's attention. Like prisoners of war throughout history we were always talking and planning for our great escape. This was a daily occurrence in almost every hut. Most of those who had carried out their plans up to now were never heard from again. We hoped they made it home but unless they were caught quickly, near the camp, they would not be returned to the same compound. If they had gone far from the camp they didn't want information they may have gained from the experience passed on to the rest of us. It kept us from building a store of knowledge that may assist us in later escape attempts. Because of this we seldom knew if any attempt had been successful. Each time it happened we were all given a very stern lecture on the subject by our captures.

I now sat up with more authority, noticing more than passing interest in the other guys. I began to address the entire group rather than just Don.

"Seriously, fellows, I've been giving this some serious thought. I've been reading from some selected Commie material, and I think I have a plan that will work.

"Well, come on boy, don't keep us all in the dark," Don smiled. "Give us the details. How do you propose to pull it off?"

"Look at it this way," I began to explain. "We've always relied on just two ways to escape. Either head for the coast and hope to get picked up by one of our ships, or head south through the hills. Now as far as we know, no one has made it either way. You can't count on too much help at the coast because the civilians are afraid to even talk to us and we can't carry anything worth trading with them. And if we go south we wouldn't stand a chance of passing unnoticed through all the Chinese and North Korean troops between here and the front lines.

"That makes sense, but what other route is there?" Don asked.

"We go into the hills and wait it out."

"And starve to death in the meantime," someone scoffed.

"No, you wouldn't have to starve. And I'm not saying we should do it now, but it would be the best way to survive if the war really heats up again."

"Don't be foolish. You couldn't live in the hills. What would you use for food? And how would you stay warm?" On came the barrage of questions from everyone in the hut.

"Wait a minute, wait a minute!" I interrupted. "I told you I have been doing some reading. I know how to make it work."

Some of the boys started laughing at that, and one of them said, "Listen to this guy, he reads a few books and thinks he can do anything. Just like that."

"Just listen to me for a minute and I'll tell you how," I said. "After all people are living in those hills now, aren't they? Yes, I've read some books and they have told me how those people are able to live in the unforgiving climate of those hills. Besides, look, I've already got a lot of stuff hidden." Going over to a secret hiding place I had constructed under my mat I exposed my stash of goods. "See I have two ax heads, a knife, and some iron to make some more tools. I have a hundred matches, six candles, a bag of nails, what the hell do you think I've been doing with all those nails I've been pulling out of the walls? There is a bottle of bean oil and a mirror."

Now they all seemed to have a little more faith in this crazy scheme I dreamed up.

"What? Where the hell did you get all that stuff," Don asked.

"Never mind where I got it, I got it and that's all that matters. If I have to go alone I will. I don't stand a chance of making it through a trip to another camp in my condition, this is my only way out."

"Yeah, but it won't work as easily as that, George," Don continued. "You still have to have something to eat."

"Like I said, I'll go into the hills. I'll also get some seeds from the garden down the road and anything else I might need right away. I would select a location that had few, if any, Chinese but was close enough to a Korean village to steal a few things now and then."

"I'd use the seeds to set up a little farm. I could always sneak down to the village and snatch some vegetables from their gardens, maybe a chicken or two now and then. The way the Chinese have been stealing from them for years they won't be too suspicious about a few items now and then."

"I'd dig me a deep hole and bury my food in it, just like the Koreans do. Hell, during the winter it would be just like a deep freeze. I'd keep the chickens alive so I could have some eggs, only killing one every few months."

"I would also build me a small shelter, we sure have had enough practice fixing this place up. There are always plenty of trees, stones, and mud to use as building materials. I already have some tools, nails, and figure I could make just about anything else I might need."

"After about three weeks I should have the place fixed up well enough to wait it out for a long while. From then on I would just sit there and wait. If any of our planes were to come by low enough to see me I would signal them with the mirror. Other than that I would just wait until our troops got far enough north to reach me in my new home. You know as well as I do that if an all out war broke out again our guys would be right back up to the Yalu River within a matter of months. See? No sweat!"

As I surveyed the faces around the hut I could tell they liked the idea. After answering few more excited questions from the crowd I soon had recruited enough volunteers to make a small village in the hills. Now my concern turned from not having any, to having too many.

Over the next few days we took the basic plan as I had outlined it and added some refinements to the details. We began to stockpile more equipment, matches, nails, knives, and more oil. The Chinese were not suspicious although they were becoming more interested in our use of the oil. With the power plant still out of action they were issuing us the oil to use for lighting. We would soak cotton in the bean oil and twist it into the form of a wick. It generally provided enough light for us to make our beds up at night, but little else. They couldn't figure out how our hut was going through it so fast.

Yes, now we were ready. If the peace talks failed and the war resumed, the men in this hut would not go on another march. We were all set to turn native and await rescue by the U.N. troops. We had absolutely no doubt that our plan would succeed.

Of course, escape wasn't just something we talked about. Many of the boys tried it. If they were caught in or around the camp the Commies would put on quite a production, if the escapee still lived. If they were killed in the attempt all we got were vague, ugly, rumors. Those who made it out of the area were never heard from again, one way or the other.

Those who survived the attempt, only to be caught around the camp grounds would spend the next two or three weeks getting worked over pretty good by the guards before we got to see them. After that the re-captured soldier would make a public confession. It took quite a bit to make some of them confess. After all it wasn't the cowards that took the risk. Whatever they did to those poor guys I can tell you one thing, they weren't a pretty sight when they came out to make their confessions. The camp officials hoped that the sight of these bruised and beaten men would deter any thoughts of escape by the rest of us. While I must admit that it did have a psychological affect on us, they were wasting their time on most of us.

Once they were in jail their life was a living hell. One of our Master Sergeants, Raymond, from Rochester, New York, was one of my close friends in Camp No. 4. He had been caught in an escape attempt and was serving his jail term. During the winter months jail was even more of an ordeal. The hard labor they were under became almost intolerable. He was having a real rough time of it. But through it all, true to his character, his spirit never wavered.

On one of the coldest days we had seen so far this winter Raymond was out working on the banks of the river loading rocks onto a cart. He had been slaving away at this for hours and appeared to be close to exhaustion. There were a few guards assigned to watch the prisoners and a few Chinese soldiers just lounging around.

A Korean mamasan, with he baby strapped to her back, was in the process of crossing the ice covered river. Suddenly the ice gave way and she tumbled, screaming, into the freezing water.

The Chinese soldiers demonstrated their usual callous indifference to human pain and suffering. Their only response to this woman's desperate plight was laughter. This reaction was not unusual for them, we had seen it before. Memories of the old man watching his only valued possession, a cow, succumb to the icy water, as the guards prevented us from providing assistance, came to mind.

But surely this was different...there was a woman with a baby strapped to her back floundering in the freezing cold water of the Yalu River. But there they stood these inhuman animals were doing absolutely nothing about it, except laughing.

Ray stood it for just a moment. Then, ignoring the warnings from his guard, he dove into the icy water and struggled to reach the poor woman. Still the Chinese offered no help. He was finally able to pull her now unconscious body to the safety of the rivers edge. Her baby was dead, washed under the ice by the force of the strong current.

Alone, Ray pulled the poor lifeless woman's body up the side of the bank and began artificial respiration. After many anxious minutes she began to convulse and regained consciousness.

By now most of the Korean civilians from the nearby village had heard the news and came running to the scene. They brought blankets for him and the woman along with some hot soup. They were waving their hands up and down in admiration for his gallant efforts. He was truly a hero in their eyes, the greatest they had ever witnessed.

The Chinese guards had enough of this display of admiration and had long since stopped laughing. After all here was an American prisoner being cheered by the North Koreans. They chased the civilians away at gun point. Ray was ordered back to work on the rock pile, soaking wet clothes and all.

Later that night someone in the camp hierarchy heard the news of his heroic act and Raymond became the only prisoner ever to win a reprieve from his jail sentence.

Even more than winning his release his selfless act of heroism gave added strength to all of us. It reaffirmed to us that neither the time nor the circumstances are important in instances such as these. Even after all these months in captivity, subjected to the most inhumane treatment imaginable, we could still act with our deep-rooted conviction and do what is right. It would take a lot more than this prison camps to change our concept of humanity.

As the time pasted during this winter there would be more and more escape attempts. While we had faith in ourselves, our faith in the long winded peace talks was waning.

I remember two other the guys who tried to escape that winter. They had talked over their plans with some of us before they left. The plan wasn't very imaginative. It was basically a rehash of many other escape attempts that had taken place both here and back in Camp No. 1. Simply stated it amounted to get out of the camp and head for the coast. This conversation like many others ended with the understanding by all in the room that once you left, you were strictly on your own. While this sounds like a cruel policy it was absolutely necessary. If anyone still in the camp were caught having knowledge of the escapees or their plot, let alone providing any assistance, they would be tortured for the information needed to secure the capture of the offenders. Because of this, anyone discussing escape plans were bound by the same code - protect each other by protecting ourselves. Only divulge the specific details of locations and time frames with those taking part in the escape. The penalties usually given out to instigators of the escape plot were typically from three to five years in jail. Another good reason for being so self protective in these matters.

When we finally received word that these two were caught we were all very concerned. After all they had been gone for days and were surely some distance from the camp when they were found. Why were they brought back here? That wasn't the way they normally handled these situations. They should have been sent to one of the other camps. It could only mean one of two things, either they were really going to make an example of these two or they knew others in the camp had knowledge of their plans, and we all were going to pay.

The first thing they did was to have a two hour formation in the parade field. The told us every move the two had made in making their escape. They traced every move, from the time they left camp until they were apprehended. They had a team of speakers bragging about the skill of their intelligence in such matters. They told us how the men had slipped through the gate guards, how they spent days moving through the area between the camp and the coast. They told us how they got their food and clothing. They were also very sure to tell us of the fate of the few Koreans who had given them some assistance. They spoke of a little North Korean boy who spotted them as they were stealing a boat. They also took the time to inform us that it would have been useless for the two to have taken the boy with them since they knew about the boat and were waiting off the shore to pick them up anyway.

It seems that the communist officials realized the old tactic of personal confessions by a badly beaten comrade would not deter our attempts. This was to be their new strategy. Give us step by step details of the aborted escape to prove to us that their information gathering system was sufficient to find us, anytime, anywhere. They wanted to instill in us a sense of futility about the chances of a successful escape. They did indeed make the prospects of future escapes appear very discouraging.

What was even worse than the news we had just gotten was the waiting to see what would happen to the men. For a while they simply disappeared amid all sorts of rumors. Then came word that there would be a public self-criticism in this case. But when? We waited for days, then days turned into weeks, still no sign of them. Finally a formation was called and we went to the parade field to listen.

To our surprise the men looked clean and well fed. They even managed smiles as they made their confessions. You could tell from their eyes that their heart wasn't in it. They were simply actors playing their parts without a hitch.

"We are sorry we broke the impartial and humane rules imposed by the Chinese People's Volunteers," they had said. "We will never try to escape again."

They sounded just like robots, and I guess at that point in time they were.

This was how all escapee situations were to be treated now. With each such incident our spirits sunk a little lower. Gone was another chance to get the truth out to the free world beyond these walls that so cruelly confined us. Gone was another opportunity to get a message out to our loved ones, a message not subjected to the rigid communist censors. Gone were all hopes built on the possibility of escape by those who were just awaiting the right time. These shows put on by the communists made a lot of men stop and give their plans of escape a second look.

There were many times in the next few months that we felt like we would soon be involved in World War III. We heard so much about how the "imperialistic United States was deliberately delaying" the truce talks that we felt sure the Chinese were looking for an excuse to start a full fledged war.

As each day passed we expected to hear that the United States had finally lost patience with these bandits. We kept looking for the unmistakable sign of an atom bomb on the horizon. We felt sure that if the hostilities resumed in earnest the bomb would be dropped. But no such mushroom shape cloud appeared over the hills.

We had the strategy all laid out. It seemed simple to us. All they have to do is break through the lines, clobber all the Chinks on the flanks and herd the rest of them into the big plateau near Hamhung. Then drop the bomb. Poof - no more war.

CHAPTER 20

The Price of News

While the grapevine did a fine job of informing us of what was taking place within the camp, and even to some extent in the village, it was news of the war, of home, of our families that we really needed. Not the communist brand of news, but news like we were use to. Honest, truthful news, sometimes good, sometimes bad, but always honest.

What little news we did receive in the form of lectures, newspapers, or letters from home, were either developed by the communists or subjected to their censors. This of course meant that we heard, saw, and knew only those things they wanted us to.

Don't get me wrong when it came to letters from home they were cherished. Even if the censors took nine tenths of the information out of them they were precious in our eyes. Not only for the news from our loved ones but also as small tangible proof that the life we had left so long ago still existed. Nothing motivated us more than news from home. We would do anything for word from our families, sometimes to the extent that we put our safety on the line, even for another person's letter.

One day I got word through the grapevine that Joe had received a letter from home. One of the guys spotted a sergeant from my hut and passed the word to him. Once he told me I headed for the commissar's hut to ask permission to visit the Seven Company compound were Joe lived.

After gaining admittance to his office, I asked, "Mr. Hue, I would like permission to visit Seven Company. I understand one of the guys there received a letter from his wife which concerns me."

"In what way does it concern you?" he demanded.

"His wife has been in contact with my wife, and I just want to find out what my wife had to say, that's all," I answered.

"I'm sorry, no visiting today," he said smugly using his hand to dismiss me.

"But, Mr. Hue, visits have been allowed before, haven't they?"

"Yes, but...no, no visits today. I will have to look into this matter."

"Awe, that's not fair. Everybody else can visit as long as they ask permission. Why can't I?" I urged.

"You come and ask on Sunday. Then I will let you go."

"Oh, okay," I grumbled. I knew it was useless to try to change his mind. "I guess a few more days won't make much difference." I said as I walked out of his office.

That night I decided to take my chances and sneak across the road to Seven Company to read the letter. Just seeing my wife's name in print made the risk worth it. I reread the part of the letter that spoke of her a dozen times, searching for hidden meanings in each line. That was the only way to get the true meaning across to one another and past the censors. I asked Joe to have his wife call Ann and have them get together to compare notes. Luckily I made it back to my hut undetected.

When Sunday came around I still made my formal request to visit Seven Company. If I didn't they were sure to become suspicious.

"I'm sorry Sgt. Matta, it is too late for a pass," Mr. Hue replied.

"What do you mean, too late, you told me to come on Sunday and get a pass. And here I am..."

"Sergeant," he interrupted, "You know it is against regulations to visit another company after six o'clock at night. Now get out of here. I said it was too late."

I didn't have a thing to argue back with. He was right there was a regulation prohibiting visitation after six. I guessed it would do no good to mention that his guards had kept me so busy with details all day that this was my first chance to ask for permission. I stomped out in anger.

I was too mad to return to the hut. I didn't want to have to explain to the guys how he had baited me in his trap so I remained outside the commissar's hut to cool down. A short time later one of the guys from the company walked inside and returned a couple of minutes later.

"What's up?" I asked.

"Nothing," he replied, "I just got a pass to visit Seven Company for a half hour."

"Who the hell gave you that pass?" I demanded.

"My own company instructor gave it to me. No trouble at all. See you later," he answered with a puzzled look on his face.

That was all I needed to hear. My blood was boiling once again. I headed into Mr. Hue's office and barged right in.

"Mr. Hue," I began, "I want a pass to visit Seven Company."

"Sergeant, what is the meaning of this?" he demanded.

"Look," I said, "Didn't you tell me there was a regulation about visiting another company after six o'clock?"

"Yes," he said questioningly.

"Well then, doesn't a member of the Chinese People's Volunteers have to publicly criticize himself for breaking a regulation?"

"What do you mean by that?" he asked.

"A soldier just got a pass for a half hour to visit Seven Company and he asked for it after I did. It was given to him by his company instructor. Now I want my pass. If he can get one, I can too. And by God if there is a regulation that says that you can't do it, then that instructor has to criticize himself, doesn't he?"

"Sgt. Matta, you get out of here right now," Mr. Hue insisted. "Or I'll have you put in jail."

"No," I replied, "I want a pass to visit Seven Company. All I want to do is go over there and read a letter my buddy got from his wife. I am not going to hurt anyone or anything. I want to go now and you said the other day I could."

What bothered me so much wasn't the fact that I couldn't get to the letter, after all I already read it. It wasn't even the fact that someone else was allowed to do something that I couldn't. I was glad the guy got his pass. What made me so mad was the prospect of having to play out this little game every time I wanted to get news about Ann from a member of another company. Either I fought this thing through once and for all now or I would always be at their mercy.

"No," he replied, "You can not go. Now get out of here."

"Hue, you are no damned good!" I charged. "Nobody can talk to you or tell you anything. You think you know it all, don't you?"

That really got to him.

"Come over here," he commanded, walking behind his desk. He reached down into a drawer and pulled out a pad of paper and a pen.

"Here sit down and write out a criticism sheet."

"What for?" I asked. "I haven't done anything but ask you for a pass."

"You have cursed the Chinese People's Volunteers," he said. "Now you will be punished by criticizing yourself."

"No, sir, I won't do it," I said. "I wasn't cursing the Chinese People's Volunteers, I was cursing you. And you are not the Chinese People's Volunteers, you're just one damned man."

"When I talk to you I represent the entire Chinese People's Volunteers. And when you curse me you are cursing all the volunteers. Now sit down and write out a confession."

"Ha! Brother if you represent all the volunteers in China, then, by God, I represent all the people of the United States. And when you curse Truman, MacArthur, and Ridgway and all the rest you are cursing me. You tell me I am a student and not a prisoner. Well, if I'm a student why don't you stop cursing me and the people I represent."

I wound up by saying, "It goes both ways. If I have to be careful about what I say to you or be accused of offending the whole Chinese Army then you had better be careful about what you say to me and stop talking about things I don't want to hear, like germ warfare, the warmongers, and how the United States is holding up the peace talks..."

He interrupted coldly with, "Sergeant, when you were sick we took care of you and gave you medicine..."

It was my turn to interrupt. "The hell you did, you gave me nothing. Besides when you captured us you were either suppose to treat the wounded or release us back to a point were we could get proper treatment. You killed most of them."

"Oh, we will not kill you," he said.

"No, not now that the peace talks have started, now you know you may be held accountable..."

"Sergeant," he ordered, "Sit down and write your confession that you have cursed the Chinese People's Volunteers."

"I will like hell."

I could tell he was tiring of our little game. "Then you go back to your squad and wait. When tomorrow morning comes you come back and write your confession. You understand. Now go. Get out of here." He shouted so loudly I'm sure everyone in the area heard him.

I headed back for my hut, realizing for the first time just how close I had come to landing in jail.

When I got back I found out that our little argument had been heard by the whole gang and they had already packed up my things in anticipation of my punishment.

The next morning nothing more was said about our incident the previous day. He didn't get his confession and I didn't get my pass.

On March 6th of 1953 we got the first bit of timely news we had heard in weeks. It wasn't from any of our usual sources. It came to us in the form of black arm bands which were being worn by many of the camp staff. Stalin had died the day before. It had no affect on us as prisoners, or in how we were treated but it did seem to affect the true die hard communists in the camp.

Soon I was to find out about one of the best kept secrets in the camp. A secret that could provide all of us with a valuable source of news from the outside world.

Since revealing my hidden stash of equipment during the explanation of my proposed escape plans a few months earlier I had developed a well known reputation as a pack rat. I had set up a few local arrangements for trading off worn out shoes to the needy Koreans in exchange for tobacco, matches, or metal from which we make items we couldn't obtain otherwise.

Given a little time, I could generally conduct enough trades to put the old barter system to shame. The more the guys learned of my operations the more dependent they became on me. The storage area for this growing hoard of supplies was the hospital latrine, somewhere the guards did their best to avoid.

Some of the boys had more money, but I had a well established trading concession and could gain items their money could never acquire. Their money came from a number of different sources. Some was picked up after new prisoners were searched, some was left by enterprising soldiers who had skillfully hidden the script during their shakedowns. Eventually over the years most of the money had accumulated into small banks owned by some of the most profitable gamblers among us.

One of the Marine sergeants, a guy we called Muscles, had gathered just about all the money in our company in card games and other forms of gambling. He was a one man Bank of American and I was a one man Sears and Roebuck Company. My wealth was in the form of usable material, some of which I hoped to use in case escape became a requirement instead of an option.

That same month I was contacted by a British sergeant who seemed very anxious to talk to me.

"Hey, Matta," he called. "Can I talk to you a moment."

"Yeah, sure...what's on your mind?"

"They tell me you got contacts with the locals."

"It depends...what's on your mind?"

He carefully looked about to make sure we were not being watched, then whispered, "We need a replacement for this." He was holding up a radio tube.

"Wow!" I exclaimed, "Who's got the radio?"

"Shhhh," he warned.

I lowered my voice and queried, "What's the deal? Where's the radio? Where did you get the tube?"

"Never mind where we got it, we got it." he replied.

I'd heard that one before.

"Can you get us one like this that works?" he asked.

"Gosh, I don't know...does the radio work?"

"No, it doesn't, but we figure this is the only tube that's blown. One Wing and Stanley have been trying to get the damned thing to work for months. They have everything they need except this tube. Whatta you say? Can you help us?"

"Gee, I don't know. This is a pretty backward society, most of them have never seen a radio let alone a radio tube. But I can try."

One Wing was the squad leader of the crippled squad. There were ten men in the squad and all were incapacitated in some way. He had been hit right on the spot where he wore his wrist watch and still had parts from the watch embedded in his arm. He had use of the arm but every few months he would have to remove a sliver of his shattered bone as it worked its was to the surface of his wound. The Chinese of course were of no help to him. Another of the guys in the crippled squad was Stanley. He was from New York and had lost most of the heels of his feet along with five of his toes due to frostbite.

After some heavy trading I was one transaction away from getting my hands on the right tube from a Korean. A watch for the tube, not a bad deal. But before I could complete the trade the Chinese found out about the radio. One Wing and Stanley broke it into little pieces and burnt it in an attempt to protect themselves. Unfortunately a few of the pieces were found by Stanley's mat.

As Stanley hobbled past our hut on his way to jail he called to me, "Hey, Matta, tell the guys in the company I got five years in jail. Tell them to be careful, I think somebody down there is a snitch."

Before I could get to him to find out the details the guard pushed him into his cell.

News was as important to the communists as it was to us, but for entirely different reasons. They were masters at using news, either real or imagined, to control both us and their own people. The camp officials had a deep and all consuming fear of any source of information other than those they provided. We fueled that fear by our constant need to find avenues that offered us the real news, facts rather than fiction. Those of us involved in the struggle to gain information at any cost, such as Stanley, understood the risks, and accepted the penalties.

CHAPTER 21

Operation Little Switch

After so many long months of hoping for a break in the terrible stalemate at the peace table it was hard to think that it really could be coming to an end. We had heard so many times before how the communists were getting ready to begin releasing some of us to boost their propaganda efforts at the talks. It never happened. Why should we believe it now.

"I'm telling ya it's the straight scoop. They are going to let a few of us go home," one of the guys began saying.

"Don't be crazy," I answered, "They wouldn't dare. Look I'm sick and tired of the rumors, it's nothing to get all excited about, just another rumor. Do you think for a minute that these jokers would let a few of us go back to tell the whole world about the treatment we have been getting in their camps. No way. They wouldn't dare release just some of us. The public outcry in the states would be enough to get our army moving not only up to, but across, the Yalu River to free the remaining prisoners. No, if they release any of us they would have to let us all go very quickly."

He thought for a moment and then responded. "Yeah, I suppose you're right, but there sure are a lot of stories going around. Something must be up. This ain't like the other times, there is too much going on, too much is stirring."

"Well, there may be a lot going on, but you can bet your ass they won't dare let just a few of us go back...I wonder who they would pick, though, that is, if they are sending some of us back?" I said.

"Probably the progressives would go back first."

"I don't think so. Look at it this way, there aren't enough of them to make a very big splash back home or in the press. And most of them are marked men back in the states because of the part they have played in the communist films and propaganda sheets. Any lies they could tell about the Commies simply wouldn't be believed. They gain nothing from releasing the progressives," I responded.

We lay back on our mats and contemplated how wonderful it would be to make it back to freedom.

The very next morning the instructor came to pay me a visit. As he headed my way I thought, "Something's up, this guy doesn't come around unless there is trouble."

"Good morning sergeant," he smiled.

"Hell," I muttered still half asleep. "What's with you?"

"What is with me?" he repeated, "Why nothing, I just thought you and I could take a walk...there is something I would like to discuss with you."

"As if I have a choice," I said grimly, getting to my feet, "Okay, come on, let's get it over with." We walked outside and he guided me over to a secluded spot by a grove of trees and he invited me to sit down.

"How do you feel?" he asked.

"Oh, so - so, why?" I replied.

"Have you been getting mail from home," he continued, finally beginning to notice my hostility to his friendly advances.

"Yeah, I'm getting it...as if you didn't know. Or have you forgotten reading them during the censorship process you put them through before giving them to us?"

"Now, sergeant, let's don't be unpleasant," he smiled once again, "I'm just looking out for your welfare, you know."

"Yeah, welfare," I replied, "That's a good one."

"Why, sergeant, I am surprised at you. You had a good dinner yesterday, didn't you?" he asked.

"Well, yes, it was pretty good," I admitted, "For that matter it was the best Sunday dinner we have had in some time. How come?"

"My but your suspicious today, sergeant. Tell me, when you were captured, what did the guards take from you?"

"You bet I'm suspicious. Living in these camps for two years makes a person suspicious. You have the audacity to ask me what they took from me after my capture. I'll tell you in two words. My life! That's what they took from me, my life," I exploded.

He was very patient with me for some reason and said, "No, sergeant, what I mean is, what personal items did they remove from you?"

I thought for a minute, "Gosh, something big is going on, this is a new pitch." Then I answered with, "They took my watch, two rings, and a wallet. Why?"

He carefully wrote each item down in his notebook and then looked up and said, "I will see if I can get them returned to you."

He must have seen the surprise reflected in my expression because he asked, "Tell me, sergeant, what is your attitude toward the Chinese people?"

I was slow to respond. "Who do you mean...the Chinese people or the Chinese soldiers? I guess I've thought about what I think of the soldiers each and every day I've been here...."

"What do you think of the soldiers?" he interrupted.

"Look," I replied, "I'll tell you. You're over here fighting for your country and I'm over here fighting for mine. The difference is how we choose to conduct that fight. Not much can be done about that. It was apparently my misfortune to spend most of this war in prisoner of war camps. I'm not bitter about that, but I am bitter about the men I have seen dying needlessly. Now why don't you leave me alone."

That was how our conversation ended that day, but it sure marked the start of a whirlwind of activities that kept us jumping for days.

A doctor, for the first time a fully qualified doctor, came in and gave us a thorough examination. This guy knew his business and spoke very good English. He checked each of us and made extensive notes on our condition. He took extra care and time with those prisoners in need of hospitalization or surgery.

We got the word the next day. They called a formation and explained a new program to us. The program was to be given the name "Little Switch." The excitement became contagious. Out of all the thousands of rumors that had come and gone without any appearance of truth, it seemed that this one was about to materialize. We could talk of nothing else, Little Switch was the only thing in our minds and on our lips. To conclude the formation they called out the names of five men. These would be the first five to return to freedom, to go from hell to heaven.

People who had become stagnant, who's minds had become dormant, were rejuvenated by the news of Little Switch. Lethargy was replaced by a new fascination at every word that was spoken. Eyes which had dulled over the months from pain, fatigue, and monotony, were suddenly clear and bright. Yes, Little Switch brought a complete transformation in all of us. It gave us our first real bit of hope in the last two years.

The first group of men to be selected received a great feast before their departure. They had twelve different kinds of food...wine, beer, canned fruit, the first they had seen since their capture. They even had all the accompaniments, tables, chairs and glasses. We later discovered that this farewell party was compliments of the North Korean civilians.

Each of the ones making the return trip were able to bring a guest along with them to the party. As always the Commies had a reason for this. The entertainment during the meal was a lecture on what to tell the folks back home. Instructions were given to tell the people back home that the Chinese want peace. Tell them to fight for peace back home and not forget the buddies we left behind in the camp. They said we should write everyone and tell them of the wonderful treatment we received at the hands of the Chinese Peoples Volunteers.

"Yeah, sure we'll tell em!"

The night after the first group departed those of us left behind couldn't eat much. We prayed, almost constantly, that our name would soon be called as one of the lucky ones. We didn't sleep all night...we tossed and turned and had pleasant thoughts of home.

As the operation continued the barbaric nature of the communists came through once again. In explaining the procedure to us we were told that the prisoner exchange would include the sick and the wounded, they would go first. Of course we all were in agreement about that. And while they held true to their word, selecting only the sick and wounded so far, we noticed that many that should have already gone still remained.

Soon it created some ill feelings among the men.

"Why do you suppose he is going?" would be whispered from man to man. It is true that he was sick, but his bunk mate would be without an eye, or a limb, or perhaps be in desperate need of immediate attention. We soon figured out the answer.

"These guys can't even be honest with themselves," I said. "Here they are picking out the sick and wounded and they deliberately skip some of those who would be entitled to go. What do they expect to gain by that?" Suddenly I realized the key to figuring it out was understanding that the answer lie in the fact that they had to gain something out of it. "They never miss a chance at propaganda. By sending back only those sick and wounded that appear to be in good health they hope to convince our side that they had provided good treatment to our men. If they let the others go now, the ones who are in bad shape simply because they hadn't received proper attention it would blow the image they wanted the world to see. Obviously some of those left behind would never have lost their arm or leg if they were in a real hospital with competent doctors."

"Yeah, but do they think they can keep us from talking? Do they think they can keep us from telling the whole world about the conditions in this place? Do they think that we will simply be so overjoyed at our release that we will forget about all those we have buried in these damned Korean hillsides? Do they honestly think we won't scream from the highest pulpit about the atrocities we have witnessed? Can we forget the neglect, poor food, forget how we have lived like dogs for two years? How we were forced to listen to their bull about how bad our government is, how oppressed we are at home, how we are being exploited. Do they think we can't convince our friends and families of the need to fight communism in any form, in any location, and die fighting before we allow ourselves to be taken prisoner ever again."

"They would have to cut my tongue out to keep me from talking"

To a man, everyone in the hut felt the same way, nodding their approval.

The feelings of most in the camp were summed up very nicely by one of those who should have left under Little Switch long ago. He said, "They way I figure it, there should be anywhere from 500 to 600 guys back in the states right now. Take a look around camp and you still see many sick and lame individuals. Buddy, when you get back tell them we're still waiting, will ya. Tell them the rest of us want to come home too."

We were all happy to hear that One Wing was one of those selected to be returned in the next group released.

While we knew things were winding down, there was still no word of peace as these small groups of men were repatriated. As I had pointed out many times, it didn't take much to set off a flood of rumors. Now that the releases had begun the main rumor had become the rumor of peace. Until the beginning of April 1953 we didn't realize how little foundation these rumors were built on. Finally it seemed that the real McCoy was about to hit.

It was about eleven at night and for most of the evening there was a steady stream of Chinese army brass coming into the camp. Even the old general who commanded all of the Chinese POW camps had arrived. Each of the individual camp commanders had also shown up. Something was definitely up.

A "This Is It" rumor began as a small squall and soon turned into a full fledged tornado. It was gaining momentum by the minute, especially when one representative from each squad was ordered to report to headquarters.

"The general wants to hear any complaints the prisoners might have about their treatment," we were told.

"Oh, brother, that's for me," one shouted. Fist fights almost broke out to see which lucky man would be able to get two years of torment out of his system. Finally it was decided to send the squad leaders. They were instructed to really pour it on, don't spare the horses.

The story of what occurred went bussing around the camp for days. The general made it clear that he was interested in learning of all our complaints. The squad leaders were told there would be no retribution, there was nothing to fear. "Tell us what is wrong and we'll fix it."

The first thing that was mentioned was the food. The gave the general an ear full about how we were eating nothing but soy beans and turnips. How our company was being cheated out of about seven bags of flour each week, despite the fact we are the largest company in camp. He heard about the times a pig was killed and we were lucky to get one meal out of it, a small meal at that. How the camp officials were always cutting down our ration of oil and sugar.

Then they turned their attention to the work details. They discussed the fact that we were forced to carry wood for all of the personnel in camp, not just for the prisoners use, a direct violation of the Geneva Convention. How the guards would steal logs from our piles.

Next came the subject of mail. Our mail was held back and sometimes not delivered at all. How we had been instructed to ask for certain items in the letters home and then they refused to mail the letters. How it took 90 days for the mail to get from Panmunjom to the prison camp.

He also was told of the basic needs that were never attended to by our captors. Pans, wash basins, clean clothes, medical supplies, and other items considered common by most standards.

The squad leaders were also able to relay our distaste for the segregation that was imposed upon us. The story was told of the wall we were forced to build between us and Seven Company, "to keep the wind out."

After the meeting the squad leaders burst back into the huts, their eyes bright with happiness. Not only had they registered our complaints but had lived to tell about it.

The promise that something would be done came when the general's reply to the complaints spread through the camp. It was another great boost to our morale.

The general told our representatives that he would personally see to it that there was an improvement in the food we received. The delivery of our mail would be sped up, and certain supplies would be issued to us. From now on there would be no more work details unless the work was being accomplished for the benefit of the prisoners. But we had listened to

Chinese lies for too long. Could we trust this general or not, after all he is Chinese.

The answer to that question seemed to come when the general added the statement that "the stone wall will come down and the Chinese soldiers would be the ones to take it down and carry every last rock back to the river." That hit us like a bombshell. That did more to assure us than anything else could have.

Now there was no doubt that the peace talks were well on their way to a successful conclusion. Within a week the general's promises bore fruit. We were issued new mats, tea, teapots, wash pans, bread boxes, and towels. We also enjoyed being spectators, watching the Chinese soldiers dismantling the stone wall.

We were riding high.

Operation Little Switch continued over the next week. Small numbers of men leaving for the south and freedom. The rest of us continued to sweat it out. Still no official peace had been declared. We hoped upon hope that something wouldn't happen to halt the progress that had been made.

We knew all it would take is for one guy to hit the wrong target, kill the wrong person, move in the wrong direction, and it could all explode in our face.

We began to debate the order in which we would be selected to receive our freedom.

"You ain't got a chance. There are lots of guys here in much worse shape than you and they've already been skipped over."

I realized, like everyone else in camp that the tensions were getting a little uneasy.

It was now April 16th, more than two years since my capture. We were called for another mass formation in the field.

"You all know what we called you out for today. We wanted to say a few words to you today," he droned on. We winced at the thought of another dry lecture. His next few words, however, brought a buzz of excitement.

Striding back and forth in front of us he shouted.

"Several more of you men are being sent back to South Korea today." That was the first time they had ever acknowledged that South Korea even existed, preferring to think of it all as their Korea. "When I call your names, go back to your rooms, pack your things and report to company headquarters. Then you will go to regimental headquarters for a big farewell party. After that you will be taken on trucks to Pyongtong where you will depart for home," he continued.

There was a great lump in our throats as we waited for the names.

"Sgt. Johnson"

"Sgt. Christianson"

"Sgt. Tomlinson"

"Sgt. Matta"

I closed my eyes and tried to hold back the tears. I had dreamt of this moment for so long that I still wasn't sure if this was for real. Did he really say it or is my mind playing tricks on me? The answer came as I felt myself being hoisted into the air. I was on the shoulders of some of my buddies and their were loud cheers. Please, God, don't let them change their minds, let me go home.

For a long time I cursed my luck at receiving the blows to my head which caused me so much pain and agony. Ironically, now it was those very blows that allowed me to regain my freedom.

With the tears blurring my vision I shook the hands that were stretched out in front of me. I thought, Gee, I wish you could all come with me. It would be hard to leave this group of men behind. Some of these guys had been with me the entire two years of our hell. It creates a bond stronger than any other I had ever encountered.

It was no surprise that these guys were as happy about my ticket to freedom as I was. Yet I couldn't help feeling their disappointment and sadness at being left behind.

I tried to pack, but with the entire hut assisting me, we made a mess of it. I didn't care, I was going home. I made it a point not to say goodbye to anyone, that seemed to final. Instead I simply said, "So Long," I knew I would see them again as free men, someday.

As I took a last look at the men I had been so close to I couldn't help but think. Give them a handful of M-1s and a few clips of ammo and they'd get themselves back to Freedom Village – and there would be a hell of a lot of dead Chinese along the way. They are all itching for a fight.

At the headquarters we were met by the camp commander. He passed out some tasteless Chinese cigarettes and candy. After a last shakedown we departed for regimental headquarters.

There we were escorted to the mess hall for the best meal we had eaten in more than two years. We had great food, eggs and meats of all kinds, wine, beer, and 170 proof so ju. After having nothing but rice and turnips for so long I was almost afraid to start eating. It was marvelous.

It was a four hour trip by truck to our next stop at Pyongtong. As the jolting truck lurched through the night we were all silent. We had talked ourselves out long before. We were, almost by force of nature, a quiet lot. Verbalizing our thoughts only in an effort to break the mental monotony. It wasn't necessary to talk any longer. We were going home to freedom and nothing more need be said.

After our arrival in Pyongtong we had another big meal. This meal consisted mainly of wine and beer. By the end of it most of us were feeling no pain - except in our hearts. I held up a bottle of amber liquor and said to no one in particular, "If they'd done this back in '50 and '51, there would be a lot more Americans still alive right now."

All of a sudden we had gone from having nothing to having too much. Instead of the one razor blade per month per ten prisoners, we now were each given five of our own. There was plenty of cigarettes, soap, combs, mirrors, everything. The Chinese were confused over our reaction.

As I said they allowed us to bring one guest to the party with us. I chose Carlie. Before he was led away I had packed his clothing full of cigarettes, soap, and blades to take back to the guys in the camp. One of the other men being released gave his loot to another prisoner, Pappy Noel an Associated Press photographer. Pappy put the items in his camera bags, promising to distribute them as he toured the POW camps and awaited his repatriation. Pappy was taken from camp to camp and allowed to take staged photographs that were sent back to the states. We all willingly gave up all our new found treasures, after all where we were going we could get plenty more, and plenty better.

After each meal we were left with a bad taste in our mouths. Not from the food itself, but from the thought of all those we had seen die from the lack of it.

It was just as if we had entered another world. All of a sudden these tormentors who hated taking care of us just days earlier, couldn't do enough for us. Why couldn't they give some of the others a break now. After all it was over. It would have been so easy to save many who were no longer with us. I wish I could remember how many had died over the past few years, but even the communists themselves didn't know that number. Maybe it was for the best that I couldn't remember.

CHAPTER 22

The Final Journey

Once again we were loaded onto the trucks for another ride south. They played "Long Live Peace" as we left this morning. Can you imagine, a band out at 5:30 in the morning playing that song? I wonder if they really thought they could make us forget the hell they had put us through for so long. They sure were trying their best. You would think they would have learned by now.

We took stock of our condition. I felt as if my back would break, but I was glad to be a passenger anyway. I wondered how Joey was making out. If this ride doesn't kill him nothing will.

Suddenly I remembered the souvenirs we were given just before our departure this time. I searched through my pockets and pulled them out. Pictures, pictures of prisoners playing games. No wonder they insisted we take them with us. Well, here are some that won't make it back. I tore them into little pieces and let them fly.

Oh, this damned road.

I remember being surprised to see the bridges and railroad lines in operation. They must have been rebuilding them as fast as our jets were knocking them out.

Some jets came low over the convoy at one point. We were parked beside some anti-aircraft batteries at the time. Noticing the precious cargo aboard the trucks below the pilots dipped their wings in recognition. We cheered loudly. It was now the 19th of April 1953. After a long days ride we stopped just south of Korni-ri in a North Korean hospital. It was just a group of mud huts, but they had bunks that held you off the floor, and mattresses. These were the best accommodations we had seen in quite a while.

At dawn the following morning we took our now familiar positions on the trucks where we were shaken all day long. We arrived in Pyongyang at 5 o'clock that evening. All of the now weary travelers fell asleep immediately. During the night our sleep was disturbed by the glow of the truck's lights each time a jet was heard overhead. They shined the lights on the large red crosses on the huts, comfortable in the knowledge that our pilots would not engage those targets as their pilots did.

All night long the sound of trucks and trains could be heard in the distance. They gave us each a bottle of wine to calm our nerves later that night.

They later regretted this act of kindness after a Turk, who had consumed more than his share, tried to beat the hell out of a Chinese officer. The Turk was just as calm as anything as he told the officer, "You are no damned good and I've got a mind to cut your throat right here and now." Luckily for him his buddies grabbed him before too much damage had been done and quickly got him out of the way.

I thought, Boy, don't blow it now. Just one stupid mistake and back you go. After being this close to freedom I couldn't take the shock of going back to prison now.

We were glad to hear the next morning that his would be the day of our release. It was now the 21st of April and we boarded the trucks for the last time. By afternoon we should be back to our side. The days drive was interrupted only once, at about 1 o'clock when a couple of American jets buzzed the line of trucks. They were obviously checking on our progress. They banked and headed back south after we were spotted.

It wasn't until around five that evening that we finally pulled into Kaesong. Now only five miles from Panmunjom and freedom. The trucks came to a stop in front of an old temple. The next shock came when about fifty boys, all dressed in white, came marching out in columns of two. They were assigned to carry our bags for us. They were instructed to tend to our needs and wait on us hand and foot. Another desperate attempt on the part of the communists to make up for the many lifetimes of misery they had put us through.

We were becoming concerned as we stayed at this location for three days. We should have been released by now according to what they had said earlier. Had something gone wrong? Please, not now!

We began being sent forward to freedom at the rate of twenty-five per day. Those left waiting were not allowed to remain idle, oh no, they still had a number of propaganda tricks up their sleeves. First there were requests to pose for pictures, then special meals, and always more wine and beer.

"Maybe you would not mind making a tape recording telling us how you have been treated on this trip?"

Word spread quickly that nothing about life in the camp was allowed to be said, only our treatment during the trip was to be discussed. There were no takers.

I was now only an hour away from my long awaited freedom. We had been issued new clothes, had a good breakfast, bathed, and sprayed for lice. We were ready. On the 25th of April I climbed into a Russian ambulance for the final journey.

We arrived at Panmunjom at 9 o'clock on the dot.

We were all leaning out of the ambulance waiting for our first glimpse of an American, a free American. As the Chinese driver backed up, we spotted him. An American military policeman. He was very sharply dressed. We were yelling so much we soon became hoarse. When we scrambled out of the ambulance we spotted the white line on the ground.

What a strange time we live in that a small white line, insignificant in size compared to the rest of the world, could mean so much. On one side of the line the world we were leaving. A world of starvation, despair, suffering, and imprisonment. On the other side was the world we departed years ago. A world of families, homes, and most importantly, freedom. A world not without it's share of problems, but our world none the less.

We left the new blankets in the ambulance. We no longer needed them. As we were loaded into the American ambulances some of our soldiers were throwing packs of Camel cigarettes to us. These packs became treasured symbols of our freedom. It was a pleasure to hear the officer call off our names as we headed for Freedom Village.

We were finally rid of our communist shackles removing the last vestige of captivity by changing from the blue uniforms to the OD green of the U.S. Army. I couldn't resist the urge to stand proudly once in the uniform of a United States fighting man.

When coffee and soup were first offered to us we went straight for the coffee. We hadn't had a real cup of coffee in so long.

We were given the opportunity to talk to the Chaplain. This more than anything those first few hours gave us a sense of peace.

Over the next few days they conducted a check of our records, set up meetings with members of the press, and there was a lot of bustle and excitement. It was a time of joyous confusion that has dimmed to a blur with the passing of time.

We devoured the papers taking note of all the events that had taken place in our absence. The Stars and Stripes, booklets with a message from General Clark, all were eagerly read, cover to cover.

The real Red Cross couldn't do enough to keep us happy and make us feel at home. When they took us to a room filled with beds and four inch mattresses we were afraid to lie on them, afraid we might never wake up. Or worse yet, wake up and find it had all been a dream.

The cokes, the malts, the milkshakes...which to chose from? And that steak. Try as we would we couldn't help but let our thoughts drift to those left behind. They would have given up all their worldly possessions for a meal such as this.

The pilot of the helicopter that flew us to Seoul promised he was heading south rather than back up north. At the hospital there was no talk of sleep, there was so much to do.

The first song we played was "The Hottest Baby In Town," it was the first and last time I heard that song.

That first shower I went through a whole bar of soap. I was determined to wash away every bit of the two years of dirt and misery I experienced. When our sleep finally did come, it was a very restful sleep.

Next we boarded a C-47 Globemaster for the trip to Tokyo. We were taken in a Cadillac ambulance to the Tokyo Army Hospital. From there the Red Cross gave us the opportunity to send free telegrams and place free phone calls. We also met some of the guys who were released before us. They looked considerably better than the last time we had seen them. The sight of an American flag, whether on a flag pole or on a cake, was wondrous to us.

There was an inspiring farewell at Haneda Airport in Tokyo. A stop on Midway for a meal and some fuel and then off for Honolulu. The best sight there being the hula girls who placed leis around our necks. We spent time at Tripler Army Hospital for more check-ups, and then were headed for Travis Air Force Base in California were there was a spectacular welcoming. We felt both gratitude and humility.

The last leg of our long journey to freedom was to Murphy Army Hospital and then our homes.

As the C-47's wheels touched the ground at the Bedford Airport, I got my first glimpse of the tremendous amount of planning that had taken place to provide me with a magnificent reception. There as part of the welcoming committee was the mayor of Brockton and another 150 residents of my home town.

To this day I am eternally grateful for the wonderful treatment afforded me on my return. I thought that it would be impossible to express the full measure of my appreciation. I'm sure the looks on my face as I finally embraced my loved ones displayed a small part of it.

The thrill of riding down Main Street in Brockton in a motorcade and seeing the banner spanning the road which read "Welcome SGT Matta"; of reading the lead editorial in the Brockton Daily Enterprise which acclaimed the city's pride in my efforts; the dinners; the parties; the meetings; the interviews; the first visit to the church; were all exhilarating.

We were given a thirty day furlough and attended a great number of festivities, far more than we deserved.

I had some wonderful personal experiences. My family and I were guests of Rocky Marciano, my childhood friend from Brockton, who invited us to attend his heavyweight championship bout in Chicago.

Those days also included speaking invitations from local civic groups. Plans for a parade featuring me as the honorary marshal were announced. A visit by the Governor of Massachusetts, my promotion, and the dramatization of my story on the radio added to this awe inspiring welcome home.

My family and I were also to receive a complimentary letter from then-Senator John F. Kennedy. To this day one it remains one of my most valued treasures.

But without a doubt the single most meaningful item I was to receive was a letter from a Chicago High School student, Edward Biehl, in which he wrote,

"I have just finished reading about your hardships while held as a prisoner of war. I am also a Catholic, and having read of what you did and said when the Commies wanted to take away your Rosary, I was deeply impressed."

"With guys like you setting the example, I don't see how any of our younger crowd are going to let down, or become afraid when and if the time comes for us to die for God and country."

There were some serious moments as well. I called and visited a number of parents. To some I was able to offer hope, to others the final shocking realization that for them, there would be no homecoming. In several cases I brought the first news they had of their loved one's fate and they lit up with the news that their prayers had been answered. Their sons and husbands were still alive.

I also spent many more days in hospitals suffering from blackouts caused by my head wounds. But I was alive.

Several months after our release I was asked to testify on Senator Charles E. Potter's Committee on Korean War Crime Atrocities. There a number of us were to take a proud stance during the Senate hearings on the communist mistreatment of prisoners of war.

At the hearings General Ridgway, Army Chief of Staff said, in part; "Brutality in actual combat can sometimes be expected, and while it cannot be excused or condoned, its stigma can be somewhat lessened by the common knowledge of all military men that violent combat can still the emotions of participants to the point where, for a time, they cease to control themselves. But a studied and calculated course of criminal misconduct, extending over a period of nearly three years and carried out with such callus disregard of human life and suffering as to indicate a design on the part of the communist leadership to exterminate prisoners of war in one way or another, should not be expected, cannot be excused or condoned, and not a word can be said in defense or extenuation of it..."

"There is some evidence which indicates that the communists suddenly realized, with the inception of the truce talks in 1951, that the living prisoners in their hands were valuable hostages and could be exploited to strengthen their bargaining position with the United Nations. Such is the sole plausible explanation for sparing the lives of any of their captives..."

"The communists had also made every effort by despicable means to secure military information from their prisoners. They inaugurated a full scale campaign with bribes of good treatment, and threats of punishment, torture, and even murder to convert prisoners to communism for propaganda purposes. That they failed is due to the native courage of our gallant men, their undying faith in our free way of life, and the discipline and manliness that were the fruits of their training..."

Thinking back to that April day in 1953 I can't honestly remember exactly how I felt as I crossed that small white line. We've talked it over many times since then, but there are no words, except possibly, "Thank God," that can adequately express our feelings. How would you feel?

It is still the little things that we remember.

We were lucky. We were among the 4,631 Americans returned by the communists. Yes, we were lucky, we were not counted among the more than 6,000 Americans murdered by the communists in captivity.

Of those who came back in operation Little Switch, and later under the expanded operation Big Switch, some came back whole; some were missing limbs; some lost their sanity during captivity; and some were swayed by the propaganda. Most of these few who did sway and returned to the states soon found that the beliefs instilled by their communists friends would prove false once again. Maybe it would be a movie, a kiss from their girlfriend, a shot of whisky, or just a good look around at home and making a comparison to what they had seen in Korea. But sooner or later they would see the error of their ways.

I know there is room for confusion, after all many stories have been told over the years. Some talk of hardships, punishments, indignities, and tortures, as described here. They contend that the best communists had to offer us was worse than they ever expected to endure.

Other say, "It wasn't too bad." They say the food wasn't too bad. That the Chinese gave them the best possible treatment under the circumstances. They say they can not substantiate the stories of brutality, lack of medical facilities, of deliberate neglect, and other stories of the horrors.

Still others take the middle of the road, saying, "Well it was pretty rough, but it could have been worse."

Receiving News of His Promotion Upon His Release

These apparent inconsistencies and contradictions are not easily explained, but there is an explanation. All three points of view are entirely correct. It depended largely on where a man was captured, how long he was held, in which camps he was imprisoned. Along with the specific aims of the communists with whom he had contact. Each of these played a part in how he would be treated. Since many different combinations of conditions were possible, it is not surprising to hear the views expressed along these three main themes.

It would be easy to end this story with a brief note that Sergeant First Class George J. Matta returned to his home and family, after the usual hospitalization, and went on to complete a twenty eight year career serving his country and the cause he had seen so many pay the ultimate sacrifice for. But there is much more to this man I call my father.

He went on to serve a tour of duty in Vietnam where he would see more of his comrades fall defending what some at home thought was an unjust war. He was a man deeply affected by returning from that "conflict" to a country that greeted him by literally spitting in his face rather than as the hero he was. A divided and hurting country that no longer respected the sacrifices made by him and many more like him.

One of the few times I ever remember this man being moved to tears occurred shortly after his return from Vietnam. He was advised by the base personnel office not to wear his uniform off the post unless it was absolutely necessary. The effect on him was devastating. To ask him not to wear the uniform of his profession; the uniform he found so much pride in upon his release from the Chinese; the uniform that bore the medals attesting to his contributions to his country; it was asking too much. That is when I realized that a uniform isn't simply a way to identify which country or branch of service a man belonged to. No it is something much more, it is a symbol that reflects the beliefs and character of the man who wears it.

He often thought back to the words expressed in the letter from that young student only sixteen years earlier and wondered what had happened. What had made patriotism, honor, duty, and love of country so wrong? Why was the fight for freedom of another Southeast Asian people being lost on the college campuses and in the streets of Chicago and Los Angeles? Why were the news organizations doing more to separate the citizens than unite them, as they had done in the past?

Yes, having grown up with this man as a major influence in my life, I can tell you that there is much more to his story than simply the uncommon experiences of a common man. While I was not yet born during the time he was a POW, there is no mistaking the fact that the man who won his freedom that April day in 1953 was a different man than the one who left years earlier in the defense of his country and its ideals.

Having committed my fathers notes and memories to paper I now have a better understanding of the man who raised me. His staunch patriotism; his stubborn defense of what he feels is right; his mood swings; his need to isolate himself from other people; his deep hatred of anyone who professed the communist point of view; the constant headaches; all these are clearer to me now. I now understand how he could feel so close to his creator without feeling the need to do it from within the confines of a church or chapel.

There were many days during my childhood that I couldn't help but think of what could make a man react to life with such passion and fervor. Many times I would wonder why my father was not like many of the others I knew. There were many questions. Why was my mother so worried that day when a baseball hit him in the head at an American Legion baseball game? Why did my father curse the President so defiantly when he announced the amnesty of the Vietnam conscientious objectors and deserters?

He was not the perfect father, if there is any such thing. He was a man who had his share of problems just as any other man. But he was a man who never stopped dreaming of a better life. He desperately wanted his children to have a better life than the one he had lived. In this endeavor he has proven to be a complete success.

What I am today, I am, due to a large degree, because of him. Some of his experiences during those years in Korea have instilled a unique sense of values and morals in me. The drive to succeed, to come to the aid of the underdog, to fight for the right, have all been passed to me.

I am incredibly proud of him for having the courage to survive his ordeals and the guts to stand by his country and it's ideals in the face of such unthinkable horrors. I realize that many of us have him, and men and women like him, to thank for the freedom we enjoy today. Come to think of it maybe he was the perfect father, considering what he had lived through.

Korean War POW/MIAs

It is not an all inclusive list of every POW/MIA from the Korean War. This list was compiled from documents, newspaper articles and personal letters written during the time of the Korean War. These documents were discovered during the research conducted for this book and are now a part of the author's personal collection. Although the author and publisher have exhaustively researched all sources to ensure the accuracy and completeness of the information contained in this list, we assume no responsibility for errors, inaccuracies, omissions or any inconsistency herein.

Last Name	First Name	Rank	City	State	Camp(s)	Status
Abbott	Robert N.	Lt Col	Rochester	NY		Repatriated
Abbott	William H.	Cpl	Beallsville	Oh	5	Repatriated
Acevedo	Bienvenido L.	PFC	New York City	NY		Repatriated
Achee	Edward R.	Pvt	Detroit	Mi		Repatriated
Adams	Clerance C.	PFC	Memphis	Tn		Stay Back
Adams	John L.					Unknown
Adams	Ralph S.	PFC	Auburn	Me		Repatriated
Adkins	Louis L.	Sgt	Darien	WV		Unknown
Aicken	Andrew	Pte	Larne	N. Ireland		Unknown
Aikin	Herbert P.	Cpl	Port Jefferson	Oh	5	Repatriated
Aitken	Hugh	Cpl	Harrogate	UK		Unknown
Allen	Clifford	Capt			2	Unknown
Allen	Ellis E.	Sgt	Daltis	Mo		Unknown
Allen	James M.	Pfc	Portersdale	Ga		Unknown
Allen	Millard	Capt				Unknown
Allen	Robert W.	Pfc	Newport News	Va		Unknown
Alley	Ronald E.	Capt	Bar Harbor	Me		Repatriated
Allred	Boyd	Sgt	Liberty	NC		Repatriated
Amador	Louis E.		Mathis	Tx		Repatriated
Anderson	Clarence L.	Capt	Long Beach	Ca		Repatriated
Anderson	Douglas R.	Capt				Unknown
Anderson	E. G. (Andy)	SFC	Ft. McClellen	Al		Repatriated
Anderson	Philip R.	Cpl	Cornish	Me		Repatriated
Andrews	Nathan O.	Sgt	Clarkston	NC		Repatriated
Aramino	Nicholas J.	PFC	Leroy	NY		Repatriated
Arias	Unknown	Lt		Ca		Unknown
Arran	William H.	Sgt		Ar		Unknown
Artesani	Richard J.	Sgt	Allston	Ma		Repatriated
Ascue	Joe J.	Cpl	Bluefield	WV		Repatriated

Last Name	First Name	Rank	City	State	Camp(s)	Status
Atkins	Roy	Cpl	Brooklyn	NY	4, 5	Repatriated
Aubrey	Carl L.		Visalia	Ca	5	Unknown
Augliera	John C.	PFC	Arlington	Ma		Repatriated
Avjian	James R.	PFC	Malden	Ma		Repatriated
Baglan	Louis B.					Unknown
Bagwell	Ralph	Lt	Quonset Point	RI		Unknown
Bailey	Richard E.	Sgt	Pasadena	Md		Repatriated
Bajo	Emiliano	M/Sgt		Phillippine		Unknown
Baker	Jack	Sgt	DeKalb	Il		Unknown
Baker	Rodney J.	Sgt	Ayer	Ma		Repatriated
Ball	James L.		Eau Claire	Mi	5	Unknown
Ballum	Ronald					Unknown
Banks	Clerance C.	PFC	Colorado	Co		Repatriated
Banks	Robert I.	Cpl	Cambridge	Md		Repatriated
Banuelos	Samuel E.	Pfc	Fresno	Ca		Unknown
Barber	James H.					Unknown
Barbour	Hugh	Cpl	Londonderry	N. Ireland		Unknown
Barczylowski	Stephen W.	PFC	Wilmington	De		Repatriated
Barker	Eldo		Redwood	Fl	5	Unknown
Barnard	Earl C.					Unknown
Barnes	Richard	Pfc				Unknown
Barrett	Franklin E.	Pvt	Kansas City	Ks		Repatriated
Bartholomew Jr.	Stanley F.	Pfc	Tacoma	Wa		Unknown
Bartlett	Wilmer A.	Cpl	Hartord	Ct		Unknown
Basham	Edward	Cpl	London	UK		Unknown
Bassett	Keneth J.	PFC	Perry	Me		Repatriated
Bassett	Richard M.		St Augustine	Fl	5	Unknown
Batchelor	Claude J.	Cpl		Tx	5	Unknown
Bathou	Robert L.					Unknown
Baudoin Jr,	Theo		Dickinson	Tx	5	Unknown
Baxter	Sydney F.		London	UK		Unknown
Bayes Jr.	Thomas					Unknown
Bayliff	Matthew		Binghampton	NY		Unknown
Baylor Jr.	Page T.	PFC	Washington	DC		Repatriated
Beadleson	Howard J.		Walnut Creek	Ca	5	Unknown
Beale	George W.	Lt	Myrtle Beach	SC		Unknown
Beard	Harold					Unknown
Beasley Jr.	Leonard	PFC	Gary	In		Repatriated
Beaudry	John H.	PFC	Willimantic	Ct		Unknown
Beaupre	Jacques	Sgt	West Depre	Wi	5	Repatriated

Last Name	First Name	Rank	City	State	Camp(s)	Status
Beck	Earl L.	PFC	Wheeling	WV		Repatriated
Beckerley	Edward G.		Wellingboro	UK	5	Unknown
Bednarz	Joseph T.	1st Lt	Gilbertville	Ma		Repatriated
Bedrosian	Raymond N.	PFC	Albany	NY		Repatriated
Beeson	Jack	Capt	South Hadley	Ma		Unknown
Belhome	Albert					Stay Back
Belhomme	Albert C.	Cpl	Ashland	Pa		Unknown
Bell	Lester	SFC	Toledo	Oh		Repatriated
Bell	Ortho G.	PFC	Olympia	Wa		Repatriated
Bellah	Morgan	Cpl	Ft. Worth	Tx		MIA
Bennett	James W.		San Antonio	Tx	5	Unknown
Bennworth	Thomas E.	L/Cpl	Portsmouth	UK		Unknown
Benoit	Clifford E.	Cpl	Cambridge	Ma		Repatriated
Bentley	John K.	Pvt	Whites Burg	Tn		Unknown
Bergin	Jeremiah		Kilkenny	Ireland		Unknown
Berkheimer	Blythe I.	Sgt	Los Angeles	Ca		Repatriated
Berman	Bernard I.	PFC	Lakewood	NJ	1	Repatriated
Bernard	Charles		Atglen	Pa	1	Unknown
Bernier	Gerald F.	Cpl	Smithville	Ga		Repatriated
Berry	Waldron	Lt	Seymour	In		Unknown
Berube	George E.	Cpl	Fort Kent	Me		Repatriated
Best	Oscar	Sgt	Warsaw	NC		Repatriated
Beyl	William M.	Cpl	Baltimore	Md		Repatriated
Biesterwald	Thomas C.					Unknown
Biever	Arie	Sgt	Hague	Netherlan		Unknown
Birchard	Spencer	Sgt				Unknown
Bishop	Lester	Cpl				Unknown
Blackburn	Otis G.	Pfc	Pikeville	Ky		Unknown
Blackburn	William Ira	PFC	Monroe	Wa		Repatriated
Blakeley	Robert	PFC	Higganum	Ct		Died In Camp
Blanton	Paul O.	Pfc	Brodhead	Ky		Unknown
Bley	Roy	Maj	Cabool	Mo		Repatriated
Blodgett Jr.	Irving D.	Cpl	Claremont	NH		Repatriated
Blowers	Omar	Cpl	Swain	NY		MIA
Boaz	Arron		Chicago	Il		Unknown
Bolton	Harry					Unknown
Boodreay	Theodore	PFC	Wareham	Ma		Unknown
Booth	Nathaniel	Pfc	Bassfield	Ms		Unknown
Boothroyd	Albert E.	PFC	Rockville	Ct		Died In Camp
Boreelli	Frank	Cpl	San Francisco	Ca		Repatriated

Last Name	First Name	Rank	City	State	Camp(s)	Status
Borer	William F.	Sgt	Jersey City	NJ		Repatriated
Borie	Harry	Sgt	Philadelphia	Pa		Repatriated
Boudreau	Philip	Sgt	Lawrence	Ma		Repatriated
Boulduc	Charles					Unkown
Bourgoin	Joseph A.	Sgt	Waterville	Me	1	Repatriated
Boutwell	Norman L.	PFC	Billerica	Ma		Unknown
Bowens	Charles D.	Sgt	Lake City	SC		Unknown
Bower	Lahman L.	Cpl	Berkley	Mi		Repatriated
Bowling	Matthew	Pvt	Dew Drop	Ky		Unknown
Boyd	William O.	PFC	San Diego	Ca		Unknown
Bozarth	Howard R.	Sgt	Hays	Ks	1	Unknown
Bradford	Dennis E.	Pvt		UK		Repatriated
Bradley	Eldon R.		South Bend	In	5	Died In Camp
Brady	John T.	PFC	Somerville	Ma		Died In Camp
Bramanti	Joseph F.	Pvt	Boston	Ma	1	Repatriated
Bramente	Joseph	Cpl	Boston	Ma		Repatriated
Brander	Donald S.	Cpl	Attleboro	Ma		MIA
Bray Jr.	Walter E.	Sgt	Carlstadt	NJ		Repatriated
Brazee	Frederick D.	PFC	Terryville	Ct		Unknown
Brazee	Frederick J.	PFC	Boston	Ma		Unknown
Breton	Joseph E.	Lt	Rochester	NH		Unknown
Brewton	Leonard	Pvt	Toledo	Oh		Repatriated
Brichard Jr.	Spencer	Sgt	Norton Hieghts	Ct		Repatriated
Briere	Randall J.	Sgt	Taunton			Repatriated
Brisland	Sidney J.	Sgt	Berkley Glos.	UK		Unknown
Britton	John D.	Pfc	Surgoinsville	Tn		Unknown
Brockes	John T.	Sgt	Great Falls	Mt		Unknown
Brooks	Arnold W.	Pvt	Wilton	Me		Repatriated
Brooks	Clifton	PFC	Smyrna	De		Unknown
Brooks	Robert I.	PFC	Reidsville	SC		Repatriated
Broom	Leroy	PFC	Albany	Ga		Repatriated
Broomhead	Unknown	Lt				Unknown
Broussard	Roy L.	PFC	Crowley	La		Repatriated
Brown	Bill Allen	PFC	Houston	Tx		Repatriated
Brown	Gerald	Lt Col	Phoenix	Az		Unknown
Brown	Harled M.					Unknown
Brown	Harold T.	Cpl	New York City	NY		Unknown
Brown	Marvin L.	PFC	Oklahoma City	OK		Repatriated
Brown	Robert A.	PFC	Jersey City	NJ		Repatriated
Brown	William B.	PFC	Clayton	NJ		Repatriated

Last Name	First Name	Rank	City	State	Camp(s)	Status
Brown Jr.	James J.	Sgt	Durham	NC		Repatriated
Bruce	Alexander	Pte	Dundee	Scotland		Unknown
Bryant	John D.	1st Lt	Baldwin Park	Ca		Repatriated
Bryant	William J.	SFC	Decatur	Ga		Died In Camp
Bryant Jr	Charles	PFC	Cincinnati	Oh	Pyoktong	Repatriated
Buchanan	Billy J.	Cpl	Atlanta	Ga		Repatriated
Buli	Bernard	Cpl	Wilkes-Barre	Pa		Repatriated
Burdelas	James J.	Cpl	Baltimore	Md	5	Repatriated
Burrell	Leonard G.		Holt Norfolk	UK		Unknown
Burrows	John K.	1st Lt	West	RI		Died In Camp
Burton	Charles A.	Cpl	Scottsburgh	Va		Repatriated
Burton	George R.	PFC	Orono	Me		Died In Camp
Busbee	Lawrence A.	Sgt	Ruskin	Fl		Repatriated
Butler	Charles H.	Cpl	Gibsland	La		Repatriated
Buttery	Linton J.	Capt	Nashville	Tn		Repatriated
Buttrey	Linton	Capt	Nashville	Tn		Repatriated
Buzbee	Lawrence A.	Sgt	Ruskin	Fl		Repatriated
Byers	Lester W.	Sgt	Moscow	Id		Unknown
Byrd	Roy T.	Lt	Winnetka	Il	2	Repatriated
Cabacar	Heren					Unknown
Caine	John T.	M/Sgt	Birmingham	Al		Repatriated
Calvin	Don H.	Cpl	Chicago	Il		Repatriated
Camden Jr.	William A.	PFC	Bar Mills	Me		Unknown
Cameron	Hayward H.	Lt	Kiln	Ms		Unknown
Cameron	Owen J.	Sgt	South Athol	Ma		Died In Camp
Campbell	Billy J.	Cpl	Loraine	Tx	Pyoktong	Repatriated
Campbell	Harry	PFC	Las Vegas	Nv		Repatriated
Campbell	Howard	Sgt	Brooklyn	NY		Unknown
Campbell	Unknown		Liverpool	UK		Unknown
Campbell	Walter E.	Sgt	Inongate	Va		Unknown
Canavan	Bernard C.	Pte	Belfast	N. Ireland		Died In Camp
Cantillo	Dominic J.	Cpl	Roxbury	Ma		Repatriated
Cantwell	Samuel H.	2nd Lt	Bedford Village	NY		Repatriated
Capurro Jr.	Umberto	Cpl	San Fransisco	Ca		Repatriated
Carne	James P.	Lt Col				Repatriated
Caroland	Thomas M.	PFC	Cedar Hill	Tn		Unknown
Carpenter	Evertt H.	Sgt	Verda	Ky		Unknown
Carter Jr.	LeRoy	Cpl	Oklahoma City	Ok		Unknown
Carver	Donald J.	Cpl	Waupaca	Wi		Repatriated
Carver	Roy	Pfc		Tn		Unknown

Last Name	First Name	Rank	City	State	Camp(s)	Status
Castle	Hermon			Ky		Unknown
Caterbury	Kimball O.	Cpl	Monroe	La		Repatriated
Catoe	Milton L.	Sgt	Pensacola	Fl		Repatriated
Caulder	Unknown		Little Rock	Ar		Unknown
Cavagnaro	Gerald	Cpl	Haverhill	Ma	1, 2, 3, 5	Repatriated
Celusniak	Frank					Unknown
Chagnon	Jack R.	Cpl	West Suffield	Ct		Unknown
Chambers	Walker	Pvt	Harrisburg	Pa		Repatriated
Champman	Virgil E.	Sgt	Hoisington	Ks		Repatriated
Channell	Jennings R.	Cpl	Girard	Oh		Repatriated
Chapman	Franklin J.		Bisington	Mi		Unknown
Chappell	Robert J.	PFC				Unknown
Chevere	Hermenegildo	PFC	Ciales	P.R.		Unknown
Chiarelli	Leonard	PFC	Brooklyn	NY		Unknown
Chisholm	James		McComb	Ms		Unknown
Christensen	Floyd C.	Cpl				Repatriated
Christensen	Martin	Sgt	Libertyville	Il		Repatriated
Cinar	Halil Ibrahim			Turkey	4	Repatriated
Clairmont	Cleveland	Pvt	Mission	SD		Repatriated
Clark	Billy E.	Cpl	Dallas	Ia		Unknown
Clark	David T.	Pte	Aldershot	UK		Unknown
Clark	Vernon W.	PFC	Brooks	Me		Unknown
Clarke	Keith (Nobby)		Lancaster	UK		Unknown
Clements	Paul E.	Pvt	Indianapolis	In	3	Repatriated
Clevenger	Edward E.	PFC	Dayton	Or		Unknown
Cline	O. J.	Cpl	Lumber Bridge	NC		Unknown
Clinton	Ernest	Cpl	Bowerham	UK		Unknown
Clinton	William	Sgt	Pine Bluff	Ar		Unknown
Cloutman	Rodney F.	Capt	Athol	Ma		Died In Camp
Clyde	D.					Unknown
Cobb	Richard P.	Cpl	Fulton	NY		Repatriated
Cockfield	Graham	M/Sgt	Savannah	Ga		Repatriated
Cocks	Ronald A.			UK		Unknown
Colbalis	Vincent J.					Unknown
Cole	Milton		Desloge	Mo		Died In Camp
Cole	Thomas W.	PFC	Brooklyn	NY		Unknown
Colgate	Thomas S.	Pfc	New Haven	Ky		Unknown
Collins	Edward R.	A2C	Jackson	Mi	1	Repatriated
Comeau Jr.	Benjamin L.	Cpl	Mystic	Ct		Repatriated
Condron	Andrew M.	British	West Lothian	Scotland		Unknown

Last Name	First Name	Rank	City	State	Camp(s)	Status
Cones	Richard L.	Sgt	Cedar Rapids	Ia	1	Repatriated
Conley	Benjamin	Sgt	Columbus	Oh		Repatriated
Connacher	Kenneth H.	PFC	Altoona	Pa		Repatriated
Connally	James M.	PFC	High	Tx		Repatriated
Connally	Mark	Pvt	Medford	Ma		Died In Camp
Conner	Connie Mack	Pvt		Wi		Unknown
Connolly	Mark	Pvt	Medford	Ma		Died In Camp
Connor	Norman P.	Sgt	Merrimack			Died In Camp
Conrad	George E.	Sgt	South Boston	Ma		Repatriated
Consbruck	Jerome (Red)					Unknown
Coogan	James J.	Pvt	Philadelphia	Pa	2	Repatriated
Cook	Allan	M/Sgt	Honaker	Va		Repatriated
Cook	Jessie B.	Cpl	Somerville	Al		Repatriated
Cooke	Charles L.	PFC	Mathews	Va	5	Repatriated
Cooper	Estle L.	PFC	Winfrede	WV		Repatriated
Cooper	Frederick J.	PFC				Unknown
Copeland	Harry C.	Cpl	Muncie	In		Unknown
Copeland	Robert B.	Capt	Tulsa	Ok		Unknown
Corbine	Donald	Cpl	Canton	NY		Unknown
Corden	Richard G.	Sgt	East	RI		Unknown
Cordero	Hector	1st Lt		P.R.		Unknown
Cormier	Ernest P.	PFC	Malden	Ma	5	Repatriated
Cormier	Leo A.	Cpl	Fall River	Ma		Repatriated
Costlow	William T.	Cpl	St. Michaels	Pa		Repatriated
Cottle	Wayne T.	Pvt	Preston	Id		Repatriated
Couk	Harold	W.O.	Littleton	Ma		Unknown
Covington	Clarence B.	M/Sgt	St. Louis	Mo		Unknown
Cowart	William		Dalton	Ga		Repatriated
Cowell	John J.	Pte	Middlesex	UK		Unknown
Cox	Tully	PFC	Gadsden	Al		Repatriated
Coxe	Dwight	W.O.	Fresno	Ca		Repatriated
Cram	Bruce H.	Capt	South	Vt		Repatriated
Crawford	David	L/Cpl	Belfast	N. Ireland		Unknown
Crawford	Norman		Columbus	Ga		Unknown
Crawford Jr.	Robert E.	PFC	Carthage	Mo		Repatriated
Creeson	Calvin C.	Msgt	Winston-Salem	NC		Repatriated
Crespo	Candido O.	Pvt	New York City	NY		Unknown
Crompton	Peter C.	Sgt	Bournemouth	UK		Unknown
Cruz	Ruben D.	PFC	Detroit	Mi		Repatriated
Curry	James	Capt	Mount Vernon	Oh		Repatriated

Last Name	First Name	Rank	City	State	Camp(s)	Status
Curry	James R.	Lt	Rockford	Il		Repatriated
Curtin	Francis R.	Cpl	Chicago	Il		Repatriated
Curtin	John J.					Unknown
Curtis	William E.	Pvt	Hyde Park	Ma		Repatriated
Cushing	Jess M.	PFC	Bradford	Ct		Died In Camp
Cuthbertson	Bernard R.					Unknown
Cutshaw	Worley	Pfc	Greenville	Tn		Unknown
Cutting	Harry A.	Sgt	Belleplain	Ia		Repatriated
Cuttings	Henry S.					Repatriated
Cydrus	Ronald E.	Cpl	Springfield	Oh		Repatriated
Dabbs	James		Essex	UK		Unknown
Dahms	Lawrence P.	PFC	South Portland	Me	5	Repatriated
Dalmazzi	Robert J.	PFC	Providence	RI		Repatriated
Danao	Jaime D.	Cpl		Phillippine		Unknown
Dandero	Vincent	Cpl	Swampscott	Ma		Repatriated
Daniels	Clifford J.	PFC	Oakland	Ca		Repatriated
Daniels	James	Sgt				Unknown
Daniels	Willie L.	PFC	Berkeley	Ca		Repatriated
Dantzler	Earl	Sgt	Richmond	Va		Unknown
Darnell	Melvin W.	Pfc	Sinai	Ky		Unknown
Darrow	Kenneth R.	Sgt	Charles City	Ia		Repatriated
Daujat	John	Maj	Richmond	Ca		Repatriated
David	Leroy	Sgt	Peoria	Il		Repatriated
Davies	Tom	Pte	Essex	UK		Unknown
Davis	Charles R.	Sgt	Mt. Vernon	Il		Repatriated
Davis	Harold W.	Sgt	Russell	Ar		Unknown
Davis	James	Sgt	Mullins	SC		Repatriated
Davis	James NMI	Cpl	Bradshaw	Md		Repatriated
Davis	Prestee	Sgt	Durham	NC		Repatriated
Davis	Richard K.	Pfc	Cambridge City	In		Unknown
Davis	Richard M.	Cpl	Booneville	Ak		Repatriated
Davis	Truman	Sgt	Heber Springs	Ar		Repatriated
Davis	William H.	PFC	Hearne	Tx	Pyoktong	Repatriated
Dawson	Thomas	Sfc	Akron	Oh		Unknown
Dean	William F.	Maj			5	Repatriated
Dean	Zachary W.	Capt	Douglass	Ks		Unknown
DeBord	Billy A.	Pvt	Dayton	Oh		MIA
Dee	Ivor J.	Sgt	Kent	UK		Unknown
Degrow	Bobby R.	Pvt	Portageville	Mo		Unknown
DeLong	Denton	PFC		Wi		Unknown

Last Name	First Name	Rank	City	State	Camp(s)	Status
DeLong	Jim		Eberson	Pa		Unknown
Demirdelen	Ismail	Pte		Turkey		Unknown
Derzern	William	Sgt	Durham	NC		Repatriated
Desautels	Richard G.	PFC	Shoreham	Vt		Unknown
DeSilva	Ralph H.	Capt	Taunton	Ma		Repatriated
Deumas	Unknown	Ukn				Repatriated
Deveau	Albert J.	Cpl	East Millinocket	Me		Repatriated
DeWeese	Jerry W.	Cpl	Detriot	Mi		Repatriated
Dibble	Donald	Sgt	New Britain	Ct		Escaped - Unk
DiCato	Joseph	PFC	Everett	Ma		Repatriated
Digan	Vana	Cpl	Muncy	Pa		Repatriated
Dillon	William K.	Cpl	Bluefield	Va		Repatriated
Dimmelow	Bernard	L/Cpl	Stoke-on-Trent	UK		Unknown
Dixon	Albert	Cpl	Manchester	Ga		Repatriated
Dixon	James	Sgt	Hampton	Va		Repatriated
Dixon	James W.	Sgt	New York City	NY		Repatriated
Dixon	John L.	Cpl	San Jose	Ca		Repatriated
Dixon	Walter	PFC				Repatriated
Dobson	James G.	Pvt	Alcoa	Tn		Repatriated
Doll Jr.	Martin	Pfc				Unknown
Domenech	Jamie O.	Cpl	New York City	NY		Unknown
Doran	Carl L.	PFC	North Fork	Ca		Repatriated
Dorsey	Marvin E.	Cpl	Winter Garden	Fl		Repatriated
Douglas	Rufus E.	Cpl	Cashmere	Wa		Unknown
Douglass	Richard F.	PFC	Hanover	NH		Unknown
Dougless Jr.	Rupert L.	PFC	Oklahoma City	Ok		MIA
Douthitt	Charles J.	Cpl	Shelbyville	Ky		Repatriated
Downey	John					Unknown
Doyle	Vincent F.	M-Sgt	Fall River	Ma	3	Repatriated
Drake	Brady H.	Sgt	Coraopolis	Pa		Unknown
Dugger	Carl		Durham	NC		Unknown
Duggins	Unknown					Unknown
Duke	Paul	SFC		Al		Repatriated
Duke Jr.	Paul	Sgt	Essex	Ma		Unknown
Dukes	Ollum	Cpl	Easley	SC		Repatriated
Dumas	Roger					Unknown
Dunbaugh	Franklin P.	2nd Lt	Hubard Woods	Il		MIA
Duncan	Solon W.	PFC	Ft. Myer	Fl		Repatriated
Dunham	Wallace L.	Cpl	Covington	Ky		Repatriated
Dunlap	Junior E.	SFC	McCorkle	WV	5	Repatriated

Last Name	First Name	Rank	City	State	Camp(s)	Status
Dunn	Harold M.	Cpl	Baldwinsville	NY		Repatriated
Dunn	John R.	Cpl	Baltimore	Md		Stay Back
Dunn	Robert	Cpl	Muskogee	Ok		Repatriated
Dunning	Ernest	2nd Lt	Clayton	NJ		Unknown
Dutra	Joseph F.	M-Sgt	Fall River	Ma		Repatriated
Dwyer	Leo E.	Pvt	Lawrence	Ma		Unknown
Eaton	Ivan Q.	PFC	Seabrook	NH		Repatriated
Eckenbarger	John	PFC	Stafford	Ct		Repatriated
Edson	Robert L.	Cpl	Patterson	NJ		Repatriated
Eichhorn	Thomas J.	Sgt	Milwaukie	Or		Repatriated
Ekenbarger	John	Pvt	Stafford	Ct		Unknown
Eleftheratos	Salvatore T.	Pfc	Binghamton	NY		Unknown
Ellis	Alfred O.	Maj	Waldoboro	Me		Unknown
Elwell	John M.	Sgt	Baldwinville	Ma		Repatriated
Enbom	Walter					Unknown
Englehart	Robert M.	Cpl	Roxbury	Ma		Died In Camp
English	Vernon R.	Sgt	Groton	Ma		Died In Camp
Enoch	Kenneth	Lt	Youngstown	Oh		Repatriated
Enos	Andrew E.	Cpl	Honolulu	Hi	1	Repatriated
Erickson Jr.	Edwin W.	Cpl	Somerville	Ma		Repatriated
Escobar	Federico M.	Cpl		Phillippine		Unknown
Esensten	Sidney	Capt	Minneapolis	Mn		Unknown
Esenston	Sidney	Capt	Minniapolis	Mn		Unknown
Espelin	Oscar E.	Lt Col	Hartford	Ct		Died In Camp
Espinosa	Floyd E.	Pfc				Unknown
Estabrook	Wilbert R.	Sgt	Potland	Me		Repatriated
Estell	Howard D.	PFC	Columbus	Oh		Repatriated
Esterbrook	William R.	Cpl	Gloucester	Ma		Unknown
Evans	Bob	L/Cpl	W. Cumberland	UK		Unknown
Evans	Edward R.	PFC	Racine	Wi		Repatriated
Evans	Jess E.	Maj				Unknown
Evans	Unknown					Unknown
Ewan	Alexander	Cpl	Perth	Scotland		Unknown
Factor	Kenneth J.	Lt	Wewoka	Ok		Unknown
Fajardo	Adolfo J.	Cpl				Unknown
Falconeiri	Donald L.	Sgt	Middleboro	Ma	5	Repatriated
Farley	Roy E.					Unkown
Farmer	Clyde R.	Cpl	Flat River	Mo		Unknown
Faulkner	James	Sgt	Monroe	NC		Repatriated
Faust	Edward J.	PFC	Norristown	Pa		Repatriated

Last Name	First Name	Rank	City	State	Camp(s)	Status
Fawcett	Eric		Bradford Yorks	UK		Unknown
Fecteau	Richard					Unknown
Ferah	Ali	Pvt		Turkey		Unknown
Ferguson	Charles E.	Pfc	Lowville	NY		Unknown
Ferreira	William	PFC	Fall River	Ma		Repatriated
Fichtner Jr.	Harry	Pfc	Hyndman	Pa		Unknown
Fink	Gerald	Capt	Chicago	Il		Repatriated
Fischer Jr.	Harold E.	Capt	Swea City	Ia		Unknown
Fisher	Edward	Sgt	New Bedford	Ma		Repatriated
Fisher	William	Cpl	Royal	Ak		Repatriated
Fitzgerald	Dennis J.	Sgt	Durham	UK		Unknown
Fitzpatrick	Bobby F.	Cpl	Clifford	Ky		Repatriated
Flaherty	Michael W.	PFC	North Adams	Ma		Died In Camp
Flanagan	Thomas	L/Cpl	Glasgow	Scotland		Unknown
Fletcher	Robert	Pfc	Ypsilanti	Mi		Unknown
Flook	Grady H.	PFC	Alhambra	Ca	Pyongyang	Died In Camp
Floyd	Delmar F.	Sgt	Minden	La		Repatriated
Flynn	John P.	Capt	Colome	SD		Repatriated
Fogle	Robert E.	Cpl	Dorset	Oh		Repatriated
Foley	Charles T.	Cpl	Woburn	Ma		Died In Camp
Foliweiler	Clair	Pvt	Bownamstown	Pa		Repatriated
Fontaine	Joseph A.		Gonic	NH		Repatriated
Foote	Zachariah H.	PFC	Baltimore	Md		Unknown
Ford	John E.	Pfc	Jeffersonville	In		Unknown
Fort	Walter		Chicago	Il		MIA
Foshee	Billy B.	Capt	Bowling Green	Ky	2	Repatriated
Foss	Sheldon H.	1st Lt	Hampton	Me		Repatriated
Foulsham	George E.	Pvt	Boston	Ma		Repatriated
Fox	Louis	Cpl	Dallas	Or		MIA
Francois	Gerald A.	Cpl	Jersey City	NJ	5	Repatriated
Franklin	Henry R.	Sgt	Fitchburg	Ma		Repatriated
Frantz	David	Cpl	Bridgewater	Ma	3	Repatriated
Frederick	George	Unk	Southhampton	England		Repatriated
Friday	James F.	Cpl	Torrington	Ct		Unknown
Fronapfel	Charles L.	PFC	Alliance	Ne		Repatriated
Frost	Elmer	Cpl	Heidelburg	Ky		Repatriated
Fuentes	Moises P.	Pfc	Puerto de	P.R.		Unknown
Fulk	James W.	Cpl	Reelsville	In		Repatriated
Fulk	Lester E.	PFC	Elk Creek	Mo		Unknown
Gagnon	Jack R.	Cpl	West Suffield	Ct		Repatriated

Last Name	First Name	Rank	City	State	Camp(s)	Status
Gaither	Edward M.	PFC	Philadelphia	Pa		Unknown
Gale	Frederick	Pfc	Chicago	Il		Unknown
Galt Jr.	Robert L.	Pfc	Baltimore	Md		Died In Camp
Gambocurta	Henry	Cpl	Robertsdale	Pa		Repatriated
Garneaux	Moses F.	Pvt	White River	SD		Unknown
Garza Jr.	Fred	Cpl	Gary	In		Unknown
Gauldine	Jack E.	PFC	Ashburn	Ga		Repatriated
Gaylet	Thomas B.	Cpl	Old Forge	Pa		Unknown
Gaylets	Thomas B.	Cpl	Old Forge	Pa		Unknown
Geisendorfer	Lew	Cpl	Denver	Co		Repatriated
Gennaro	Harry C.	Cpl	Rockford	Il		Repatriated
Geolzer	James C.	Msgt	New Albany	In	3	Repatriated
Ghinazzi	Mario R.	Pfc				MIA
Ghyers	Robert H.	PFC	Caruthersville	Mo	5, 7	Repatriated
Giannini	Michael A.	Cpl	Huntington	NY		Repatriated
Gilbert	John A.		Littleton	NH		Repatriated
Gilday	Patrick	L/Cpl	Renfrew	Scotland		Unknown
Gillette	Robert J.	1st Lt	West	Ma		Repatriated
Gilliam	Thomas J.		Philadelphia	Pa		Unknown
Gilmer	Robert K.					Unknown
Ginn	Robert A.	Cpl	Columbia	SC	Death	Repatriated
Girdano	Anthony	PFC	Pittsburgh	Pa		Repatriated
Giroux	Frederick J.	Capt	Brattleboro	Vt		Died In Camp
Glass	Cecil Robert	Pvt	Louisburg	Mo		Escaped Died
Glowacki	Steve	Pvt	Brooklyn	NY	Pyoktong	Repatriated
Godburn	Donald M.	Cpl	Cannan	Ct		Repatriated
Godewski	Richard W.	PFC	Bayonne	NJ		Repatriated
Godlewski	Richard W.	PFC	Bayonne	NJ		Repatriated
Gollewski	Richard W.	PFC	Bayonne	NJ		Repatriated
Gonzales	Reinol J.	Cpl	New York City	NY		Repatriated
Goodreau	Theodore	PFC	West Wareham	Ma		Repatriated
Gordon	Lewis L.	PFC	Blairsburg	Ia		Repatriated
Gorka	Earl D.					Unknown
Gorn	John W.	Lt Col	Ann Arbor	Mi		Repatriated
Gorr	Robert R.	PFC	Sheboygan	Wi		Repatriated
Gorski	Raymond A.		Milwaukee	Wi		Unknown
Grabusky	John	Sgt	Chester	Pa		MIA
Graham	Elwood H.	Pvt	Fieldsboro	NJ		Repatriated
Granger	Ralph M.	Cpl	Hallsboro	NC		Repatriated
Graveline	Ernest	Capt	Pawtucket	RI		Died In Camp

Last Name	First Name	Rank	City	State	Camp(s)	Status
Gray	Freddie H.	Cpl	Augusta	Ga		Repatriated
Gray Jr.	Roy C.	Capt	Franklin	Ky		Unknown
Green	George E.	Pte	Birmingham	UK		Unknown
Green	Jack	Cpl	Westwoodside	UK		Unknown
Green	John T.		Doncaster	UK		Unknown
Green	M. W.	Capt	Lawton	Ok		Repatriated
Greenwell	Wallace J.	Pvt	Webster	Ky		Unknown
Greenwood	Alva E.	Cpl	Uhrichsville	Oh		Unknown
Greer	Samuel H.		Belfast	N. Ireland		Unknown
Gregory	Arthur	Cpl	Mt. Vernon	Il		Repatriated
Grenier	Richard	PFC	Howland	Me		Repatriated
Griffiths	John		Connerton	Pa		Unknown
Griggs	Lewis W.		Jacksonville	Tx		Repatriated
Grimmett	Shirley	Pvt	Rita	Wva		Repatriated
Grudge	Peter					Unknown
Guidetti	Charles G.	Cpl	Philadelphia	Pa	1, 3	Repatriated
Guidy	Peter J.	Cpl	Lafayette	La		Repatriated
Guinter	Dorland F.	Cpl	Montoursville	Pa		Repatriated
Hadden	George L.					Unknown
Hagerup	Erion T.		North	Me		Unknown
Hale	Jack M.	Sgt	London	UK		Unknown
Hale	Norman S.	PFC	Cullman	Al		Repatriated
Haley	Richard A.	M/Sgt	Auburndale	Ma		Escaped Died
Hall	James K.	Cpl	Amelia	Va		Repatriated
Hamdi	Okten					Unknown
Hamilton	Ronald	PFC	Middletown	Oh		Repatriated
Hamilton	Tommie	Cpl	Chicago	Il		Repatriated
Hammersmith	Robert W.	Cpl	Lynwood	Ca		Repatriated
Hammond	Glen D.	Cpl	Ganesvoort	NY		Repatriated
Hammond	Harold M.	Cpl	Belvidere	Il		Repatriated
Hampton	Tommie	Cpl	Chicago	Il		Repatriated
Hancke	Robert H.	PFC	Springfield	Ma		Escaped - Unk
Hancock	John W.	Pfc	Hamboldt	Tn		Unknown
Hanke	Robert H.	PFC	Springfield	Ma		Escaped - Unk
Hannaway	James		Belfast	N. Ireland		Unknown
Hansen	Calvin C.	Sgt	South Braintree	Ma	1	Repatriated
Hansen	William C.	Cpl	Long Island	NY		Repatriated
Harder	Jesse T.	PFC	Louisa	Va		Repatriated
Hardy	Robert	PFC	Chelsea	Ma		Unknown
Harlan	John C.	Maj	Institute	Wva		Repatriated

Last Name	First Name	Rank	City	State	Camp(s)	Status
Harper	Archie G.	Cpl	Avondale	Az	5	Repatriated
Harper	Fred	Cpl	Wayland	Ky		Repatriated
Harr	Vernon E.	Pfc	Morehead	Ky		Unknown
Harris	Clerance	PFC	Detriot	Mi		Repatriated
Harris	Edward R.	1st Lt	Marblehead			Repatriated
Harris	Theodore R.	Lt (AF)	Van Nuys	Ca		Repatriated
Harris	Walter R.	Maj	Glen Ridge	NJ		Repatriated
Harrison	Thomas D.	Lt Col	Clovis	NM		Repatriated
Hart	Edward				5	Unknown
Hart	Ted		Ilkestone	UK		Unknown
Hartman	Bobby		Ganite Quarry	NC		Repatriated
Harvey	William R.		St. Paul	Mn		Died In Camp
Haskins	Ernest E.	PFC	Beckley	WV	5	Repatriated
Hastings	Donald W.	Lt	Newton	Ma		MIA
Hatano	Billy K.	Pvt	Sacramento	Ca		Repatriated
Hatcher	J.C.	PFC	Trion	Ga		Repatriated
Hatter Jr.	Jesse	Cpl	Eldorado	Ar		Unknown
Havener	George	PFC	Gloucester	Ma		Repatriated
Havener	Stanley J.	PFC	Glouster	Ma		Repatriated
Hawksworth	Henry	L/Cpl	London	UK		Unknown
Hawley	Leroy J.	Pfc	Armour	SD		Unknown
Head	Carl R.	Cpl	Evansville	In		Unknown
Hearn	Charles F.	Cpl	St. Louis	Mo		Repatriated
Heath	Richard C.	SFC	Arlington	Va	Pyongyang	Died In Camp
Heaton	Donald W.	Cpl	Maryville	Tn		Repatriated
Hedlund	Harry F.	Capt				Unknown
Heitkamp	Kenneth	Cpl		Wi		Unknown
Heminger	Lawrence J.	Pfc	Gulliver	Mi		Unknown
Hemric	Kenneth M.	Sgt	Yadkinville	NC		Repatriated
Henning	Vernon	Cpl	St. Cloud	Mn		Repatriated
Henry	Robert C.	Capt	Chicago	Il		Repatriated
Herbert	Edwin	L/Cpl	Cheshire	UK		Unknown
Hernandez	Abraham R.	Pfc	Waco	Tx		Unknown
Heron	William H.	Cpl	Durham	UK		Unknown
Herrman	Frederick C.	Cpl	Evansville	In		Repatriated
Heslop	Jack	Pte		UK		Unknown
Hess	Raymond D.	Sgt	Honaker	Va		Repatriated
Hettinger	Richard H.	Sgt	Joplin	Mo		Repatriated
Hibberd	Winthrop B.	Pfc			1	Unknown
Hickox	Robert H.	PFC	Syracuse	NY		Unknown

Last Name	First Name	Rank	City	State	Camp(s)	Status
Hikida	Roy					Unknown
Hilgart Jr.	John M.	Pvt	Park Falls	Wi		Unknown
Hill	Clyde H.	Cpl	Joplin	Mo		Repatriated
Hill	George H.	Cpl	Chance	Ky		Repatriated
Hill	J.	Sgt	Clochester	UK		Unknown
Hill	James A.	PFC	Burlington	Vt		Repatriated
Hill	Lemon S.	Cpl	Hugheston	WV		Repatriated
Hill	Oscar C.	Pvt	Nuyaka	Ok		Repatriated
Hill	Philip J.	Pvt	Worcester	Ma		Unknown
Himpel	Carl E.	PFC	Bloomer	Wi		Repatriated
Hinton	Edgar J.	PFC	St. Louis	Mo		Repatriated
Hodge	Herbert B.	Sgt	New York City	NY		Repatriated
Hodges	Carroll T.	M/Sgt	San Diego	Ca		Repatriated
Hodges	James E.	Cpl	Gallatin	Tn		Unknown
Hoffman	Marvin L.	PFC	South	WV		Repatriated
Holberton	John W.	Sgt	Yorks	UK		Unknown
Holbertson	John W.	Sgt	York	UK		Unknown
Holland	Billy J.	Pfc	Fort Smith	Ar		Unknown
Holland	Charles			UK		Unknown
Hollinger	Bernard R.	PFC	Lebanon	Pa		Repatriated
Hollis	Thomas H.J.			Australia		Unknown
Holman	John		St Paul	Mn		Died In Camp
Holmes	William D.		New York City	NY		Unknown
Holmquist	Richard A.	Cpl	Boone	La		Repatriated
Hoper	Peter J.	Sgt	Dorset	UK		Unknown
Hopkins	Stephen	Cpl	Philadelphia	Pa		Repatriated
Horsfall	Ronald F.	Pte	Portsmouth	UK		Unknown
Hotson	Wayne O.	Cpl	La Crosse	Wi		Unknown
House	Carl W.	PFC	Columbia	Mo		Repatriated
Howell	Bobbie J.	Sgt	Detroit	Mi		Unknown
Hrobak	Charles		Acmetovia	Pa		Unknown
Hubbard	William H.	Pvt	San Antonio	Tx		Repatriated
Hubener	Wayne E.	Pvt	Saxonville	Ma		Repatriated
Hughes	Hobart	Pvt	Lovisa	Ky		Unknown
Humphreys	Harold E.	Pfc	Harriman	Tn		Unknown
Hunt	James R.	PFC	Russell	Pa	3	Repatriated
Hunter	James R.	Sgt		N. Ireland		Unknown
Hussey	Donald P.	Sgt	New Canaan	Ct		Repatriated
Hutchens	Lockley H.	Cpl	Yadkinville	NC		Repatriated
Hwai	Hyun Sun			S. Korea		Unknown

Last Name	First Name	Rank	City	State	Camp(s)	Status
Inman	Eugene		Clatwoods	Ky		Unknown
Irish	Bradley	1st Lt	Danforth	Me		Repatriated
Isula	Henry J.	Sgt	Lackawanna	NY		Repatriated
Jackson	Elmer L.	Sgt	Skowheagan	Me		Repatriated
Jackson	Thomas R.	Cpl	Ottawa	WV		Repatriated
Jackson	William T.	Sgt	West Monroe	La		Repatriated
Jackson Jr.	Walter L.	1st Lt	Seymour	In		Repatriated
James	John W.	Cpl	Baltimore	Md		Repatriated
James	Russell P.	Cpl	Auburn	Wa		Repatriated
Jaramillo	Arturo J.		Pueblo	Co		Repatriated
Jefferson	Charles T.	Cpl	Popular Bluff	Mo		Repatriated
Jenkins	E. James		Tipton S. Stuffs	England		Unknown
Jenkins	Ernest T.	Cpl	Richard	NC		Repatriated
Jenkins	Roy L.	Cpl	Dallas	Tx		Unknown
Jennings	Channell R.	Cpl	Valley Head	WV		Unknown
Jennings Jr.	Lacey	Pfc	Bothwun	Pa		Unknown
Jewell	Charles W.	Cpl	Wilmington	De		Repatriated
Joel Jr.	Peter C.	Cpl	Albert Lea	Mn		Repatriated
Johnson	Alfonso					Unknown
Johnson	Booker T.	Cpl	Texarkana	Ak		Repatriated
Johnson	Calvin C.	Cpl	South Braintree	Ma		Unknown
Johnson	John G.	Sgt	La Porte	In		Stay Back
Johnson	Robert	Cpl	Palmer	Ma		Repatriated
Johnson	Spears T.	Sgt	Paris	Ky		Repatriated
Johnson	Webster L.	Cpl	Boston	Ma		Repatriated
Johnston	Robert O.	Pvt	Palmer	Ma		Unknown
Jones	Billie W.	Cpl	Kermit	Tx		Repatriated
Jones	Godfrey	Pvt	Scarburo	WV		Repatriated
Jones Jr.	Robert L.	Sgt	Syracuse	NY		Unknown
Joseph	Unknown		Eliot	Me		MIA
Joyce	Thomas	Capt	Oak Park	Il		Unknown
Kaiser	Wyman A.	PFC	Rio	Wi		Unknown
Kammrad	Melvin E.	Cpl	Sheffield	Ia		Repatriated
Kappel	Thomas	Cpl	Homestead	Pa		Repatriated
Kartye	Joseph D.	Pfc	Cincinnati	Oh		Unknown
Katzman	Ross W.	Pvt	Elkhorn	Wi		MIA
Kaver	Virgil A.	PFC	Marthasville	Mo	1	Unknown
Keck	Clyde A.	Cpl	Sparta	Mi		Unknown
Keck	Harold M.	Sgt	Bethlehem	Pa		Repatriated
Keenan	William P.	Lt	Cape Elizabeth	Me		Repatriated

Last Name	First Name	Rank	City	State	Camp(s)	Status
Keenon	Unknown					Unknown
Kelleher	Francis C.	PFC	Brockton	Ma		Died In Camp
Kelley	Ned	Sgt	Ashland	Oh		Repatriated
Kelly	Don L.	Cpl				Unknown
Kenard	Charles	Cpl		Fl		Repatriated
Keneally	Unknown	Unk	South Boston	Ma		Unknown
Kennedy Jr.	Gatherine	Cpl	Detriot	Mi		Repatriated
Kenney	Ashford R.	PFC	Boston	Ma		Repatriated
Kenney	Ashward R.	Cpl	Clark Harbor	Nova		Unknown
Kerr	Hugh	Pte	Glasgow	UK		Unknown
Keys	Frederick R.	Cpl	Greene	NY		Repatriated
Kiba	Steve					Unknown
Kilburn	Gerald					Unknown
Kilby	Thomas E.	2nd Lt	Anniston	Al		MIA
Killion	Richard E.	Cpl	Albuquerque	NM		Repatriated
Kimball	Reuben K.	PFC	Baytown	Tx		Repatriated
Kinard	Charles E.	Cpl	Quincy	Fa		Repatriated
Kinder Jr.	Arthur S.	Ssgt	Marlboro	Ma		Died In Camp
King	Joseph					Unknown
Kingston	Russell	Cpl	Kuttawa	Ky		Repatriated
Kippke	James A.					Unknown
Kirby	John R.	Cpl	Pittsburgh	Pa		Repatriated
Kirchhausen	Carl					Unknown
Kirk	Robert C.	Sgt	Kingsburg	Ca		Repatriated
Kiser	James (Jim)		Ft. Walton	Fl		Unknown
Klein	Joseph J.	Cpl	Hermosa	Ca		Repatriated
Klinger	James F.					Unknown
Knapp	John L.	Cpl	Los Angeles	Ca		Repatriated
Knott	Albert	Pvt	Nottingham	UK	5	Unknown
Koboski	Edward		Lincoln	Il		Unknown
Kohl	Robert I.		Lisbon	Ia		Unknown
Kohus Jr.	Francis E.	PFC	Norwood	Oh		Repatriated
Koroser	Richard R.	Cpl	Worcester	Ma		Died In Camp
Kostegan	Stanley J.		Back Bay	Ma		Repatriated
Kowalewsk	Joseph T.	Cpl	Buffalo	NY		Repatriated
Kreider	Lloyd	Cpl	West Willow	Pa		Repatriated
Kreizer	Alexander	Pvt	Danbury	Ct		Repatriated
Krueger	Ralph H.	M/Sgt	Black River	Wi		Repatriated
Kyle	Leland R.	Cpl	Cleveland	Oh		Repatriated
Kytys	Joseph J.	Capt	Drexel Hills	Pa		Repatriated

Last Name	First Name	Rank	City	State	Camp(s)	Status
La Pointe	Lawrence	Cpl	Lewiston	Me		Repatriated
Lacy	Roylin	Sgt	Frankfort	Ky		Repatriated
Lafleur	Roy D.	Sfc	Vancouver	Wa		Unknown
Lakin	Lloyd C.		Detroit	Mi		Unknown
Lam	Leroy V.	Cpl	Upperco	Md		Repatriated
Lambert	Arthur J.	Sgt	Leicester	Ma		Repatriated
Lambert	Joseph	M-Sgt	Worcester	Ma		Unknown
Lampkin Jr.	Miles E.	Cpl	Akron	Oh		Repatriated
Lane	Fred M.	Pfc	Syracuse	NY		Unknown
Langfitt	Ray C.	Msgt				Repatriated
Langston	Offord C.	Cpl	Colline	Ms		Repatriated
LaPointe	Lawrence	PFC	West Peru	Me		Unknown
LaRose	Arthur L.	Sgt	Lowell	Ma		Died In Camp
Lashua	Roy J.	PFC	Washau	Wi	1	Repatriated
Lauer	Robert	Sgt				Unknown
Laurent	Alfred	Sgt	Lowell	Ma		Repatriated
Lauter	Burl B.	Sgt	Effingham	Il		Unknown
Lawrence	Jack	Cpl	Mansfield	Pa		Unknown
Lawson	Kenneth		Galesburg	Il		Unknown
Leach	Louie	SFC	Columbus	Ga		Repatriated
Ledbetter	Jack W.	Lt				MIA
Lee	John	Pvt	Springfield	Ma		Repatriated
Lee	Robert M.	Sgt	Alma	Ga		Repatriated
Lefebvre	Joseph R. T.	Sgt	Morrisville	Vt		Repatriated
Legay	Donald K.	Cpl	Leominster	Ma	5	Repatriated
Leveillee	Joseph	Cpl	Coventry	RI		Repatriated
Lever	Donald J.	PFC	Bennington	Vt		Repatriated
Lewis	Wayne E.					Unknown
Lex	Charles B.	PFC	Allentown	Pa		Repatriated
Liddell	Fred					Unknown
Lide	Charles	Sfc	Baltimore	Md		Unknown
Ligue	Charles W.					Unknown
Lile	Ralph T.	PFC	Norman	NC		Repatriated
Liles	Paul V.	Lt Col	Birmingham	Al		Repatriated
Lilley	Merritt T.	SFC	Lubbock	Tx		Repatriated
Limb	Eric C.	Pte	N. Matlock	UK		Unknown
Linn	Frank M.	Sgt	Altus	Ok		Died In Camp
Lipper	Edward W.	PFC	Brockton	Ma	5	Repatriated
Locke	William Davis	Maj	High Point	NC		Escaped Home
Lodge	Walter	Cpl	Liverpool	UK		Unknown

Last Name	First Name	Rank	City	State	Camp(s)	Status
Logan	William E.					Unknown
Logan Jr.	Samuel P.					Unknown
Long	James	Sgt	Philadelphia	Pa		Unknown
Lord	Albert	Pte	Manchester	UK		Unknown
Lovejoy	Ronald	Pvt	Pilot Hill	Ca		Unknown
Lovtitt	Charles		Mononghela	Pa	1, 3	Unknown
Lucas	Pearl					Unknown
Lucas	W.A.	Sgt	Surrey	UK		Repatriated
Ludwig	Anthony R.	PFC	Cincinnati	Oh		Repatriated
Lumpkin	Billy M.	Cpl	Stockton	Ca		Repatriated
Lundquist	Carl R.	Lt	Georgetown	Tx		Unknown
Lundquist	Edwin C.	Cpl	Fitchburg	Ma	5	Repatriated
Lundquist	Unknown		Bell	Ca		MIA
Maack	Otto A.F.	Cpl	Chicago	Il		Unknown
MacDougall	Bernard A.	Pvt	Brookline	Ma		MIA
MacGhee	David F.	Maj	Tampa	Fl		Repatriated
MacLean	Robert A.	Cpl	Malden	Ma		Repatriated
MacNeil	Wilfred W.	PFC	Roxbury	Ma		Unknown
Madone	Rene	Cpl	Paris	France		Unknown
Magill	Andrew	L/Cpl	Belfast	N. Ireland		Unknown
Mahoney	Thomas R.	PFC	Worcester	Ma		Died In Camp
Maillet	Yvon J.	Cpl	Otter River	Ma	5	Repatriated
Makarounis	Alexander C.	Capt	Lowell	Ma		Escaped Home
Manring Jr.	Roy Paul		New Albany	In		Repatriated
Mansfield	L. F.	Cpl	Hamilton	Oh		Repatriated
Manuel	Donald W.	Cpl	Racine			Repatriated
Marchowsky	Martin J,	Cpl	Primrose	Pa		Deid In Camp
Marinez	Ramon	Cpl	Crystal City	Tx		Repatriated
Markham	Arnold L.	Cpl	Moncks Corner	SC		Repatriated
Marrero-Alvarez	Hannibal	PFC	Corazal	PR		Repatriated
Martelli	Paul L.	Capt	San Francisco	Ca		Unknown
Martin	John E.	PFC	Ferndale	Mi		Escaped Home
Martin	R. E.		Falls Church	Va		Unknown
Martin	Raymond C.	Sgt	Enosburg	Vt		Repatriated
Martinez	Daniel					Unknown
Martins	John	Cpl	Ludlow	Ma		Died In Camp
Maryea	George	PFC	Amesbury	Ma		Repatriated
Massie	Carles E.	Sgt	Toledo	Oh		Unknown
Mathis	Chester A.					Unknown
Matta	George	SFC	Sacramento	Ca	1, 2, 3, 4,	Repatriated

Last Name	First Name	Rank	City	State	Camp(s)	Status
Maxey	Robert	PFC	Santa Rosa	Ca		Repatriated
May	Pat		London	UK		Unknown
Mayer	Willibald J.	M/Sgt	Ayer	Ma		Unknown
Mayo Jr.	Walter L.	1st Lt	Watertown	Ma		Repatriated
Mayor Jr.	Walter L.	1st Lt	Watertown	Ma		Repatriated
McAbee	Fillmore W.	Maj	Framingham	Ma		Repatriated
McAuliffe	Raymond J.	Cpl	Omaha	Ne		Unknown
McCarthy	Francis A.	Sgt	Charlestown	Ma		Repatriated
McClellan	Donald J.	Lt Col	Van Nuys	Ca		Repatriated
McCloud	Arlo (LaVern)					Unknown
McComas	Estel H.	PFC	Otsego	WV		Repatriated
McCoy	John M.	Pvt	San Diego	Ca	1	Unknown
McCracken	Kenneth W.	Cpl	Rockland	Ma		Died In Camp
McCurley	Herman D.	Sgt	Pauls Valley	Ok		Repatriated
McDonnell	George F.	Capt	Attleboro	Ma		Repatriated
McDonough	Martin F.	PFC	Brighton	Ma		Repatriated
McDonough	Thomas F.	Cpl	Philadelphia	Pa		Repatriated
McDougall	Bernard		Brookline	Ma		Unknown
McGhee	Benjamin F.	PFC	Phoenix	Az		Repatriated
McInerney	James P.	Cpl	Holyoke	Ma	1	Repatriated
McIntyre	Harold F.	PFC	Presque	Me		Unknown
McIntyre	Herbert J.			UK		Unknown
McKee	Cecil		Belfast	N. Ireland		Unknown
McKell	Allan (Jock)	L/Cpl	Glasgow	Scotland		Unknown
McKeown	John	Cpl	Philadelphia	Pa		Repatriated
McKibben	Harold L.	Sfc	Tacoma	Wa		Unknown
McLaughlin	John N.	Maj	Savannah	Ga	2	Repatriated
Mclean	Unknown	Cpl				Unknown
McLellan	Donald	Lt Col				Unknown
McManus	Edward H.	Cpl	London	Uk		Unknown
McManus	Marion C.	Sgt	Lancaster	SC		Repatriated
McMillan	Fred	Pte	Belfast	N. Ireland		Unknown
McMillen	James J. K.	Cpl	Pittsburgh	Pa		Repatriated
McMurtrie	Thomas H.	Pfc	Pottsville	Pa		Unknown
McNeil	Alfred W.	Cpl	Framingham	Ma		Repatriated
McNeil	Joe		Brooklyn	NY	1, 3	Unknown
McNeill	John J.	PFC	Brooklyn	NY		Repatriated
McNichols	Henry	Lt	St. Louis	Mo		Repatriated
McPherson	Lester V.	PFC	Rumford	Me		Unknown
McQuade	Alfred	PFC	Maine	NY		Unknown

Last Name	First Name	Rank	City	State	Camp(s)	Status
McRoberts	James (Jim)			Wi	1	Unknown
McTaggart	William C.	Capt	East Brady	Pa		Unknown
Meanley	A. J.	Pvt	Wolverhampton	UK	5	Unknown
Medcalf	Walter	Pfc	Winchester	Ar		Unknown
Megesi	John J.	PFC	Farrell	Pa		Repatriated
Mello	Ernest	Cpl	East	RI		Repatriated
Menzia	Conrad C.	Pfc	Roscoe	SD		Unknown
Merrill	Delvin B.	PFC	Casco	Me		Unknown
Merworth	Lee E.	Sgt	Midland	Tx		Repatriated
Metz	Henry X.		Newton	Ma		Repatriated
Meyers	Edwin R.	Sgt	Baraboo	Wi		Repatriated
Meyers	Robert E.					Unknown
Michaud	Lionel E.	Sgt	West Mystic	Ct		Repatriated
Milano	William L.	Cpl	Philadelphia	Pa		Repatriated
Miller	Delmar G.	Pfc	San Diego	Ca		Unknown
Miller	Elmer L.	PFC	Olathe	Ks		Repatriated
Miller	Henry	PFC	Magnolia	Ms		Repatriated
Miller	Herbert A.	Sgt	Pulaski	NY		Repatriated
Miller	James E.	Sgt	Granite City	Il		Repatriated
Miller	John W.	Cpl	Clarkrange	Tn		Repatriated
Miller	Loris R.	Lt				Unknown
Miller	Robert (Bob)	Lt	San Pedro	Ca	Pyongyang	Unknown
Mills	Raymond E.	Sgt	West Palm	Ca		Repatriated
Mines	Charles W.	Sgt	Sparta	Il		Repatriated
Minietta	Charles	Lt	Brooklyn	NY		Unknown
Mitchell	Edwin L.	PFC	Auburn	Me		Died In Camp
Mitchell	James L.	Cpl	Frankfort	Ky		Repatriated
Miyamura	Hiroshi	Sgt	Gallup	NM		Repatriated
Moats	Robert E.	Sgt	Morgantown	WV		Repatriated
Molitor	John A.	Sgt	Fayetteville	Oh		Repatriated
Monroe	Franklin		LeJunior	Ky		Unknown
Montanaro	Richard		Stoney Brook	NY		Unknown
Montgomery	James H.	PFC	Weston	Wva		Repatriated
Montgomery	Joseph L.	Cpl	Trenton	NJ		Repatriated
Montgomery	Patrick	Pte	Londonderry	N. Ireland		Unknown
Montgomery	Robert P.	Cpl	Indianapolis	In		Repatriated
Montoya	Celso J.	Cpl	Albuquerque	NM		Repatriated
Moore	Martin J.	Pvt	Colfax	In		Unknown
Moore	Quincy O.	Cpl	Farmerville	Ca		Repatriated
Moore	Ronald	Sgt	Mooresville	NC		Unknown

Last Name	First Name	Rank	City	State	Camp(s)	Status
Mora	Rafael R.	PFC				Unknown
Moreland	Harry D.					Unknown
Morgan	Jerry	Sgt	Columbus	Ga		Repatriated
Morgan	Joseph W.F.	Cpl	Connersville	In		Repatriated
Morgan	Lynn H.	Pvt	Powell	Tn		Unknown
Morgan Jr.	Charles		Springfield	Ma		Unknown
Morman	Carlton G.	Cpl	Portland	Ar		Repatriated
Morrison	Joe	Pfc	Kansas City	Mo		Unknown
Morrison	Louis R.	Cpl	Hartford	Ct		Died In Camp
Morrison	Richard	Cpl				Unknown
Mosnicka	Francis J.	Pvt	Tomah	Wa	1	Repatriated
Moss	William H.	SFC	North Adams	Ma		Died In Camp
Muise	Eric E.	PFC				Unknown
Muldrow	Frederick N.	Ar		Prescott		Repatriated
Mullins	Orville R.	Sgt	Covington	Ky		Repatriated
Murdock	Joseph J.	Sgt	Spinozzi	Pa		Repatriated
Murphy	Matthew J.	M/Sgt			3, 4, 5	Repatriated
Murray	John R.	1st Lt	Brookline	Ma		Repatriated
Murray	Thomas R.	Cpl	Baltimore	Md		Repatriated
Murray	Wesley	Cpl	New York City	NY		Unknown
Murray Jr.	Neil A.	Sgt	Danforth	Me		Died In Camp
Myer	Alan	Lt	Arlington			Repatriated
Myers	Edward L.	1st Lt	Attleboro	Ma		Repatriated
Myers	William	Sgt	Dayton	Oh	1, 3, 4	Unknown
Nable	Jack D.	Pfc	Arlington	Ca		Unknown
Nance	Donald I.	Sgt	Rockford	Il		Repatriated
Nanegre	Leo J.	CWO	Springfield	Ma		Died In Camp
Nard	Thomas A.		La Grange	NC		Unknown
Narvin	John	Cpl	Newburgh	Oh		Repatriated
Neel	Clifford L.	Sgt	Osceola	Ar		Unknown
Neff	Kenneth E.	Sgt	San Bernardino	Ca		Died In Camp
Negron	Jorge A.	M/Sgt	San Juan	P.R.		Unknown
Nevill	James F.	1st Lt	Hyannis	Ma		Repatriated
Newhouse	George E.	Pte	Gloucester	UK		Unknown
Newton Jr.	Earle C.	Cpl	Leominster	Ma		Died In Camp
Nichols	Joseph D.	PFC	Clinton	Ma		Repatriated
Nicholson	Thomas H.	Cpl	Norfolk	Va		Repatriated
Nielsen	Henry L.	Lt	St. Joseph	Mi	2	Repatriated
Noble	Jack D.	PFC	Riverside	Ca		Unknown
Noel	Frank (Pappy)				5	Repatriated

Last Name	First Name	Rank	City	State	Camp(s)	Status
Nolan	John	M/Sgt	Fall River	Ma		Died In Camp
Nothstein	Edward E.	PFC	Layton	Pa		Repatriated
Novobilski	Thaddeus F.	Pvt	Simpson	Pa		Unknown
Nutter	Lewis G.	Sgt	Whitman	Ma		MIA
Nystram	John	1st Lt				MIA
O'Boyle	James M.		Pittsfield	Ma		Died In Camp
O'Brien	James P.	Cpl	South Boston	Ma		Repatriated
O'Donnell	George F.	Maj	Quincy	Ma		Repatriated
O'Hara	William P.M.	Sgt	London	UK		Unknown
O'Keefe	John J.	Sgt	Wakefield	Ma		Repatriated
O'Leary	James P.	Cpl	Acushnet	Ma		Died In Camp
Oakley	Jerry L.	Cpl	Shelton	Wa		Repatriated
Oakley	L.	Pfc	Albany	Or		Unknown
Obenauer	Ira J.	Cpl	Bonne Terra	Mo		Repatriated
Oberle	Edward F.	M/Sgt	Medford	Ma		Repatriated
Obroff	Fred	PFC	Wheelwright	Ky		Repatriated
Ohara	Bill		London	UK		Unknown
Olazabal	Joseph O.	PFC	Long Island	NY	6	Repatriated
Oleksink	Stephen	W/O	Amarillo	Tx		Unknown
Oliver	Glenn J.	Sgt	Ramona	Ok		Repatriated
Olson	William H.					Unknown
Omerzo	Louis	Cpl	Friedens	Pa		Repatriated
Orteza	Dioniscio	PFC	Pangnsinan	PR		Repatriated
Osaski	Edmund	Cpl				Unknown
Osborne	Chester M.	Capt	Minneapolis	Mn		Unknown
Packard	William	Cpl	Sterling	Ma		Died In Camp
Pantazis	Emmanuel N.	PFC				Unknown
Paquette	Joseph G.	Pvt	North	Ct	Mining	Repatriated
Parker	Clifford A.	Sgt	Houston	Tx		MIA
Parman	Joseph		NW Palm Bay	Fl		Unknown
Parris	Unknown					Unknown
Patchowski	Edward J.		Scranton	Pa		Repatriated
Pate	Arlie	Cpl	Carbondale	Il		Stay Back
Patriquen	Leighton	Cpl	Needham	Ma		MIA
Patterson	Lewis J.	Pvt	Brookings	SD		Unknown
Patterson Jr.	Joe N.	Pfc	Corpus Christi	Tx		Unknown
Payne	Euell B.	Pfc	Bremen	Ga		Unknown
Payton	John	Capt	Burlington	Ia		Repatriated
Peach	Edwin	Riflem	Walsall	UK	5	Unknown
Pearman	Charles E.	Cpl	Athens	Tn		Repatriated

Last Name	First Name	Rank	City	State	Camp(s)	Status
Pecoraro	Anthony	Capt	South Windham	Me		Unknown
Pedicone	Henry A.	Lt				Unknown
Pegler	John H.	Sgt	Stroud Glos.	UK		Unknown
Pelletier	Joseph N.	PFC	Berlin	NH		Died In Camp
Pelser	Frederick	Lt	Apponaug	RI		Repatriated
Pemble	Unkown		Peoria	Il		Died In Camp
Penn	Billy R.	HM2				Repatriated
Pennington	George	PFC	Augusta	Ga		Repatriated
Pentz	Howard E. H.	Cpl	Everett	Ma		Unknown
Perez	Richard	SFC	San Jose	Ca		Repatriated
Perkins	Albert	Cpl	Bristol	UK		Unknown
Perreault	George A.	PFC	Burlington	Vt		Died In Camp
Perry	Jack E.	Capt	Laguna Beach	Ca		Unknown
Peterson	Clerance	Cpl	Edensburg	Pa		Repatriated
Peterson	Richard A.	Pfc	Ishpeming	Mi		Unknown
Petitt	Hershel C.	Cpl	Dayton	Oh		Repatriated
Petrey	Clifford L.	Sgt	Rockhold	Ky		Repatriated
Pettit	William R.	T/Sgt	Warwick	RI		Unknown
Petty	James H.					Unknown
Pfannenstiel	Victor J.	Sgt	Haysville	Ks		Repatriated
Phillippi	Robert P.	Sgt	Abington	Va		Repatriated
Phillips	Kenneth A.	Pvt	Danielson	Ct		Unknown
Phillips	Raymond El	PFC	Wheatley	Ak		Repatriated
Phipps	Cecil E.	Pfc	Fort Dodge	Ia		Unknown
Pickering	Fred D.	Capt	Rockford	Il		MIA
Pierce	Richard P.	PFC	Brockton	Ma		Presumed Dead
Pietrasiewicz	C. L.	Pvt				Esacaped - Unk
Pina	Frank J.	Cpl	Roxbury	Ma		Died In Cptivity
Pingree	John Preston	Sgt	High Grove	Ca		Repatriated
Pitho	Andrew F.	Pvt	Cleveland	Oh		Unknown
Plum	Gary W.	Cpl	Tunnelton	WV		Repatriated
Poirot	Don		Bellevue	Il		Repatriated
Polee	William	Cpl	Sun Valley	Ca		Unknown
Pool	Willard	Sgt	Columbus	Ga		Repatriated
Porter	Fred W.	PFC	Los Angeles	Ca		Repatriated
Potvin	Joseph E.	Sgt				Unknown
Pough Jr.	Albert	SFC	Detroit	Mi		Unknown
Powazi	John	Pvt				Unknown
Powell	John W.	PFC	Brighton	Ma		Repatriated
Powell Jr.	Roosevelt	Cpl	Okmulgee	Ok	Pyoktong	Repatriated

Last Name	First Name	Rank	City	State	Camp(s)	Status
Powers	Elmer C.	PFC	Clintwood	Va		Repatriated
Preola	Joseph W.	Sgt	Bayonne	NJ		Repatriated
Prestridge	Wyatt E.	Cpl	Nauvoo	Al		Repatriated
Prewitt	James W.	Cpl	Louisville	Ky		Unknown
Price	Richard	Sgt	Stuart	Fl		Repatriated
Prokip	Alois	Pvt				Unknown
Provencher	Conrad J.	2nd Lt	Methuen	Ma		Repatriated
Publicover	Urban F.	Sgt	Cambridge	Ma		Repatriated
Purvis	Harry E.	Cpl	York	SC		Repatriated
Qualls	Ted E.	Sgt	Stillwell	Ok		Unknown
Quarles	D. E.	SFC	Fresno	Ca		Unknown
Quarles	Frank		Hopkinsville	Ky		Repatriated
Quinn	John	Lt	Altadena	Ca		Repatriated
Quinn	Pat					Repatriated
Radanovich	Harry J.	Pfc	Rockford	Il		Died In Camp
Ragland	Dayton W.	Lt		UK		Unknown
Ramirez	Andres	Sgt		P.R.		Repatriated
Ramirez	Joe E.	Cpl	Houston	Tx		Repatriated
Raup	Carl J.	Cpl	Franklin	Pa	Pyoktong	Repatriated
Ray	Vernon		Venice	Fl		Unknown
Raymond	Robert L.	Sgt	Westwood			Unknown
Read	Raymond F.	Cpl	Winona	Mn		Unknown
Reeder	Dale L.	Cpl	Waukon	Ia		Repatriated
Reedy	Doyle L.	Sgt	Chelsea	Ok		Repatriated
Reekie	Douglas R.	Sgt	Essex	UK		Unknown
Reese	Richard		Woodside L.I.	NY		Unknown
Reeves	Henry L.	Pfc	Port Arthur	Tx	1	Unknown
Reid	Eugene W.	PFC	Warrenton	Va		Repatriated
Reid	Troy L.	Sgt	Fitchburg	Ma		Unknown
Reilly	Eugene R.	Cpl	New York City	NY	3	Repatriated
Renouf	Bernard R.	Cpl	Hartford	Ct	1	Repatriated
Revezzi	Joseph	Cpl	Worcester	Ma		Repatriated
Rhoden	Berry F.	Sgt	MacClenny	Fl		Repatriated
Rhodes	William H.	PFC	Cumberland	Md		Repatriated
Rhoton	John B.	Sgt	Sweetwater	Tx		Repatriated
Richards	George	Cpl	Sussex	UK		Unknown
Richardson	Arthur	PFC	Fall River	Ma		Died In Camp
Richardson	James W.	Cpl	Philadelphia	Pa		Repatriated
Richie	Preston		San Antonio	Tx		Unknown
Ricks Jr.	Jack	Cpl	Macon	Ga		Repatriated

Last Name	First Name	Rank	City	State	Camp(s)	Status
Riddle Jr.	Robert	PFC	Johnson City	Tn		Repatriated
Ridlington	Jack H.		Essex	UK		Unknown
Riley	Donald J.					Unknown
Rittenberry	Billy L.	PFC	Mount Pleasant	Tn	5	Repatriated
Rivers	Bernard	Tsgt	North Oxford	Ma		Repatriated
Rix	Lawrence					Unknown
Roach Jr.	Paul R.	Lt	Las Cruces	NM		Unknown
Robb	Arlo G.	Sgt			1	Unknown
Robbins	Edward P.	PFC	Fall River	Ma		Repatriated
Roberts	Edward P.	PFC	Fall River	Ma		Repatriated
Roberts	Gene L.	Cpl	Leakay	Tx		Repatriated
Roberts	Martin R.	1st Lt	Jeannette	Pa		MIA
Roberts Jr.	Albert J.	T/Sgt	Apponaug	RI		Repatriated
Robertson	Allen B.	Sgt	Phoenix	Az		Unknown
Robertson	Dewey E.	Cpl	Rome	Ga		MIA
Robinette	Casey J.					Unknown
Robinson	Johnnie		Belmont	NC		Unknown
Robinson	Marshall	Cpl	Toledo	Oh		Repatriated
Robinson	Robert	Pfc	Muscatine	Ia		MIA
Rodriguez	Johnny		Jackson Hgts	NY		Unknown
Roese	Unknown		Pomeroy	Ia		Unknown
Roesse	Paul R.	Pvt				Unknown
Rogers	Clayton V.	Cpl	Little Rock	Ak		Repatriated
Rogers	James T.	Lt Col	Greenwood	SC		Repatriated
Rogers	John S.	Cpl	Arlington	Ma		Repatriated
Rogers	William	Sgt	Mattapan	Ma		Repatriated
Roman	Joseph J.	SFC	Worcester	Ma		Died In Camp
Roosevelt	Lunn	Pfc	Baltimore	Md		Unknown
Rosario	Camilo	PFC	Santurce	P.R.		Unknown
Rose	Junior B.	Cpl	Morgantown	Wva		Repatriated
Ross	Ernest	Pte	Co. Derry	N. Ireland		Unknown
Ross	Ulysses	SFC	Roxbury	Ma		Died In Camp
Rothwell	Floyd	Pvt	Chicago	Il		Unknown
Roush	Eugene P.	Sgt	Columbus	Ga		Repatriated
Rovezzi	Joseph	PFC	Worcester	Ma		Repatriated
Rowden	Thomas W.	Sgt	Lewiston	Me		Died In Camp
Rowley	Peter		New Barnet	UK		Unknown
Royster	William H.	Sgt	Skirwith	Va		Unknown
Ruben	Tibor	PFC	Brooklyn	NY		Unknown
Rudd	Willie J.	Pvt	Los Angeles	Ca		Repatriated

Last Name	First Name	Rank	City	State	Camp(s)	Status
Rudo	Willie J.	Pvt				Unknown
Ruest	Joseph	PFC	Beverly	Ma		Repatriated
Rush	Scott					Stay Back
Russell	Roy H.	Capt				Unknown
Ruth	Gerald		Beattyville	Ky	1, 4	Unknown
Rutherford	Virgil A.	PFC	Ochalta	Ok		Repatriated
Ryan	John E.					Unknown
Ryan	Patrick	Riflem	Clonmel	Ireland		Unknown
Ryder	Donald F.	Cpl	Harwichport	Ma	1	Repatriated
Salerno	Frank	Pvt	New York City	NY		Unknown
Salerno	Stefano	Cpl	Rochester	NY		Repatriated
Sallabank	Dennis W.	Sgt	Guernsey	UK		Unknown
Sanders	James	Sgt				Unknown
Santini	Nazeruo	Sgt	South Bound	NJ		Repatriated
Santora	Bert	Maj				Unknown
Scahill	James P.	Cpl	Rochester	NY		Unknown
Scales	Leslie E.	Cpl	Folsomville	In	5	Repatriated
Scherer	James H.	Sgt	Sayres	Pa		Repatriated
Schlusser	Harrison J.	Cpl	Carlisle	Pa		Unknown
Schmitz	Gordon M.	Sgt	LeMars	Ia		Repatriated
Schnur Jr.	Paul F.		San Francisco	Ca		Repatriated
Schwable	Frank	Lt Col	Arlington	Va		Repatriated
Schwarts	Frederick	Pfc	Shawand	Wi		Unknown
Scoggins	Vernon	Cpl	Richmond	Va		Repatriated
Scott	Eugene L.	PFC	El Paso	Tx		Repatriated
Scott	Gerald D.	Sgt	Wakefield	Ma		Died In Camp
Scott	Ishmael D.	Sgt	Mecrory	Ar		Unknown
Scott	James J.	Sgt			1, 4	Repatriated
Scott	Mickey K.	PFC				Unknown
Sebastian	Henry H.	Sgt	Mystic	Ma		Died In Camp
Serafin	Chester	PFC				Unknown
Serenelli	Mario J.	Pvt	Trenton	NJ		Repatriated
Serra	John					Unknown
Serran	Eligio	Pvt				Unknown
Shabbee	Lloyd		Abbottstown	Pa		Unknown
Shadduck	Melvin		Oldtown	Id		Unknown
Sharland	Henry	PFC	Dorchester	Ma		Unknown
Shaw	Robert W.	M/Sgt	Vancouver	Wa		Unknown
Shearer	Roy D.	Cpl	Haverhill	Oh		Repatriated
Shedd	George F.					Unknown

Last Name	First Name	Rank	City	State	Camp(s)	Status
Sheffield	Horace R.	Cpl	Tallahassee	Fl		Repatriated
Sheppard	Robert F.	PFC	Brockton	Ma	2, 3	Repatriated
Sherrick	Donald V.	Cpl	Sioux City	Ia		Repatriated
Shipes	D. P.	Pfc	Columbia	SC		Unknown
Shuppan	Frederick W.	PFC				Unknown
Sibaya	Lamberto P.	Pvt				Unknown
Siebert	Arnold					Repatriated
Silva Jr.	Manuel	Cpl	East	RI		Repatriated
Simonetti	Vincent G.	PFC	Cleveland	Oh		Repatriated
Sinnett	Harry D.	SFC	Kingman	Ks		Unknown
Sirk	Kenneth L.	Pfc	Clarksburg	WV		Unknown
Sisson	Maryln K.	Pvt	Lennox	SD		Unknown
Sitler	Harold E.	Cpl	Mt. Morris	Il		Unknown
Skelton	John C.					MIA
Skinner	Eric (Von)	Pte	Halifax Yorks.	UK		Unknown
Skinner	Lowell		Akron	Oh		Stay Back
Skinner	William		Clarksburg	WV		Unknown
Skipper	William J.	PFC	Galivants Ferry	SC	Pyoktong	Repatriated
Slagle	Donald L.	Sgt	Narka	Ks		Repatriated
Slater	Harold K.	Maj				Unknown
Smith	Bill	Pvt	Suffolk	UK		Unknown
Smith	Billy J.	Cpl	Dallas	Tx		Repatriated
Smith	Dale S.	PFC	New Plymouth	Id		Repatriated
Smith	Edward T.	Sgt	Fresno	Ca		Repatriated
Smith	Edwin S.	W.O.				Unknown
Smith	Fred Albert	Capt				Unknown
Smith	George W.		Rotherham	UK		Unknown
Smith	Herman	Pfc	Mousie	Ky		Unknown
Smith	James	Pfc	Crossgill	Tn		Unknown
Smith	James B.	Lt	Franklin	In	Pyongyang	Escaped - Unk
Smith	James W.	Pvt	Kansas City	Ks		Unknown
Smith	Paul R.	PFC				Unknown
Smith	Robert B.	Cpl	Pittsfield	Ma		Died In Camp
Smith	Robert D.	Cpl	Indianola	Ok		Repatriated
Smith	Unknown	Cpl	Pittsfield	Ma		MIA
Smith	William H.	Cpl	Gloucester	UK		Unknown
Smith	William J.	Cpl	Xenia	Il		Repatriated
Smotherman	Calvin B.	Cpl	Peterburgh	Tn		Repatriated
Smythe	James W.	Sgt		Ireland		Unknown
Snipan	George					Unknown

Last Name	First Name	Rank	City	State	Camp(s)	Status
Snyder	Daniel	Sgt	Bedford	Ma		Repatriated
Snyder	Jesse		Mill Creek	Pa		Repatriated
Sobieck	John		Astonia - Long	NY		Unknown
Soble	Eugene R.	Sgt	San Pablo	Ca		Repatriated
Spackman	Thomas M.	PFC				Unknown
Sparks	Ronald M.		Cambridge	Ma		Unknown
Speer	Fred L.	Capt				Unknown
Spingda	Kenneth E.	Cpl	Seattle	Wa		Unknown
Spivey	John	Sgt	Washington	DC		Repatriated
Stahlman	Harold E.	1st Lt	Niantic	Ct		Unknown
Stamer	Francis	M/Sgt	Arlington			Unknown
Stanley	George A.	Sgt	Glenallen	Va		Repatriated
Stanley	Milford W.	Capt	East Orange	NJ		Unknown
Stavrakes	James	Lt	Medford	Ma		Repatriated
Steege	Leonard	PFC	Medford	Me	5	Repatriated
Steele	Charles H.	PFC				MIA
Stegall	Jack L.	Cpl	Desloge	Mo		Repatriated
Stevens	William H.	Cpl	Baltimore	Md		Repatriated
Stevenson	James J.	PFC	Kushequa	Pa		Repatriated
Stockley Jr.	Stephen	Cpl				Repatriated
Stokes	Henry		Wilson	NC		Unknown
Stone	Clovis (Ray)		West	Tx		Unknown
Stone	Floyd L.	Pfc	Langton	ND		Unknown
Stone	James	1st Lt	Hot Springs	Ar		Repatriated
Stone	Willis	Pfc	Eldon	Mo		Unknown
Stonesifer	Raymond	Cpl	Empire	Or		Repatriated
Stopf	Don		Belleville	Il		Unknown
Stough	August F.	PFC	Valley Park	Mo	1	Repatriated
Stravrakes	James	Lt	Somerville	Ma		Repatriated
Stringer	Bobbie P.	Sgt	Arlington	Ca		Repatriated
Stupa	Joseph	M/Sgt	Anahola	Hi		Repatriated
Su	Kim Ail			S. Korea		Unknown
Sub	Andrew	Pvt				Unknown
Sugrue	Daniel	Pvt				Unknown
Sullivan	James	2nd Lt	Dorchester	Ma		Unknown
Sullivan	Larance V.	Sgt	Omaha	Ne		Stay Back
Surridge	Arthur		Roydon Herts.	UK		Unknown
Swartz	Donald L.	Pfc	Lacrosse	Ks		Unknown
Sweeney	Ronald J.	Cpl	Allentown	Pa		Unknown
Sykes	Arthur B.	Sgt	Essex	UK		Unknown

Last Name	First Name	Rank	City	State	Camp(s)	Status
Sykes	Leroy James	Cpl	Savannah	Ga		Repatriated
Talbot	Edgar H.	PFC	Cambridge	Ma		Died In Camp
Tates	Howard T.	Sgt	Detroit	Mi		Repatriated
Taylor	George J. R.	Sgt	Fordingbridge	UK		Unknown
Taylor	John	Cpl	South Boston	Ma		Died In Camp
Teal	John H. F.	Pvt	Hartford	Ct		Repatriated
Tenneson	Richard R.	PFC	Alden	Mn		Stay Back
Teriera	Pedro	Cpl		PR		Repatriated
Thomas	John L.	Pfc	South Hill	Va		Unknown
Thomas	Nathaniel S.	PFC	Alliance	Oh		Repatriated
Thomas	Solomon	Cpl	Macy	Ne		Repatriated
Thompson	Haljmer E.					Unknown
Thompson	James T.	PFC	Horatio	Ak		Repatriated
Thornton	John	Lt	Philadelphia	Pa		Unknown
Thrash	William G.	Lt Col	Atlanta	Ga		Repatriated
Timpanaro	Joseph	Cpl	Lyndhurst	NJ		Repatriated
Todd	Blanton	Sgt	Orlando	Fl		Died In Camp
Tolan	Joseph W.	PFC	Port Carbon	Pa		Unknown
Tolley	Kenneth R.			UK		Unknown
Tondreau	George A.	Cpl	Salem	Ma		Died In Camp
Tooley	Frank N.	PFC	Greer	SC		Repatriated
Toomey	Joseph	Lt	South Boston	Ma		Died In Camp
Tower	Maynard A.	Cpl	Corning	NY		Repatriated
Towne	Charles E.	Cpl	Poultney	Vt		Died In Camp
Trammell	David	Sgt	Winfield	Tn		Repatriated
Trarrington	Edward M.	Sgt	Richmond	Va		Repatriated
Travers	Joseph	Pvt	East Taunton	Ma		Died In Camp
Traynham	Robert L.	Pfc	Charleston	SC		Unknown
Treffery	Wnedell H.	Cpl	Westfield	Me		Repatriated
Tumbleston	Raymond E.	Sgt	Miami	Fl		Repatriated
Tupper	John	Sgt	Brockton	Ma		Repatriated
Turner	Robert R.	PFC	Oslaloosa	Mo		Repatriated
Turner	Sammy	Pvt	Evarts	Ky		Repatriated
Tutino	James V.	Pvt	Brooklyn	NY		Unknown
Underwood	John		Bournemouth	UK		Unknown
Underwood	Tom			UK		Unknown
Unknown	"Slick"					Disappeared
Uzulmez	Kadir			Turkey		Unknown
Vadala	Guy T.	Sgt	Stoneham	Ma	1, 3	Repatriated
Van Dala	Guy T.	Cpl	Stoneham	Ma		Unknown

Last Name	First Name	Rank	City	State	Camp(s)	Status
Van Leuven	Otis A.	Cpl	Sussex	NJ		Repatriated
Van Wees	Ronald					Unknown
Vanderkooi	Charles C.		Galion	Oh	1, 3	Unknown
Vanryn	Arie	PFC				Unknown
Vasapolli	Gene	PFC	Woburn	Ma		Repatriated
Vaughn	Donald W.	Cpl	Raleigh	NC		Repatriated
Veautre	Jacques	Sgt			5	Repatriated
Veihdeffer	Kenneth D.	Pfc	Hyde	Pa		Unknown
Veneris	James G.		Hawthorne	Ca		Stay Back
Vidalo	Guy	PFC	Stoneham	Ma		Unknown
Vieu	Herman J.	PFC				Unknown
Villegas	Elias B.		San Antonio	Tx		Repatriated
Vincent	Robert E.	PFC	Raymond	NH		Repatriated
Viscuso	Andrew	PFC	Phoenixville	Pa		Repatriated
Vitale	George A.	Pvt	Stoneham	Ma	5	Repatriated
Vollers	Edwin W.	Sgt	Houston	Tx		Repatriated
Voss	Richard G.	2nd Lt	Osborne	Ks		Repatriated
Wagner	Arthur	Capt	Chino	Ca		Unknown
Wagner	Kenyon Lewis	Cpl	Detroit	Mi		Unknown
Waiau	Oliver		Oahu	Hi		Unknown
Wakefield	Gerald					Escaped - Unk
Walintukonis	Joseph A.	Cpl	Waterford	Ct		Repatriated
Walker	George E.	PFC	Swanton	Vt		Repatriated
Waller	Donovan D.	PFC	Creston	Ia		Repatriated
Wallter	Donovan D.	PFC	Creston	Ia		Repatriated
Walton	John	Sgt	Fall River	Ma		Repatriated
Warren	Vernon L.	Cpl	St. Louis	Mo		Unknown
Warsawski	Joseph	Sgt	Turners Falls	Ma		Repatriated
Waters	John L.	Sgt	Washington	DC		Repatriated
Watkins	Alfred	Sgt	Tacoma	Wa		Unknown
Watkins	Curley					Unknown
Watkins	Samuel K.					Unknown
Watling	James T.	PFC	Los Angeles	Ca		Repatriated
Watson	George	PFC	Springfield	Ma		MIA
Watson	John W.	Lt	Medford	Ma		Unknown
Watson	Leo T.	Cpl	Thomaston	Ga		Repatriated
Watson	Martin R.	Cpl	Deep River	Ct		Repatriated
Watson	William C.	Lt	Hickman Mills	Mo		Unknown
Watters	John L.	Ssgt	Washington	DC		Repatriated
Weem	Carl	Sgt	Back Bay	Ma		Repatriated

Last Name	First Name	Rank	City	State	Camp(s)	Status
Weinel	Carey H.	SFC	Hickman Hills	Mo		Repatriated
Wentworth Jr.	Lloyd G.	Lt	Sanford	Me		Repatriated
Wheeler	Bernard L.	Cpl	Masontown	Pa		Unknown
Whitaker	Mickey A.	Sgt	W.	Ky		Unknown
White	Robert E.	PFC	Commerce	Ok		Repatriated
White	Unknown					Unknown
White	Victor F.	L/Cpl	Somerset	UK		Unknown
White	William C.	Cpl	Kansas City	Mo		Unknown
White Jr.	R. C.	Capt	Monroe	La		Repatriated
White Jr.	Thaddesus C.	Cpl	Woodland	Me		Unknown
Whiting	Walter		Huddersfield			Unknown
Whorton	Marcus E.	PFC	Gadsden	Al		Repatriated
Wienel	Carey	Sgt	Kansas City	Mo		Repatriated
Wignall	Harry	W.O.	New Bedford	Ma		Repatriated
Wilkins	James V.	Capt	Worcester	Ma		Repatriated
Wilkins	Robert M.	Sgt	Detroit	Mi		Repatriated
Williams	Edward	Sgt	Vicksburg	Ms	5	Repatriated
Williams	James C.	Sgt	Kinston	NC		Repatriated
Williams	Kenneth	Pte		UK		Unknown
Williams	Lester E.	Cpl	Kemah	Tx		Repatriated
Williams	Peter	Cpl	Bradford Yorks	UK		Unknown
Williams	Roosevelt	Sgt	Chicago	Il		Repatriated
Williams	Walter R.	Cpl	Alleyton	Tx		Repatriated
Williams Jr.	John	Sgt	Oakland	Ca		Repatriated
Williamson	Kenneth E.	Pvt	New Hope	Pa		Unknown
Willis	Unknown					Unknown
Wills	Morris		New York	NY		Stay Back
Wilmeth	Leonard	Cpl	Ft. Worth	Tx	5	Repatriated
Wilson	Glen C.	Cpl	Rolla	Mo		Repatriated
Wilson	Harold	Cpl	Mobile	Al	5	Repatriated
Wilson	Joseph	Pvt				Unknown
Wilson	Louis	2nd Lt				Unknown
Wilson	Robert	Pvt	West Chester	Pa		Unknown
Wilson	William C.	Lt	Hickman Hills	Mo		Unknown
Winter	Frederick	Maj				Unknown
Witt	James R.	Lt Col	San Antonio	Tx	2	Unknown
Wolfe	Charles J.	PFC	Wallace	WV	1	Repatriated
Wolz	Henry D.	Lt				Unknown
Wood	Robert	Lt	Washington	DC		Unknown
Woodley	Perry F.	Sgt	Jasper	Al	1	Repatriated

Last Name	First Name	Rank	City	State	Camp(s)	Status
Woods	David	Sgt	St. Louis	Mo		Repatriated
Woodson	Unknown				Pyoktong	Unknown
Wooldridge	Larry K.	PFC	Lynchburg	Va		Repatriated
Worley	John R.	Sgt	Tulsa	Ok	Puck-Dong	Repatriated
Wozniak	Joseph W.	Sgt	New Haven	Ct		Unknown
Wright	C. L.	Cpl	Memohis	Tn		Repatriated
Wright	Carroll	Lt	Falls Church	Va		Unknown
Wright	William E.	Sgt	Elmore City	Ok		Repatriated
Wyatt	Robert L.	Sgt	Baltimore	Md		Repatriated
Wyman	Kenneth L.	PFC	Kansas City	Mo		Unknown
Yacko	Peter	Pvt				Unknown
Yang	Pak Wun			S. Korea		Unknown
Yates	Allen W.	Pfc	Lexington	Tn		Unknown
Yesko	Daniel D.					Unknown
Young	James R.	Cpl	Queens City	Tx	1	Repatriated
Younge	Barney M.	Sgt	Clevelad	Va		Repatriated
Yung	Jiuh Hyung			S. Korea		Unknown
Yurukoglu	Zeki	Pte		Turkey		Unknown
Zacherle	Alarich	Lt Col	Tacoma	Wa		Unknown

A POW DIARY - My Father's Struggle
Order Form

"A POW DIARY - My Father's Struggle" documents the long march into captivity and over 800 days of desperation, treachery and brutality. It is presented in a manner that allows the reader to understand the human side of captivity. You will learn how each of the men coped with the knowledge that for them, the war was over and they may never get home again.

Understand for the first time the affect the Chinese entry into the war had not only on the prisoners, but the North Korean civilians as well.

To order this gripping, vivid and powerful true life story of the daily struggle to survive in the Prisoner of War (POW) Camps during the Korean War, fill out this form and mail it in today along with a check or money order.

Watch for the companion book **"Letters from the Heart - The Victims at Home"** coming soon. This is a compilation of the actual letters written by the POWs and their families. The letters are a time capsule back almost fifty years and provide an insight into the era, the family ties, and the heartbreak caused by the uncertainty and loss of control over their lives.

===

Complete, Clip and Mail with Payment

A POW DIARY - My Father's Struggle	$ 12.00
Shipping and handling	$ 3.00
Al. Sales Tax(if applicable) 4% (.48)	$

Total Enclosed	$_______

Please Print

Name:________________________ **Mail To: DarRyan Press**
Dept. B
Address:____________________________ **P.O. Box 361582**
Hoover,AL 35236
City:_____________________ **State:**____ **Zip:**___________

Please Notify Me When "Letters from the Heart" is Published - Circle One: Yes No

Bulk Purchase Inquiries Welcome